SECOND-HAND
DOGS

With Adopters' Stories of their Special Rescue Dogs

Compiled and Written
By

PAULA JONES

Expert Advisors: Dr Susannah O'Hanlon, PhD MSc
Helen Howell, BSc (Hons) in Canine Behaviour Management
Ryan Dillon, BSc (Hons) in Animal Behaviour and Welfare, MSc

SECOND-HAND DOGS

Copyright 2024 Paula Jones

All rights reserved

No part of this book may be reproduced, stored in a retrieval system, or transmitted in any form, or by any means electronic, mechanical, photocopying, recording, or otherwise, without express written permission of the author.

ISBN : 978-1-917367-65-3

This book is dedicated to my beloved mum and dad – thank you for giving me my first experience of a dog's love, and especially to my long-suffering partner, Neil, for taking that initial brave step to open up his world to the company of rescue dogs.

TABLE OF CONTENTS

Acknowledgements	xi
Introduction	xiii

PART I: RESCUE DOGS' HAPPY TALES

Words of Wisdom: Lloyd Alexander	3
Max – Maria Glazier	5
Pablo and Scooby – Brenda Ditchfield	13
Miss Gracie – Rosemary Bryant	16
Words of Wisdom: George Graham Vest	19
Josie – Gesa	20
Rocco – Bob Machin	22
Words of Wisdom: Mahatma Gandhi	29
Benji and Scout – Lara Naqvi & Jasmin Strothmann	30
Our Poochie Princess – Rob & Julia Roberts	38
Words of Wisdom: Unknown	41
Tommy 1 – Jean Rose	42
Gina	44
A Special Breed: Patricia Brown	46
Mickey: We were sent an Angel – J Rahner & N Frach	48
From Mickey to Polly: A World of Difference – J Rahner & N Frach	51
Words of Wisdom: Albert Payson Terhune	54
Doraimon	55

The Wolfman Cometh – John Clothier	56
Wilma – Fastest Tail in the West	60
Words of Wisdom: Unknown	63
Hobo – From Drifter to Sofa-Surfer	64
Pepper's Story – Paul Kendall	70
Rosie's Story – Donna Morris	74
Words of Wisdom: Mark Twain	79
Dolly	80
Amara & Remi's Stories – Marjon Van Wateren	82
Nessie, The Patchwork Pup – Jonathan Wittenberg and Nicola Solomon	84
Words of Wisdom: Diogenes	86
Ruby – Angie Stone	87
Lucas	89
Words of Wisdom: Albert Payson Terhune	92
When Freya Joined Us – Ramona Noack	93
Words of Wisdom: Unknown	103
Angel	104
Jack and Cherry	106
The Diva – Neva	108
Dobby and Cookie – Clem Hall	113
Sir Dougie	117
Words of Wisdom: Unknown	119
Katla: A Very Special Dragon – Raquel Carceles	120
Barney	124
Scorrie's Story – Richard & Heather Lorimer	125
Gizmo – Nick & Lily	128
Rondie	133
Words of Wisdom: Lynn Van Matre	135
Mia The Minx	136
Chan – Dorinda Watson	141
Mongrel Dogs are Truly Unique	144
Tasha – Thanks so much – Maya	146

Words of Wisdom: Woodrow Wilson	149
Puma	150
In Memory – Little Tommy - Kim & George Baker-Blakemore	151
Poochie Princess Pt.2 – Julia Roberts	155
Twinkle – Nicola Cherry	157
Dave – Daisy Merrell	160
Words of Wisdom: Eartha Kitt	164
Fleur – Kelly Mander	165
Timmy – The Shortest Tale	168
Words of Wisdom: Roger Andrew Caras	171
Little Cuddle Monster Ellie – Lisa Dunlop	172
Snow's Story – Debs and Chris Wright	175
Words of Wisdom: Horace Walpole	182
Lady	183
Claudia & Eddie – Claudia Lessander	189
Shirley & Gracie – Shirley McGillivray	195
Josh	198
Words of Wisdom: Josh Billings	201
Malaga Four:	202
• Dylan – J. Pastewsky	204
• Barnaby – Jenifer Andrews	206
• Daisy's Journey – Debbie Pryke	209
• Becky – Bärbel Wehmeier	213
Words of Wisdom: Charles M. "Sparky" Schulz	217
Cassie	218
Magic Merlin – Peter Schier	221
Kiki, Pt 2 of Becky's story – Bärbel Wehmeier	226
Words of Wisdom: Gil Schwartz	229
The Collectors:	230
• Rosemary's Fur-Babies – Rosemary Pockett	230
• Berry, Sansa & Allegra – Jill Williams	237
• The Creation of Team Litfin – Kerstin Litfin	243

Words of Wisdom: Konrad Lorenz	262
House Rules …	263
A Dog's Last Will	270

PART II: ADOPTION ADVICE

Chapter 1: So you think you want a dog?	273
Chapter 2: The search begins …	281
Chapter 3: Choosing the right dog	291
Chapter 4: Babies, Children and Dogs	301
Chapter 5: Bringing your new dog home	309
Chapter 6: Welcome to the gang	338
Chapter 7: Fearful dogs	352
Chapter 8: Learn a new language	354
Chapter 9: Training	361
Chapter 10: Why Adopt?	372
Glossary	383
Biographies	391
Contact List	395

ACKNOWLEDGEMENTS

There are so many people I would like to thank for helping to take my dream of show-casing the wonderful world of rescue dogs to this point of reality of a *book*!

Huge thanks must go to all of the rescuers for their enthusiasm and generosity in sharing their canine stars' stories and photos, and for adopting a second-hand dog in the first place. It was so amazing how quickly everyone got on board which made my mission so much easier. I sincerely hope that they are as delighted with the result as I am, seeing their beautiful dogs' lives proudly in print.

Not being imbued with an abundance of self-belief, I really appreciate all the editing suggestions and advice from my good friend, Tausha Johnson, a talented poet and writer, and ardent dog-lover. Her knowledge, guidance, belief and encouragement kept me going when spirits were flagging.

To three amazing people: Dr Susannah O'Hanlon, Helen Howell, and Ryan Dillon, who took on the task of double-checking the advice chapters for accuracy, adding pertinent advice or improvements where required. Despite never having met me and each being incredibly busy with their own careers, without hesitation they all bravely agreed to help bring this book to fruition. With their infinite wisdom and expert advice, I felt in very safe hands and am eternally grateful for their trust and patience.

To my special friend and veterinarian, Susana Perez of Petlovers Clinic in the local village of Sucina, I send my heartfelt *muchas gracias* for allowing me to pick her brains on medical issues for this book, and especially for her meticulous care of my beloved dogs.

Special thanks to my translators: Sharon Day in the UK, and Peter Trepp in Switzerland, both of whom immediately agreed to help without second asking; and to Richard Brown for bravely volunteering to proofread and edit the manuscript.

Thanks to Sue Johnstone for her help, knowledge and endless patience in dealing with the barrage of questions from a technological dummy.

And last but not least, to all those people, too many to mention, whose enthusiasm, quiet support and belief kept a total novice afloat.

Thank you, everyone for your help and support. This book belongs to all of you, but particularly to those special "second-hand" dogs who allowed their stories to be told, and who are loved to the end of the world and back.

INTRODUCTION

Second-Hand Dogs ...

… make first class pets.

For the first thirteen birthdays and Christmases of my life, I yearned for a pony. I dreamed of soaring high over jumps, winning red rosettes, grooming it until its coat gleamed … until after thirteen years of wretched disappointment, I reluctantly accepted that a pony was never going to be a part of my life. But when my mother made the fundamental mistake of asking what I'd like for my fourteenth birthday, I changed tack slightly and suggested a dog … while I might not be able to ride on their backs, well - dogs had 4 legs, and a head and tail, didn't they?

I'd obviously got Mum at a very weak moment because surprisingly, she reneged on my family's (well, my father's) total ban on pets, and while my dad was away working, we went to see a puppy that was advertised in the newspaper (this was in a different era). And I became the proud owner of a pedigree Airedale Terrier, Tara – or Shy Sharon to apply her registered IKC name.

Tara became a much-loved member of our family; even with my dad who had expressed his initial displeasure at my mother's disobedience upon his return: "Women! They never listen to you!"

But he soon discovered the joys of having a dog. He loved the way Tara participated in funny little games – she would sit pertly in front of him while he was opening his post, taking the envelope he presented back to her bed to happily shred, whereupon she returned to await the next envelope present. Another favourite was to unknot Dad's shoelaces, after which the little plastic tips had to be removed. He even admitted to my Mum (well outside of my earshot) that he wished we'd got a dog earlier, such was Tara's contribution to our family.

While Tara was a lovely, funny pet, as a total Airedale blue-blood from a rich line of champions that went back generations, she was also very slightly bonkers in a suitably royal way. The main problem was that the same champion names kept cropping up on both the male and female sides of her lineage – no doubt a by-product of a breeding programme in a small country with limited breeding stock. It also indicated a resolutely blinkered refusal on the part of breeders in the country to introduce new dogs from abroad, to strengthen the genetic pool with new DNA.

Notwithstanding her neurotic ways, Tara was a super dog that lived until she was nearly 16 despite stiff arthritic joints and a dicky heart, neither necessarily a legacy of her regal heritage. My mother and I missed her dreadfully when she did finally depart this mortal coil, her death leaving a huge hole in our lives.

Roll forward the years, past numerous travels and work in foreign parts, to when my partner and I finally retired to south-east Spain where, to stave off boredom, I became involved in dog rescue. It was only a matter of time before we were adopted by 3 mutts (word used affectionately) over a period of 6 years, when I could finally experience the non-royal version of the wonderful canine species.

And they haven't disappointed, each one displaying very individual characters combined with the little quirks or idiosyncrasies of their diverse breeding, and previous experiences, providing us with hours of fascination, fun and entertainment. Each beloved one has been a good, solid companion pet, adding – as my previously non-dog-loving partner admitted – "something" to our home. We can hardly imagine what life would have been like without each one.

Sadly, lovely dogs of "undetermined breeding" rarely get much promotion in the media. Talk to any owner of a mixed-breed dog about their pet, and these people will passionately describe the special attributes and talents of their mutt – as proud as any human parent of a super-talented child prodigy.

While owners are so delighted with and proud of the multiplicity of genes of their fur-babies, many express total irritation and frustration when strangers ask them "which breed" their dog is, rather than accepting that it is a *dog* with a unique appearance, character and ability.

It is so sad that the slick TV marketing machines produce dreamy advertisements that feature glossy-coated, pedigree blue-bloods with bright eyes, and teeth that sparkle in a special TV canine smile, running through long grass or playing in cool azul water.

Any pretty picture that might grab the viewer by the cockles of their heart and not a mixed-breed in sight!

Lovely as all of the dogs are, these advertisements are a kind of subliminal PR, gently persuading more than one potential adopter that pedigree is the only way to go.

Little chance for poor mongrel shelter dogs, then.

Sadly, there are already far too many lovely pooches with TV-ready smiles lounging in shelters, waiting for their big moment when they too can promote dog products and look gorgeous. Or just find a home where they'll be loved unconditionally.

Which is so shameful.

And let's not forget the slick media publicity pictures of Mr or Ms Celebrity and their little itsy-bitsy canine accessory. Perish the thought that these PR hounds should ever been seen with an equally cute pet that just so happens to be the result of an accidental coupling.

Much as that gorgeous fluffy pedigree or titchy little dog that fits in Ms Celebrity's handbag are very beautiful and doubtless, very expensive, it is such a shame that too few high-profile celebrities, many of whom have a priceless ability to influence their followers, will visit a shelter to adopt a dog that so desperately needs a new home, thus giving vital positive publicity to rescue dogs.

For those who really do want a pedigree animal, it shouldn't be forgotten that it is still possible to find such dogs languishing in shelters. Except they may not come with the pedigree book that adds hundreds, if not thousands of pounds, euros or dollars to their "value".

We live in a world where "perfection" appears to be the Holy Grail: the perfect body, perfect bottom, perfect skin, perfect teeth, the perfect nose. Imperfection too can be beautiful in its own unique way. Italian actress Sophia Loren was considered to be one of the most beautiful women of her era and yet her features, taken one by one, could be considered "wrong" or "imperfect". Model Lauren Hutton was the highest paid model in the early seventies and despite possessing "irregular features", still looked incredibly beautiful.

People want "designer" – the right brand-name, the right style, whatever is "in" for that very brief period in time.

This quest for perfection also seems to extend to dogs – they must in vogue – PERFECT. Not so bad when it involves a handbag but potentially devastating when it's a unique living being.

There is no doubt that all of these perfect dogs may make really nice pets, but so can one that's been unlucky in its life when a past owner was unable to look after it, or the poor animal had become an inconvenience in their life.

And so can that dog that has a wonky ear or leg, has a coat like a multi-coloured canvas of modern art, is old, blind or deaf, or perish the thought - *missing* a limb or tail. Despite possessing the ability to be sweet and loving pets, these poor animals stand little chance of getting re-homed, and live what could be a very uncertain life in a shelter.

There's absolutely nothing wrong with seeking perfection but equally there should be nothing wrong with imperfection either. Perhaps the world would be a better place if there was a little more acceptance of perceived differences, flaws or faults. The majority of the unfortunate dogs – whether pedigree or mixed-breed, that find themselves in a shelter are there for no other reason than they've been let down by humans in one way or another.

It just needs people to look beyond the "designer name" and consider each rescue dog with open minds and hearts, to see them for what they are: beautiful creatures with so much capacity to bring company, fun and love into any home.

How many Staffis, Pit Bulls, Labradors, Rotties and other pedigrees patiently wait in shelters, not to mention all those mixed-breed dogs that grow old without a home (or worse still, lose their lives)? And while they wait, people pay large amounts of money to breeders for designer dogs.

It is generally accepted that mongrel and cross-breed dogs are psychologically more stable and more physically healthy than thoroughbred dogs, with longer expected life-span. While of course it is possible to get pure-bred dogs that have perfect health and conformation, all too readily the potential medical issues of meticulously-bred pedigrees or "designer" breeds are conveniently glossed over: Pugs that can't breathe properly, Labradors and German Shepherds with dysplasia, Dachshunds with weak backs, English Bulldogs that can barely walk, let alone breed naturally, or give birth without a caesarean operation. Cocker Spaniels have developed a syndrome called Cocker Rage (strangely, this is reported to occur more commonly in golden cockers) – something that wasn't known in the breed 30+ years ago.

Where have these flaws come from if not from imprudent breeding programmes over the years? All in the name of breed aesthetics and ignored by Kennel Clubs around the world.

Not to mention those so-called pedigree dogs bought from the puppy farms, or unscrupulous or uneducated breeders that have not bred responsibly or raised the puppies to be well-adjusted and sufficiently socialised.

In buying "pedigree", one is not necessarily guaranteed perfection.

And then there are the designer dogs – the Cockapoos, Labradoodles, Dorgies, Cavoodles, Puggles and goodness knows how many more inventive descriptions. These are not separate breeds but are hybrids with a mix of more than one pedigree dog (to my mind, basically a mongrel!), that will display any combination of the characteristics of their breed genetics to a lesser or greater degree. They just come with a very hefty price tag of up to £1000 and above.

One of the large rehoming charities in the UK run a lovely TV advertisement that states that 1 in 4 domestic dogs are adopted from shelters. How great would it be if those figures actually read 3 in 4 dogs are rescues?

So much more painful to consider are all those tens of thousands of poor innocent animals put to sleep every year in shelters across the world – for no other reason than they weren't young enough, beautiful enough, they weren't the right colour, size, or breed. Or the shelter had no more space for additional dogs, or not enough volunteers to help care for them. Or no one wanted them. Such a dreadful, dreadful waste of beautiful, sweet creatures that (for the most part) were just unfortunate enough to have had fickle owners who considered them all-too-easily dispensable, but which could still have added so much joy to a home.

Owners who haul their poor pets off to a shelter for no other reason than they grew tired of them, didn't bother to train them sufficiently or they no longer fitted into their life-style, should be made to watch the trauma caused to their pet by this abandonment: how they cry pitifully in their cold kennel before eventually falling asleep, often refusing to eat or engage with the world, pining away for people who didn't care enough about them – until such time as they're dragged off for that one dreadful final "walk" … to the euthanasia room.

There may be a prevailing belief among people looking for a family pet that all rescue dogs come with problems. But they should remember that the majority of animals are there through no fault of their own, having been surrendered due to the death or illness of their owner, or the poor dog has just become "surplus to requirement" in its previous home. While a small percentage may have behavioural issues through bad breeding, past experiences, or poor ownership, far too many are there purely because of bad luck or impulsive humans and are happy, adjusted dogs that will make super pets.

It should be remembered that some of the larger rehoming agencies have the wherewithal to provide behavioural training or remedial work with those animals who may have issues, to enable them to be successfully adopted.

A genuine mongrel's genealogy may contain countless number of breeds, but they are still 100% pure dog, full of character, fun and affection. It's fascinating to try to identify the various traits a mixed-breed may display. Highly individual, they are truly unique and a one-off that no one else will have.

It is undoubtedly an adventure to adopt a rescue dog – while some may have emotional scars from traumas from their past life, the vast majority will bring huge amounts of joy to a new family, and will probably provide one of the most rewarding experiences of a dog-lover's life.

There's something so special about adopting a rescue dog; more than one adopter has told me that it's almost as if the dogs know that they're being given a second chance and give so much in return. Adopting may not suit everyone, but to see a rescue dog's dull eyes, devoid of hope, take on a special sparkle upon adoption is an experience like no other and I, for one, will be forever grateful to have been lucky enough to have been adopted by my dogs and have them share my life.

This book is designed to show off the beauty and intelligence of rescued dogs. So let's have a look at that big wide kaleidoscopic world of these wonderful creatures; enjoy their beautiful faces, eyes that hide the mysteries of their life or recount volumes of experiences. Happy, amazing dogs that can brighten up homes and lives, bringing love and companionship where needed, and occasionally rescuing their human.

The following stories are diverse – many dogs took to their new homes with little or no bother while others required varying degrees of work to try to help them to settle. A few needed incredible effort to try to help them sort out their problems.

What is so heartening is to see the extent to which those families went to try to help their troubled shelter dog, spending time with trainers or behaviourists, and really working with their pet to overcome their issues. While some are too damaged to be totally "healed", these wonderful families still love them, refuse to return them to a shelter, and have learned to live with their dog's "idiosyncrasies".

I'm sure people who adopt a pedigree from a breeder love their dogs, but those who take on a troubled rescue dog are truly adopters *extraordinaire*.

Anyone contemplating adopting from a shelter shouldn't be disheartened or put off by some of these exceptional stories and efforts; rest assured that there are still plenty of normal, adjusted dogs just waiting for their second chance of a happy home.

I should add that even though most of the following stories involve dogs adopted from Spain, this book is **NOT** designed as an advertisement for overseas adoptions. My message will always be to ADOPT – either from any of the well-known rehoming organisations or small local shelters in your home countries. Just ADOPT.

The majority of the photos included in this book are not professional nor should they be viewed as such, but are snap-shots of much-loved pets taken by adoring owners, and the majority of the stories are, for the most part, the unedited words of their proud humans.

Let's go see some beautiful dogs!

Laughing Laiko *(Photo: PeaJayz)*

PART I

Rescue Dogs' Happy Tales

She had no particular breed in mind, no unusual requirements. Except the special sense of mutual recognition that tells dog and human they have both come to the right place.

Lloyd Alexander (30 Jan 1924–17 May 2007), American author

Maria, with Nicola McNally (*Photo: PeaJayz*)

Martin: The First Night *(Photo: J. Roberts)*

Max
By Maria Glazier, UK

In 2015, my family was going through a difficult time, various things had happened and as a result my mental health was deteriorating. I had a partner, a 6-year-old daughter and we also had my partner's 9-year-old daughter (who will be referred to as J in Max's story) who came to stay with us every other weekend. I tried to continue life as normally as I could, but I was giving up. I had struggled with depression for years, but this was the worst it had ever been.

For months prior to this, my partner and daughter, Ella, had been asking if we could add a new pet to our family – they really wanted a dog. They reasoned that it would be good for me, too - sort of like a therapy dog. I was not keen on the idea, it was a big responsibility and as much as they promised to do their fair share of caring for the dog, it would all inevitably fall to me to make sure it was cared for, trained, fed and healthy and I was struggling mentally already.

I had not given them a definite answer, but I joined a few rescue groups on Facebook and dogs in need of homes would often pop up on my newsfeed as I was browsing. I would read the information given about each dog and after a few months I had not seen one that would fit our family (a good match was important as much for the dog as for us).

In October 2015, I was scrolling through Facebook as usual, when a photo of a scruffy little dog popped up. I cannot describe the feeling I had as I clicked on his photo. This little dog was described as friendly, and the post said he loved to be with people. He had long, black, messy fur, a little beard, and the most beautiful, big brown eyes. I joked that he looked like a grumpy little old man. He was found as a stray and taken to rescue shelter where he had been waiting ever since for his forever home.

As I looked at this photo, I had the strongest feeling that this was our dog. His name was Max, he was roughly 2 years old and needed a home. He was being cared for by a charity in Spain, and I immediately made enquiries – I needed to bring Max home. After a home-check, I was approved to re-home a dog and the wheels were set in motion for Max's journey to the UK.

On the 12th of November, I waited (pretty much wore a hole in the carpet, pacing) until finally at 3pm, the van carrying Max pulled up. Out came this gorgeous, scruffy, lovable little dog with whom I was already in love. I felt like I already knew him, and when I was given his passport, his estimated birth date was my birthday – talk about meant-to-be! He was led into the house when he immediately began to explore.

I had everything ready, including a quiet space I had been advised to make to allow him to settle in. He wasn't interested in this at all – in fact as soon as I opened the door to his crate he quickly disappeared from the room! Crating was clearly not for him, and this was fine with me – he made himself at home at the end of my bed and slept there every night. For the first month or so, he slept very lightly, always with one eye open. After that he began to relax more and during the first night when he fell into a deep sleep he made us jump, barking in his sleep!

We didn't even know he could bark until then – he was such a quiet, well-behaved dog. He still does this now and it makes me smile every time.

Adopting a dog from a rescue, particularly a dog I had never met, was a risk. We had no idea if he was toilet-trained or how he would behave in a completely new environment, a new country. Whatever it took, I had decided he would always be with us, if he struggled to settle, we would do everything in our power to make him happy in his forever home. As it turned out, I had worried for nothing. Max was the perfect dog from day one. He was house-trained; I can count on one hand the number of accidents he had in the house while settling in.

I threw myself into training and caring for him, and he made it easy. Now, I was no longer in the house all day, every day – my mental health had previously made me almost a recluse. I was out with Max, going on long walks, taking him to fields for training, meeting other dog owners and chatting, and I was the happiest I had been in such a long time – all thanks to this little dog.

Eight months after he arrived, I took him to an event at a local dog and cat rescue centre and he won a rosette in 'Temptation Alley' – to do this he had to walk from point A to point B – where I was standing, past all the treats that were on the floor on the way. He loves a treat, but as soon as I called his name, he ran straight past every one of them and into my arms. I was so proud of him. He was and is still my faithful little shadow.

Life continued this way, Max came on holidays, days out and on school runs. We chose dog-friendly restaurants, he was with me as much as possible. Yes! Me! The one who hadn't wanted a dog! I couldn't bear to be away from him.

He discovered ice and snow one winter, and his utter astonishment was hilarious. I remember one day I had left a water bowl in the garden, and it froze overnight. He found it in the morning and looked from the bowl to me, completely confused. I tipped the ice out and I have a video of him with this round lump of ice, pushing it and chasing it around the garden at top speed while I was laughing in the background. His personality was brilliant and his happiness infectious.

In May 2017, Max's behaviour changed towards me. My little shadow was suddenly backing off from me, preferring to be with other members of the family. When I called him, he would come, have a quick sniff and be off again. After a couple of weeks of this behaviour, I soon realised why he was so stand-offish – Max had sensed that I was pregnant, he knew before I did! We were so excited but also nervous – we had previously lost a baby during early pregnancy, so my anxiety was at an all-time high. Max was a great comfort during this time, whatever happened would happen and I knew I had him to help get us through it and make us smile.

After a few months, Max's behaviour returned mostly to normal, but things were slightly different. He was pawing at me when I sat down with him, he was barking at other dogs when on his lead on our walks. He wanted to be as close to me as he could, whenever he could. He was already an affectionate boy but became even more so. I believe he was trying to protect me and make sure I was OK during what he sensed was a big change.

Our baby, Skyla, was born in February 2018. Having spent the most of my pregnancy following me everywhere, he was no different towards the baby when we brought her home. He was never left alone with her, and we installed baby gates so that I could keep them separated if I left the room. There were a few teething problems – if a nappy or bottle was left within his reach, he would chew it which was strange for him. I Googled why he might be doing this and the only logical explanation I could find was that in the wild, animals try to destroy anything with their young's scent on so that potential predators couldn't find them. This fitted with Max's behaviour and how he was. I made sure to keep these things out of his reach.

I found myself getting frustrated when I left the changing mat out one night and saw in the morning that he had peed on it. I couldn't find a reason why my calm, toilet-trained little Max would do that. And then he became destructive if he was shut out of the room Skyla was in and I wasn't in there with her. He would chew anything he could find, it seemed to be in an effort to convey his unhappiness at being kept from the baby.

This continued for a while and as I was sat thinking during one of the night feeds having messaged the lovely lady from the rescue group for advice, I realised what a huge change this had been for him. I decided I would try to show him extra affection, make sure I took him on walks – just the two of us, and play ball with him, and basically just try to make sure he knew he was still loved and wanted, and that everything was OK. Over the next few weeks, he settled into life with his new little pack member. He was still protective – barking at any other dogs who came near  the pram on walks – but his chewing and other behaviours stopped.

As Skyla grew, he liked to sit with her while she played on the floor with her toys, and just as we had to teach him how to be around her, we had to teach Skyla the ground rules too at a young age. She learned to be gentle, not pull his little tail, and that Max's bed was off limits, that it was his space not to be invaded, especially if he was on it. In no time, they were the best of friends and still, at age 5, Skyla adores her Maxie, as she calls him.

In July 2018, we noticed another shift in Max's behaviour – however this time it was towards my partner's daughter. J was 12 years old who visited us every other weekend. She also came on holidays with us for a week in the summer. Max had been uninterested in the older two children until this point – he liked to play with them but otherwise left them alone – it was me he wanted to cuddle up to and follow around.

When J's mum dropped her off to us, he started to whine and scratch at the door until she came in. As soon as she was in, he would jump up, pawing at her and when she sat down, he sat next to her, pushing as close to her as he could, until J finally had to ask us if we could tell him to get down because he was squishing her. When the girls went to bed, he pushed their door open and jumped up on J's bed, usually waking her up. We would go and call him out, and he would then whine because he couldn't get to her.

This behaviour confused us, we couldn't work out why he was obsessive with her, he was almost frantic in his attempts to be with her. We put it down to him missing her in the two-week gaps between her visits.

That year, we took the girls and Max to our usual caravan holiday on the south coast. Max continued his unusual behaviour towards J. She had been her usual self, except I noticed she was falling over a bit more than usual, felt unwell a couple of times and had been sick. We had all had a stomach bug, so we put these things down to that, and soon returned home, dropping J off at her house with her mum and returning to normal life. In September, after more changes in J, her mum took her to see her GP, who sent them to hospital. It was there that they discovered J had a brain tumour.

At 12 years old, J had a battle on her hands and over the following weeks and months, she rose to the challenge. She had surgery, radiotherapy, and chemotherapy, along with scans, tests, transfusions and lengthy hospital stays

We were all in awe of her strength and bravery. As the tumour shrank, so did Max's obsessive behaviour towards her. He no longer fought to get to her or jumped on her bed in the night. He greeted her as he had before, and then left her alone until she wanted to throw a ball for him and play.

With Ella

It cannot be said for certain, but I truly believe that Max knew that J was unwell. How else could his strange, obsessive behaviour and subsequent disinterest after the tumour was treated be explained? He knew and he was trying to tell us the only way that he could.

As our family came to terms with all that had happened, the upheaval of having a new baby and then a horrible illness to a loved one, Max helped to keep us going. He was there for me in December 2019 when my relationship came to an end, when I wanted to give up, convinced that I couldn't be a single parent to two children who both have their individual special needs. He was there when we went into lockdown during Covid, then the next lockdown, and the next. We spent hours playing in the garden with Max joining in and making us laugh with his funny little ways.

There may have been the odd hiccup since we've had Max, I'd be wrong to say it's been 7 years of sunshine and rainbows. There is his love of eating the contents of the cat's litter tray, his initial fondness of finding sticks to chew on when on walks which led to a stomach blockage and a trip to the vet's, the hole in our old sofa when he decided to try digging through it and the times he's stolen the girls' soft toys and claimed them as his own (he does love a teddy bear). But these have all been minor things and I had to really sit and think to remember times when he has had little incidents like that.

Max, with two of his favourite girls, Skyla and Ella
(All photos: M.Glazier)

My lovely little Max is now nine years old and is sat next to me in his usual spot as I write this. He loves to chase his ball, have his belly rubbed and run around with the kids. He still loves his long walks, and is the most loving, loyal, precious dog I could ever have asked for. I knew from the moment I saw him he was meant to be a part of our family and he proved it by settling in as well as he did. He came from a rescue, so is referred to as a rescue dog.

The reality is, he rescued me.

Catalan Sheepdog Mum & Daughter, Shakira & Electra

Shakira, forever the lady *(Photos: K.Rust)*

Pablo and Best Buddy, Scooby
By Brenda Ditchfield, Spain

Two of the best dogs in the world. Wouldn't change anything about either of them. These boys love to be groomed – which is a daily task, then every three to four months they go to the groomer who makes such a fuss of them … which they love, as crazy as they are. They are the best of friends, and we love them to bits.

Big fluff-ball Catalan Sheepdog, Pablo, with his Dad *(Photo: B.Ditchfield)*

Scooby—still displaying his shelter-coat, enjoying a snuggle with Dad
(Photo: B.Ditchfield)

Becky *(Photo: B.Wehmeier)*

Miss Gracie
By Rosemarie Bryant, UK

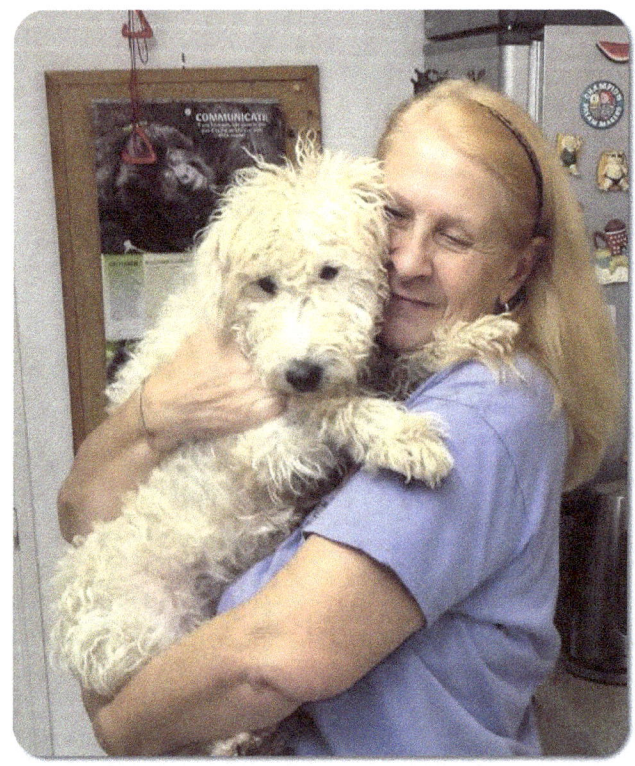

Fresh off the transporter, tired and scared

Seven years ago, Isa-Grace arrived on a van from Spain, a rescue from Asoka – thank you, Nick Moore – and the adventure began.

We've been to France and Spain, Devon to the Lake District, Wales and Scotland, all the way out to the Outer Hebrides. And, of course, your favourite places close to home: "the swan pond" (Wimbledon Common) and "the river" (Richmond Park). Countless picnics, pub lunches and dinners with your BFF's.

SECOND-HAND DOGS

(All photos: R. Bryant)

Love you, my sweet little Gracie.
Please, everyone, adopt don't shop.

Telly-Addict *(Photo: PeaJayz)*

The one absolutely unselfish friend that man can have in this selfish world, the one that never deserts him and the one that never proves ungrateful or treacherous, is his dog.

George Graham Vest (6 Dec 1830–9 Aug 1904), U.S. Politician, Lawyer

Jefferson *(Photo: C.England)*

Josie
By Gesa, UK

As a puppy, Josie was in a Spanish shelter from the end of July until November when she travelled to her new home in the UK. After my previous rescue pet passed away in September 2020, a friend contacted the adoption coordinator in the shelter and between them, it was decided that Josie would be perfect for me.

And they were so right! She is now a stunning 3-year-old girl, and an amazing companion.

Josie is a very chilled happy dog who loves to please me, I do not have to tell her off very often. She is my absolute little star! At the same time, she often makes me laugh, the way she likes to do things – for example, she loves carrying around her favourite toy (a red giraffe), or being chased by other dogs on playdates. She particularly loves to collect all her toys and bones into her bed when she retires, which looks very funny because she lies on them or has them close around her, protecting them!

Josie is also very clever as she quickly noticed that I am hearing-impaired – if she hears something unusual during the night, she needs to get out for a wee, or if I miss my vibration alarm in the morning, she wakes me up by nudging me with her cold nose until I respond. She is my very own furry alarm!

During the day, I can hear with the help of my cochlear implants, but still can miss a lot things going on around me. When Josie hears the front gate opening, she barks once and goes to the door or windows to see who is coming, but luckily doesn't bark when people pass by the house, or when the neighbours' dogs bark. So I know when I hear her barking that someone is at the door; if I don't respond, she will walk up and down in front of me until I move. If she hears someone in the back garden, she will do the same but go to the patio doors instead of the front door. It is amazing that she responds so well to sounds and guides me without any special training.

Josie didn't have any sad souvenirs of an abusive past like my previous two rescues, which helped her to settle more easily, but it still wasn't all plain and simple as there were some hurdles to overcome: things like house-training, walking on the lead, learning to play nicely with other dogs and getting her to listen to me. Some issues were worked out quickly, others took a little more time but it was definitely worth it. Josie is an amazing companion and I love her to bits. Thank you to everyone who helped to rescue her. She has settled in her Forever home and I am as lucky to have her as she is to be here.

(All photos: Gesa)

Rocco
By Robert Machin, UK

Rocco arrived in the rural Welsh Marches in the back of a transporter on a dark October night in 2017. He climbed slowly down, stiff after the long journey, trotted up to me, and I can say without exaggeration that he hasn't left my side since, other than when my work has occasionally taken me away.

He's very much a one-man dog. On those rare occasions when I'm not around he'll suffer my wife, Nicky, to feed him and take him for a walk but makes it clear this is very much second choice, something to be endured until the pack leader gets home. Nicky doesn't mind. She's no.1 with three ponies, three cats and a goat, so she's willing to allow me one loyal friend, and she loves him anyway.

We don't know much about Rocco's early life. We know he lost the tops of his ears and his tail to a farmer that had no use for him once it had been established that he only wanted to be friends with sheep, so we suspect a bit of a hardscrabble upbringing (he never talks about it). We like to think we've made up for that since he got here. I guess he has a pretty easy life – lots of walks, plenty to eat and regular treats (cheese, the occasional bit of roast chicken and the ends of our yoghurt pots are his favourites) keep him going, but we never feel taken for granted.

But Rocco's been more than a great companion. A few weeks after he arrived, I was diagnosed with a pretty serious illness that meant that much of the next few months were spent in and out of our local hospital. It was what the doctors like to call 'a tough time' but Rocco helped me through it, both just by being there, offering 24-hours-a-day company when I could barely get out of bed, and by giving me something I had to get up and do a couple of times a day. No matter how bad I felt, I could always make it to the end of our lane and back with Rocco and I'm sure that did me a power of good. I'm fully recovered now, but I credit Rocco with getting me through.

Rocco is my first dog; needless to say, I can't imagine life without one now. More specifically, I can't imagine life without him.

I often wonder: it's so easy and so rewarding to make a dog happy, how can anyone make a dog miserable?

No-ooo, Rocco! They belong to the King!!

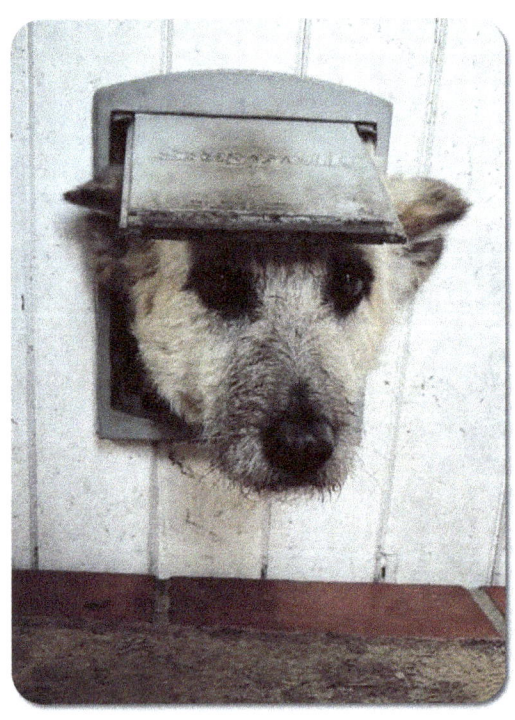

Order! Orrrrder! The Court of Rocco is now in session!

Studiously ignoring the sheep that have been patiently waiting for years for him to make his move *(All Photos: R.Machin)*

Trevor (*Photo: PeaJayz*)

Nala
Germany

No words needed

Snow-baby – on holiday in Sweden

I like cars but really hope this one isn't going to the vet!

(All photos: Philip Rose)

The greatness of a nation and its moral progress can be judged by the way its animals are treated.

Mahatma Gandhi (2 Oct 1869–30 Jan 1948), Indian Lawyer, Anti-Colonial Nationalist and Political Ethicist

Missy & Pantera *(Photo: B.Stafford)*

Missy and her best mate, Pantera, are a bonded pair of little street urchins. As the so-called owner could not be bothered to give her a name, Missy was named by caring local dog-owners. This sweet pair often tag along on walks with he and his wife, and regularly rock up at their house at meal-times, never demanding or assuming anything, sleeping in beds in the hallway of the home. As Pantera is very nervous of walking on bare tiles, a rug was put down for him to make him feel more comfortable.

Thank heavens for kind people.

The Long Journeys of Benji & Scout
By Jasmin Strothmann & Lara Naqvi, UK

Benji's Story:

Lara and I have always loved dogs, we grew up with them but we had just bought our first place together in England which happened to be an apartment, and I definitely wasn't serious about getting a dog at the time.

I remember Lara coming home and showing me a picture of this dog – "Vilko" – on Facebook, a beautiful yellow and white Staffi-mix. Lara told me that he was in Spain, approximately a year old, and he needed a home.

For those who know Lara, they will know that she had already half-planned his move to England without my even knowing, so while I debated whether or not it would be a good time, before slowly agreeing, she showed me all the forms she had filled out and what we needed to do next.

We got in touch with the dog rescue in Spain that had shared the original post of Vilko and connected with one of their volunteers. We had never adopted a rescue from abroad so she explained how it worked. First, we needed to make sure Vilko had all his injections and was microchipped. Then he needed a passport which also meant we could change his name as we just couldn't get the hang of Vilko, so that's when we named him Benji.

The rescue charity was very honest with us when it came to Benji's issues prior to adopting him, explaining that he had been muzzled due to having previously bitten someone/nipped (air-biting) and was very nervous around other dogs, when he would pull and then start biting. We decided to go ahead with the adoption as we didn't see a reason why this couldn't be worked on. So, on February 21, 2017, Benji arrived in England, using transportation recommended by the charity.

I have to admit that the first few days he was quite distant, he didn't really want to cuddle or be close to us for too long, he was a very quiet dog indoors and when we went out, seemed unsure. We had a crate but he didn't use it very much, he just lay on the floor and looked at us. So, we went for walks with him and explored everything as we weren't sure how he was around cars, cats, kids, other people …

We quickly realized that he didn't like other dogs and when he saw them would jump and toss around in the air, try and bite the leash, he would try and snap at us (unintentionally) and almost couldn't control himself. Despite being muzzled in Spain, we never muzzled him in England, we simply used a Halti which also enables us to walk in a better way without being pulled everywhere. Thankfully he was generally good around cars, loud noises and kids but realizing that Benji didn't like other dogs, pulling so hard to get to them, and then almost going into a crazy frenzy – biting and snapping – was hard.

We knew we wouldn't give up on him, so we got in touch with a dog behaviourist who spent a day with us walking Benji, who confirmed he was very anxious and needed his mind taken off those things that upset him with treats and a clicker. However, while that sounded great, the reality was that Benji wasn't that food-obsessed and having a clicker in one hand and holding a dog in the other … while safely giving him a treat … while keeping him from biting you … was just not realistic! Whenever he saw a cat, he would lunge and pull towards it, we had a real fear about what he'd do if he managed to reach it. Lara and I realized that this was another thing that would need time and patience.

So, we put the clicker away and went out to the local parks every day, we walked, we socialized and taught him the commands he needed and when it was safe to do so, we booked an enclosed park and let him off his leash.

Dreaming of Santa

Over time, he settled in a lot more, he grew to "like" us, he cuddled up, he would play with his toys and even take very peaceful naps. We knew we had to be confident in this and let him know that we would protect him – but that we were also The Boss. We had treats with us for every walk and when he did things that we thought were great, always rewarded him. We played a lot of hide-and-seek with him which taught him to always come back for us, and to look for us. We had to tire Benji out before bringing him around other dogs and eventually settled him into a doggy day-care with other dogs, went on long road trips to Germany with him and even let him meet a cat (when he was perfectly fine).

Now seven years on, Benji has just turned 8 years old. He goes to the park where he runs off-leash and plays a lot of fun games with a ball or frisbee. When he's on-leash, he might have the odd moment where he pulls when he sees a Doberman but is now generally a pleasure to walk with.

There was no quick fix to any of his problems except for patience, being calm, assertive, and consistent. Benji is the most intuitive dog we've ever had and extremely loyal which he shows when the postman comes (which is a work in progress!). But we can't imagine not having him and still can't believe that he was dumped somewhere and was possibly treated badly. We are currently working on walking him without the Halti as he is more confident now and knows what we expect, as well as our improved ability to read his body language and behaviour.

With human mums, Lara & Jasmin, Benji is now an international traveller

Play-date with former Casa del Sol resident, Lucas

Scout's Story:

Which brings us to Scout. We weren't in a position to have another dog but when we travelled to Spain in 2019 for a holiday, we found ourselves at a local horse ranch where we saw a little puppy getting smacked by local boys; immediately we marched over to tell the boys off and demanded they hand us over the puppy.

We spent the day by the pool and somehow so did the puppy, she didn't leave our side once during the 5 hours we were there, and we were starting to wonder who she belonged to. The owner of the ranch told us that she was probably about 4 months old and had been dumped there when she was a week old, but no one really looked after her and they had named her "Rose".

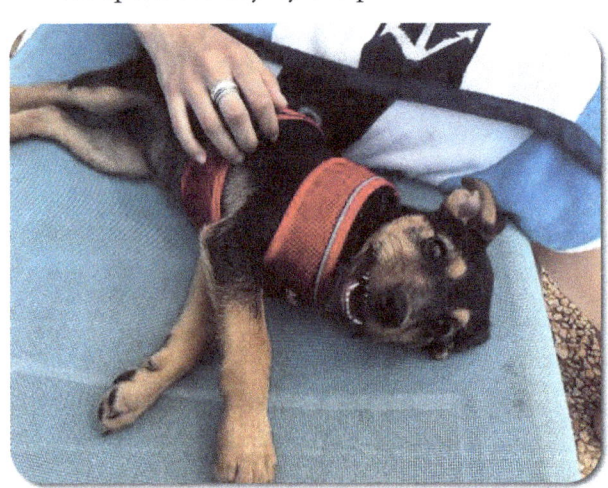

Totally sucked in by those soft little puppy eyes and how loyal she seemed, we made arrangements to adopt her. We spoke to the ranch-owner who had bought her some food and a red harness which was too big and after some negotiations, we made sure our doggy day-care back home was okay with another dog and then got in touch with the rescue charity, PAPS, which helped us to find her a foster-home so she could have all her injections and be ready to come to England, since we were only staying for another two days.

We then wrapped the little bundle up and took her straight to the vet to get her initial injections, microchip and passport (don't worry, we did check if she had a microchip already). And her name was now Scout. A foster family were happy to look after her until she could come to us, which was roughly 6 weeks later.

When we originally met Scout, she was smooth-coated, quiet, shy, and playful. When the van arrived to drop her off at our home, we found that she had grown a little, her coat was thicker and more wiry – and she now had a small beard. Over the following weeks she grew bigger than Benji and was extremely fast – she and Benji both enjoy exercise and have great fun playing in the park together.

Scout seemed very scared of most things (people, animals, children) and barked a lot when she saw them – we are still working on these issues with her, and trying to socialize her as much as possible. She goes to doggy day-care and gets plenty of walks in the park, on- and off-leash, which she enjoys. She has yet to meet a cat up close but whenever she sees one she barks like crazy, so that's something else to slowly tackle.

We are trying to teach her confidence and don't shy away from walks to help to socialize her; just the other day she was able to walk past a few cats without barking! She has settled in very well and is a big part of our family. She's the most affectionate dog and really loves Benji. It's been over 4 years since we got her and we have seen a lot of progress, and wouldn't change anything. Both our rescues are the perfect dogs for us.

Best buddies

Cute as a button!
(All photos: J.Strothmann/L.Naqvi)

Nina *(Photo: PeaJayz)*

Milo and Rosie *(Photo: E. Redfern)*

Nita – The Poochie Princess (Part 1)
Rob & Julia Roberts: Our Story, Spain

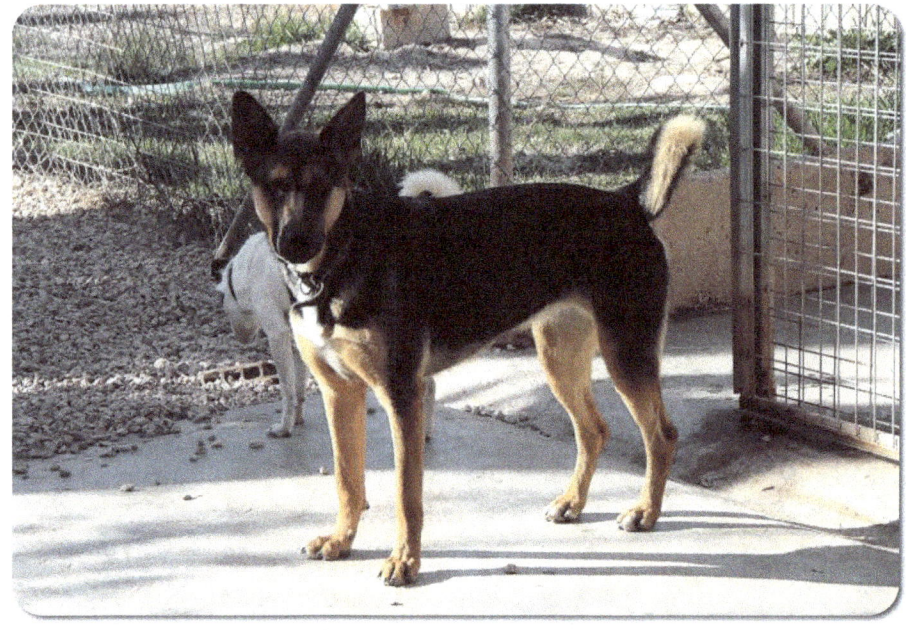

Found on a local golf resort after being dumped at 3 months old with her sister, Cilla. Sadly Nita had to wait a long time in the shelter, enduring a couple of failed adoptions along the way (through no fault of hers) before finally finding her Happy Every After.
(Photo: PeaJayz)

My husband wanted a dog (he had them growing up). I did not. I didn't dislike them, I simply had no experience.

One day a sweet little dog wandered into our garden and sat under a tree whilst Rob was gardening. He chatted to her and I observed their interaction. Later the dog went home (we have seen her since and know she's fine).

All night I lay awake thinking that it was only my reluctance and fear stopping us. The house was sorted so we could give a dog a nice home.

SECOND-HAND DOGS

The next day: "Maybe we could get a dog. We have the time and the space. A dog would like this house," I said.

And so our search began.

A week or so later we arrived at a local shelter and met all the lovely helpers there.

I wanted a small/medium-sized girl. Little did I know Rob had other ideas. He had already been on the shelter's Facebook page and simply asked to meet Nita. Off we went for a walk with this gigantic dog and that was it, Rob was in love.

Me? ... I was terrified.

"Rob, she is your dog, so these are my rules:

1. Not on the furniture
2. Most definitely not on the bed
3. Fed outside
4. She will have to go to kennels when we are away
5. Oh, and I don't really want to pick up poo."

All I can say is, I was a complete idiot.

Of course, I pick up poo.

Nita is fed in the kitchen because mummy doesn't want flies to disturb her whilst she's eating.

We have lovely friends to look after Nita in their house when we are away.

As for the bed, see for yourselves.

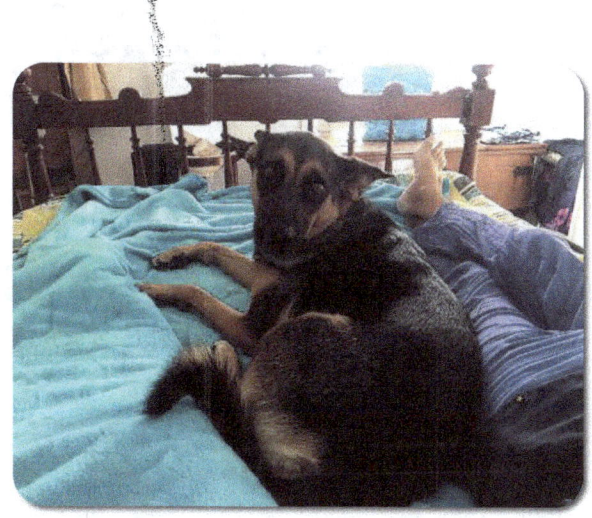

I love this dog, my Poochie Princess, with all my heart. She is a comical, playful, intelligent girl who gives us all her love and devotion and I cannot remember our lives without her in it.

I appreciate this has been a long story but I wanted to say, don't hesitate like I did.

Thank you to the rescue charity for looking after our girl, they have been fantastic.

Thank you for our Nita 🖤🐾🐾xx

(All Photos: J.Roberts)

He is your friend, your partner, your defender, your dog. You are his life, his love, his leader. He will be yours, faithful and true, to the last beat of his heart. You owe it to him to be worthy of such devotion.

Unknown Author

Rondie with Logan *(Photo: L.Allen)*

Tommy 1
Spain

(Photo: PeaJayz)

Tommy came in to the shelter with his little brother but unlike him, he struggled to find a home, being continually overlooked. While his brother had a lovely, long waving tail, poor Tommy had been born without one. It may well have been this

that put people off, which was such a shame as all they could see was the space where a tail should have been, instead of his sweet, kind nature.

Tommy had to wait far too long before someone finally fell in love with him, and applied to adopt him. And Tommy hasn't disappointed. Right from the start, he's thrived in his Forever home, Mum Jean discovered that he was an affectionate, quiet little fella that had never seen a toy before so he had to learn how to play. Jean says "He particularly enjoys his walks and lots of cuddles. We love him to bits and couldn't be without him".

Snug as a bug in a rug!

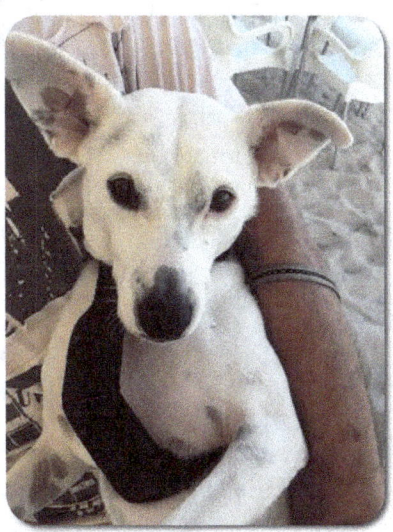

A cuddle is good at any time of the day
(All other photos: Jean Rose)

Gina
Germany

(Photo: K.N.)

(All other photos: I.Horn)

A Special Breed

I have affection for my friends, a different breed 'tis true
I've shown the many skills I have when given just a clue
I learnt quite quick the signs they make with noises they combine
But sometimes feel they find it hard to get in tune with mine

Still, on the whole, I do my job and guard the home with pride
I've come to terms with what they lack and take it in my stride
If I'm fed well and kept quite warm, I'll listen when one talks
I'll play with children and enjoy taking the adults for walks

But there are many more of us who are of similar breed
Who get the training for the work that countries often need
For it's been found with senses far beyond their human scope
That with my nose I smell much more than they could ever hope

In war zones and at airports, even searching in the snow
With partner right beside me there is no place I won't go
Policemen know that I'll be there before them when they chase
Those criminals who seem to think they can outrun my pace

All farmers need me to assist the sheep to find their way
Back to the fold and to ensure they do not go astray

SECOND-HAND DOGS

The trips to hospitals when I see the young and older folk
Give me a thrill especially when my fur they love to stroke

I'm multi-skilled and give my best to those who cannot see
And others who would not get by without some help from me
Then if it's found I respond well to showing all I know
I then become a canine star of film and TV show

As you can see, I'm everywhere whenever there is need
To do my best and fit right in is every canine's creed
So if you treat me kindly then on this you can depend
I'll offer you companionship and be your truest friend

©2020 P. Brown

Mickey – We Were Sent An Angel

By Julia Rahner and Norman Frach, Germany

The story of our adoption begins well before we knew Mickey.

During our holiday in the mountains we met the Chair of PAPS (Germany), Kerstin. We immediately got on so well and talked a lot about our dogs. At that time, we only had our mixed-breed dog, Paula.

A few months passed, during which we repeatedly admired the photos of the new arrivals in the shelter, Casa del Sol, on Facebook. In the Spring of 2018, Mickey went into the care of Yvonne, the President of the Spanish section of the charity, and she lovingly cared for the old gentleman and his woes.

SECOND-HAND DOGS

We fell in love immediately and decided to adopt him despite his limitations – sight impairment and especially, his deafness. He arrived in Germany in Autumn 2018 and immediately found a place in all our hearts. From the very first day in his new home, he was fun for everyone, he walked extremely well on a leash, and our Paula immediately became his great love.

He was a very smart little guy that learned to communicate with us and live a carefree dog-life in spite of his hearing and sight issues. He not only enchanted our family with his charm, but was always popular with everyone on his walks.

Unfortunately, Micky had only eight short months with us, his old age and ill-health bothered him and at about 13 years old, we had to let him go.

Today we hope that he looks down on us from heaven and thinks of the beautiful times we spent together.

Above all, we miss and love him to this day.

(All photos: N.Frach/J.Rahner)

From Mickey to Polly – A World of Difference

By Julia Rahner and Norman Frach

Mickey and Paula

After Mickey lost his battle with cancer on 22 June 2019 and we buried him with dignity, Paula remained as our only dog.

At first, we told ourselves that we would never get another dog. Norman casually mentioned: "If we do take another dog, then please let it be another Paula …"

It came out of the blue: just a few weeks later, a new post from Casa del Sol popped up on Facebook and hit me like a blow to the face. In fact, a dog had arrived at the Casa, whose face looked identical to our Paula. At that very moment it was obviously clear that this dog belonged to us. On that day the dog was called Anita, but it wasn't long before we finally reserved her and renamed her Polly.

Polly-Power

On 7 September 2019, Polly came to Germany with another girl, Kylie, who joined Team Litfin (you'll be reading about them later).

Polly gave her first kisses as soon as we left the van, and we just melted. On the other hand, she was not so friendly towards our dog Paula … over the course of the next few weeks, it was more like love at second sight.

Polly showed us from day one how much power she had within, fearless, loaded with energy and happy to face each new task. She quickly learned the basic commands: sit, down, stay, paw, come, no, etc, and also showed a natural talent for jogging, cycling and man-trailing.

It seemed as if she was literally waiting to discover the world. She even overcame her initial fear of water and now happily splashes around with Paula. Slowly but surely, she also learned to get along with stranger dogs; at first, she was looking for a riot, but now she can even walk in a big pack and is improving her social behaviour.

She came to Germany as a rough diamond, and is slowly growing up and turning into a cuddly dog – and a beautiful gem.

Every week we notice how her character positively strengthens, and she has settled more and more into our family.

Polly and Paula

(All photos: Julia Rahner/Norman Frach)

Any man with money to make the purchase can become a dog's owner. But no man – spend he ever so much coin and food and tact in the effort – may become a dog's Master without the consent of the dog. Do you get the difference? And he whom a dog once unreservedly accepts as Master is forever that dog's God.

Albert Payson Terhune (21 Dec 1872–18 Feb 1942), American author, dog breeder, and journalist

Two Claudias *(Photo: Courtesy of Just Moments Photography)*

Doraimon

(Photo: PeaJayz)

Found as a young stray of approximately 13 months in a local town, Doraimon arrived in the shelter in July 2016. Despite the charity's relentless efforts to find him a new home he remained in their kennels for over 4 years before finally, someone noticed him, and he was taken out on trial by potential adopters with a view to adoption.

Sadly, he managed to escape from his new home within a few days, and was found dead by the roadside four days later to the heartbreak of the shelter volunteers.

The Wolfman Cometh to England
By J. Clothier, UK

We first met "Wolfie" in October 2014 at a rescue centre near San Javier, a town in Spain's Murcia region. He was 10 months old at the time and had spent his whole life there having been dumped with his sister shortly after birth. He was reclusive at the centre and could usually be found under a pile of old timber in the grounds.

Initially we thought he was an Alsatian/Corgi mixture albeit with noticeably short legs! We were looking to adopt again having lost our beautiful German Shepherd cross earlier that year and with wife Chris having been brought up with Corgis, he seemed simply perfect.

He certainly knew how to put on a show, as if we were not smitten as soon as we laid eyes on him. His behaviour was perfect on the day we met – lots of cuddles and walks and even a demonstration that he was "cat" friendly.

We were asked to take him to our little house for a couple of days to check that this was the right adoption for the wee lad. It was a magical 48 hours – he was a delight and apart from vomiting in the hire car, did not put a foot wrong. I do not think he had ever seen car headlights before and he could not take his eyes off them when on the first night we sat outside our local bar.

A week later we were together again in England after he was couriered from Southern Spain to the Midlands where we lived at the time. For a dog prone to vomiting in a car, it must have been a gruelling journey – he certainly took to his new bed like a duck to water. He had never been house-trained but there were no "mistakes" as he quickly settled in.

We quickly realised that he was neither German Shepherd nor Corgi, although to this day other dog walkers still ask if that is the mixture. He was (and still is) tunnel-visioned when he sniffs a squirrel or rabbit which led us to look more closely at what breed he really was. Eventually it became clear that most of him is "Podenco Maneto", a recognised breed of Andalusian hound known for its hunting capabilities, particularly for smaller animals!

So, it's fine to let him off the lead in a dog-safe environment but you cannot let your concentration lapse for a moment.

In the early days he was petrified of passing traffic and of all things, dustbins. But step by step we overcame both and he is now quite happy to plod around the local streets. Having said that, he is the reason we usually walk around the huge reservoirs near our home in the Yorkshire Dales on a daily basis. He is a joy to

walk and what better fun than to scare the ducks in the water!

He loves his home – unfortunately too much! From the word go he was territorial so far as the house was concerned and the move to North Yorkshire to what for a year or so was a building site, exacerbated the problem. To say he is a good guard dog whilst in the house is an understatement – quite a ferocious little demon!

That, of course, is what you cannot possibly know when you take a rescue dog, especially one that has had no maternal training whatsoever. We have tried everything to keep him calm when people knock at the door or have the audacity just to walk or drive pass by. Nothing works.

On the other hand, we can take him anywhere and he is a good as gold – he particularly likes pubs and cafes. Coming home to his smiling face and wagging tail is wonderful. He plays very happily with his "rugby" balls which can last anything between one week and two months. His health has been first-class although he has had a few problems with sores on his rear legs – when we put the cream on, he raises whichever leg to help, which is quite endearing.

He is good in the car but the vomiting I referred to earlier was a problem overcome (eventually) by putting him in the passenger seat foot-well where he will sleep all day. Prior to that discovery it was an £6 tablet every time we went driving for more than 10 minutes! He has also developed a taste for the music of Jim Reeves which is a must in the car and whenever we leave him on his own in the house.

He needs the company of other dogs and loves nothing more than the "chase". We take him to a doggie day centre twice a week where he is a firm favourite with the other inmates and the staff. He also gets a shampoo there from time to time – little legs and mud do not mix.

SECOND-HAND DOGS

There is no doubt that "Wolf" (as he is now known) pushes the boundaries but he is a part of our lives and it feels good to know we have given him another chance after his baptism of fire to the world. He has his problems but we love him to bits, there is a bond between the three of us which is priceless.

(All photos: J. Clothier)

Wilma – Fastest Tail in the West
UK

Little Wilma made the giant step from a desolate, sun-baked field in Spain to a loving home in the UK.

Local residents don't know how long she had been abandoned but she was spotted in a ditch together with a little puppy, Bear, by Nicola, a local dog-groomer. Bear surrendered easily to his rescuers but little Wilma proved a much tougher prospect. Nicola fed her twice a day for 2 weeks, even managing to catch her twice but the little rascal managed to scarper both times. Finally, with the help of another lady who tempted Wilma with lasagne, she was caught and quickly whisked away to safety in a shelter. She was then fostered by the rescue charity's President who looked after her to build her up. Both she and Bear were in a poor state, matted coats, badly nourished and both covered in ticks and fleas. The vet estimated that Wilma was 2 and that she'd definitely had pups, leading to much debate as to whether Bear was actually one of them – an argument never resolved.

Nicola's sister-in-law Catherine came to visit and as her mum had already adopted Gracie, she was brought to the shelter. Catherine was absolutely adamant that she would not have a terrier-type dog … until she saw her, and was immediately besotted – and Wilma was soon wending her way to her Forever Home in the UK.

As soon as she arrived in the house, it was like she knew she was "home", she got on with the family's two dogs amazingly well, and indeed struck up a special friendship with Monty, who became her best buddy. Sometimes they're even spotted on the sofa, kissing!

It took her some time to lose her timidity. But she is now repaying her new family with her abundant love and happiness, displayed by a tail that whips from side to side in a continual blur. It basically hasn't stopped wagging for the past 5 years!

A very special little rescue
(All Photos: C.Demir)

The family were initially concerned about how she'd fit in as they have a little special needs boy who is also deaf, but Wilma is the only one of their dogs that responds to him when he calls her and is "so lovely and wonderful with him". She adores him, keeping an extra special eye out for him.

Lana (Photo: Ana Perez Escudero)

I hope to be the kind of person my dog thinks I am.

Unknown Author

Cuper *(Photo: Lis.Knight)*

Hobo – From Drifter to Sofa-Surfer
Spain

Hobo met me on our resort where he'd wandered after being abandoned. He and his female pal survived by raiding the community bins, hunting fresh protein via the copious rabbits on the golf course, and dining particularly well on fillet steak and the *haute cuisine* left-overs from the local restaurant. The boy wasn't starving by any stretch of the imagination but he still looked so miserable with sad, dejected eyes, devoid of any hope, that just twanged on my heartstrings.

I began to leave a bowl of water outside our front gate, and a plate of kibble in the evenings and it wasn't long before he was waiting for me on the other side of the road, virtually tapping his claws off the concrete if I dared be late. A little wag of his long tail signalled his gratitude.

To make a long story short, the water and food brought him back every evening. A night-time tryst with a nubile young Staffi around the corner led to his arrest by the *Guardia Civil* landing him in the dreaded local Kill Station – where he had only 4 days before he'd get The Needle. Desperation and fear add a great deal of urgency to one's actions and with the help of a lovely Spanish lady, we located the *Perrera*, paid the fine to break him loose and Hobo returned home to us.

It took me about 2 weeks to persuade him to come into the house which eventually he did, whereupon he proceeded to "bless" everything that didn't move until he was content that the house smelled of 'him'.

The idea was still to find him a home (much as it was becoming more and more difficult to contemplate parting with him). A man in Sweden was desperate to have him (too difficult to do the home-check there, and I couldn't bear the thought of Hobes being stuffed into a box for the plane journey). He was all lined up to go to a lovely home with an older lady in the UK (until I nixed the adoption for fear that he might be too strong and pull her over), until finally a good friend decided that she'd love to have him.

My partner declared him as the "defining member of our family." High praise indeed from someone who never wanted a dog!

To my mind, this was perfect because, living only 20 minutes away, selfishly I'd still get to see him regularly to follow his progress. The only slight problem was her beloved cat, Princess Tinkerbell. So Hobo and I duly visited the house when he and the cat studiously ignored each other, not a flicker of interest from Hobo, so we reckoned it would be ok.

The night before he left was traumatic for us, especially when my partner expressed the thought that perhaps we should have kept him. Too late to finally come to that conclusion, he was told, and Hobo was duly brought over to his new home. He got a snazzy new collar, toys of his own, a new bed (so small we had to decide which paw would fit in!), and a new name: Hobey Kinobe. His future was looking bright, especially as he was still ignoring the Princess.

He loved his new abode, and my friend and her partner adored him, enjoying taking him off for his walks along the Rio Seco, and the funny little things he did during the day. He enjoyed snoozing by their lovely pool, and as Princess Tinkerbell and he were tolerating each other, his destiny looked set. His new mum did scent transference between the two of them so they'd each get used to the other's scent, with the idea being that they'd eventually become best buddies.

At 11 o'clock on the night before Hobo's ownership was going to be transferred into my friend's name, my mobile pinged with a new text. Messages that late at night invariably are never good, and this one revealed a disaster. Hobo had been found with their beloved Tinkerbell in his cavernous jaws – he'd caught her coming out of the room where his food was stored and pounced on her. Fortunately, she was unhurt, if more than a bit put out by this indignity. But Hobo had received his marching orders. He was OUT.

As much as I was unhappy that he'd attacked Tinkerbell, my partner and I were both beyond thrilled to have him back with us, and that was that. His name went back to Hobo and he was officially HOME.

Hobo slipped easily into the rhythm of our home, quickly settling back into life with our "girlies" – two female rescue dogs. I can't say either was too thrilled to have him enter their lives as the little one feared his lumbering bulk, and blondie was upset that she was no longer Number 1 as he very adeptly put her in her place when she was getting "above her station". But all in all, they got on well with no major problems.

We reckon that he's an Irish Wolfhound-cross with his rough salt-and-pepper coat, long distinguished eye-brows like those of a sergeant-major, and wolfie beard. The vet thought he was 7 years old when he found us, an Irish Wolfhound "expert" thought he was 5 – so take your pick! I'm really hoping it's the expert who is correct which may mean that we may have him longer.

He has a "snaggle tooth" that pokes out the side of his mouth and the rest of his teeth are worn down to stubs as if he'd been chewing on stones. On the same side of his face, it looks like he suffered some kind of accident resulting in a cut that had left a V on his lower eye-lid. Some of his many mysteries! He's got a wonky knee, his hind legs are knock-kneed so his toes point out sideways and he walks a bit like Charlie Chaplin. But for us, these "flaws" are very much a part of him, adding a character that make us love him all the more.

He sleeps with his eyes open which is very strange as one never knows if he's snoozing or not. Handy for him as there's no way that anyone can sneak up on him unawares.

He's also very calm in the house, loving, and gently snores his way through fireworks or thunder-storms. The man is just amazing!

Like so many other dogs, Hobo is a total wuss when it comes to the vet clinic, with each visit having to be planned in as meticulous detail as any military operation – all staff are on stand-by to help and everyone holds their breaths when he steps in the room. He is an imposing figure – 49kgs of stubborn, furious fear-fuelled indignation when faced with impending treatment. And don't even dream of touching his tootsies – which adds even a simple dew-claw manicure to the list of perilous military action.

One thing he does love is his trip to his groomer, Nicola. In the beginning he used to fret when I left him behind – understandable for a dog that had previously been dumped, but then he discovered the joys of 3 hours of pampering. He falls asleep under Nicola's ministering hands, then happily snuggles up to her little Pug that has adopted him like a much-loved big brother.

He turned into a lethal scourge of the local cats – fortunately, we're not a cat household but he's certainly kept our garden a cat-free zone, making it easy to identify any visiting cats to the property as either tourists, or mentally deranged.

He suffered initially from a tiny bit of separation anxiety, fortunately nothing more than removing things from the table and throwing them around, or a book nibbled around the edges, but this has disappeared over time. He still likes to keep an eye on either myself or my partner, sometimes following us if we move from one room to another.

Hobo was a Thief Supremo (blame lies ultimately with us!). We've lost 2 fillet steak dinners and a couple of chicken breasts to his hungry jaws. Fortunately, he's now happy to wait in the kitchen for scraps during dinner preparation. A young visitor made the fatal mistake of leaving her much-anticipated smoked salmon lunch on the floor while she collected something from the kitchen, only to find it gone upon her return, with a very happy Hobo licking his chops. The same young lady also lost a large bar of chocolate – a present for her father – from where it had been secreted in her suitcase, which reappeared the following morning as a large chocolate-smelling pile of poo! Thankfully, the thief didn't suffer any medical ill-effects from this grand larceny.

But all of this pales into insignificance with the joy and love that he's brought into our home. After the time it took to persuade him to enter our house, now, we can hardly get him out – not even to do his evening potty! He loves the new sofa, scrambling up and getting himself as close as he can to myself or my partner, laying a rough paw against our legs, enjoying whatever attention he can get. And he warms up our bed for a few hours in the evening before we retire for the night.

I love the way his back feet dance with joy when I scratch an erogenous zone at the top of his hips, when he points his nose heavenward with sheer pleasure. Two of my favourite sounds are to hear his big contented sigh as he settles in for a sofa-snooze, and the little moans he makes when I'm stroking him – which for me, is what taking in a rescue dog is all about.

A boy's never too big to have a cuddly toy

(All photos: PeaJayz)

I never cease to be amazed that after all Hobo has been through in his life, he is still so trusting, loving and kind-natured. It's hard to define what he has brought to our lives, but we both love him to distraction and thank whoever it was who dumped him, for allowing him to come into our lives.

Pepper's Story
By Paul Kendall, UK

In the autumn of 2018, my wife Sharon and I were on our second long-stay holiday in our caravan in Spain, on a lovely site in Pilar de la Horadada. We had with us our 10-year-old black Labrador, Charlie, my retired Police search dog who went absolutely everywhere with us. Due to my job as a search dog handler for the Police, we had always had two dogs, but unfortunately we had lost Lily, our Springer Spaniel, to cancer in April that year.

We had thought about rehoming a rescue dog whilst in Spain and by chance one day we met Yvonne, the amazing lady from PAPS, who was with five dogs in a park by our campsite. We had a great chat with her, told her about Charlie who was obviously with us at the time, and mentioned that we would love a rescue dog. She told us about PAPS and left us one of her cards.

A few weeks later, at the end of November, we drove to the PAPS shelter and met Yvonne who showed us around the kennels. Sharon and I were taken to the main kennel area and saw what must have been a dozen lovely large dogs of various colours and shapes. They all ran up to the gate to say hello before running off in various directions. As we looked down to the bottom of the gate there remained the cutest little dog that Yvonne told us was called Peque and was a particular favourite of hers, though I expect all the dogs were her favourite! Sharon asked to see Peque closer up, and a few seconds later the little dog was in my wife's arms and from that moment on this beautiful little lady was always going to be coming home with us.

We renamed her Pepper on the way to the vet's to have her pet passport transferred over, and she spent time in our camper van getting to know Charlie. That was interesting as Charlie thought he was going to remain an "only child" after the loss of our Lily. Charlie tolerates Pepper, whereas Pepper idolises our big old Lab. She spent her first night with us in our caravan, sleeping soundly at the bottom of our bed. To say she settled in well the first few days is a bit of an understatement as she took to life with the three of us without any problems.

We brought Pepper back home to England at the beginning of December and our little dog from the sunshine soon had her first experience of a frosty, cold Sussex morning. She tore across the fields near our home as if to say: "If I run really fast the cold won't get to me!" Pepper met our daughter who instantly fell in love with her, but she was also surprised that Sharon and I had rescued such a small dog. Actually, compared to Charlie she is so small, but seeing the two of them together is a wonderful sight.

Our Gang of Four returned to Spain in January having driven down through France via the Newhaven ferry. Once back on our site we had a near-fatal experience with Pepper. Sharon and I had gone for a bike ride and left our dogs asleep in our caravan. Charlie being an old boy is an Olympic Gold Medal winner when it comes to sleeping, whereas Pepper obviously fancied a look around her home on wheels. We had neglected to close the door to the bedroom and our little dog decided to climb onto the bed, why shouldn't she as she spends half her life on it? and found some extra strong painkillers on a shelf. She helped herself to 8 of these, but fortunately proceeded to throw up most of them. When we got home soon after, we realised what had happened and rushed her to the vet's where she was given wonderful care, and medication and made a full recovery. Since then, everything is locked safely away from an enquiring little mind.

That scare aside, life with this gorgeous little girl has been a dream. She is a brilliant house-dog, great to walk off the lead with a lovely recall, and gets on well with other dogs, though she sometimes gets defensive when other dogs run up to us. Although small, she is quite 'leggy' and goes for a run with Sharon and I around

the countryside where we live. She loves her long walks with Charlie, and will sometimes even join him for a swim in the Cornish sea where we are currently staying for three months as we have a seasonal job on a campsite near St Ives.

People often ask us what breed she is and I tell them she is whatever she wants to be, a proper little mongrel. I also sometimes call her our little *Mestizo Español* (literal translation "Spanish half-blood"), to confuse folk as it sounds quite exotic. She loves her dinner time, eats carrots and broccoli stalks as a treat, and twice a week gets a tin of sardines in olive oil mixed in with her food. Her sleeping arrangements are varied as she sometimes sleeps on the sofa, sometimes on our bed, sometimes on Charlie's bed and every so often, on her own bed.

We have had Pepper nearly five years now and neither Sharon or I could imagine life without her. We are fortunate to only need seasonal work so spend a lot of our time in our touring caravan and our little dog is a perfect companion for us and for our Charlie, though he may disagree.

In fact, I'm not entirely sure he didn't give her those tablets!

(All photos: P. Kendall)

Best friends from across Europe: Verity (left), rescued in 2019 from Bosnia, and Dexter made his way from Spain to join her in 2020 *(Photo: A Jones)*

Rosie's Story
By Mama Donna, USA

For years of my life, I was a crazy cat lady, at one time having as many as five. As my feline family began to dwindle, I mentioned to a friend that when I got down to only one cat, I MIGHT like a small dog. I had always had a dog growing up and knew how much they had to offer. When that day came that only Mama Mia was left, my friend began sending emails from Noah's Ark Rescue, where she had adopted her dogs. I always checked them out but nothing really caught my eye or heart until I saw little Baby Ruth!

Baby Ruth, a little 6-month-old Dachshund/Chihuahua mix (Chiweenie), had been found in a ditch with her back legs and pelvis broken after either being run over by a car or thrown from a moving car. The details of her rescue are murky but it seems that a young man found her in a ditch and took her to his grandmother, who did not want to help. The grandmother then tried to take her to Animal Control in her area. Animal Control would not take her because

Baby Ruth was not found in their area. There were just a million excuses for not helping this severely injured little puppy. Finally, an ad was placed on Craig's List. A rescue group saw it and came to the aid of Baby Ruth. Funds were raised, but nowhere near what was needed. It was at this point that Noah's Ark stepped up. Noah's Ark Rescue deals with animals having severe health or abuse issues, and they do amazing work.

To make matters worse, when Baby Ruth was finally examined, she was found to have a life-threatening hernia. Baby Ruth's life was literally ticking away by the second. The hernia was right next to the Inferior Vena Cava, which returns blood to the heart from the lower part of the body. If the hernia had been any closer, Baby Ruth would have bled to death immediately. As it stood, the pressure from the hernia alone could have caused the Vena Cava to stop functioning properly. Baby Ruth had to be stabilized before emergency surgery could be done. The hernia was filled with her liver and guts. Her surgeon said it was the largest hernia she had ever seen for a dog her size.

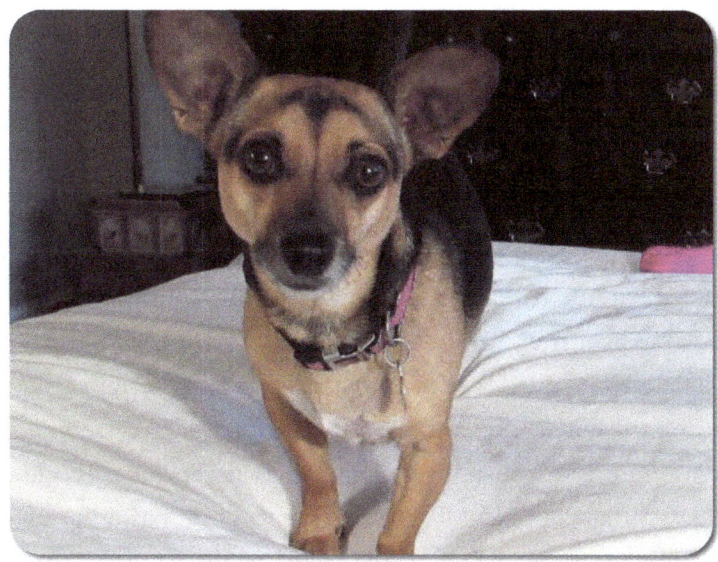

Her surgery and therapy happened slowly over the next few months with Noah's Ark posting photos of it all. I found myself hopefully following every step and seeing this small dog with a bold spirit fight her way back. As she became stronger, they announced that she was only a few weeks away from being adoptable and they were surprised that there had been no applications! I remember sitting there and thinking, "Am I ready for the responsibility of a little dog?" "Am I going to let this little girl slip away?" And then I thought, ***obviously this was meant to be***! So, I submitted the application as soon as I possibly could and was shortly informed that the adoption had been approved. I was now the mom of a little dog I'd never even seen in person! What could possibly go wrong?

Baby Ruth became Rosie and I tried to figure out what to do with a little doggie. She was mostly house broken, so that wasn't a big issue. In the beginning, she seemed hyper and chewed everything. I didn't know what to do, so I just kept things picked up off the floor and went about figuring out our relationship. Miraculously, about 4 – 6 weeks in, she just stopped chewing things. I always thought she suddenly realized that she was finally home, safe, and everything was going to be alright. She could finally settle down and relax after all she had been through.

As any dog owner will tell you, the best way to get to know your neighborhood is to have a dog, especially if she is like Rosie! She never meets a stranger, greeting everyone with loving enthusiasm. Sometimes before being allowed to continue our walk, I have to actually take her over to neighbors and tell them that Rosie wants to say hello! It warms my heart to see her make people smile … and, she knows how to work a crowd. She will go from one person to the other until I coax her away.

One of my neighbors has two grandchildren whom they frequently keep one night a week for parents to have a date night. If they see us out walking as they drive in, we can expect them to be in the driveway when we get home for a visit with Rosie. The girls decided that they would each make a sign – one was a drawing of two little girls with a dog and the other just read "We are here". When the laminated signs are posted on their grandparent's front door, Rosie and I are to stop in for a few minutes of play! That's the affect Rosie has on people. I tell folks that she has ADD – Affection Deficit Disorder! She can't give or receive enough love. That's my Rosie!

One thing you have to know about Rosie is that she does not do anything half-measure – everything is full tilt! If I throw a ball, it's a full run with a little slide to fetch it. If the doorbell rings, it's a flying jump from whatever she is on and a mad dash. Sadly, this has taken its toll and as she approaches eight years of age. She is beginning to have back issues as is common with dogs with long spines and short legs. We are seeing the doctors who dealt with her earlier injuries and doing everything we can to keep her healthy and happy. I monitor her closely and restrict her jumping as much as possible. I even have a large tag on her leash that says "Back Issues, pet gently". There was one that said "No Petting", but I knew Rosie wouldn't stand for that! She is just a little love sponge and she needs that interaction, and her love for others gives me as much pleasure as it does her!

That said, dog lovers know that we receive far more from them than we are ever able to return. Their love and devotion are pure and unconditional. I tell friends that Rosie is the best thing I've done for myself in a long time, and I mean that. I'm so glad I didn't let that little girl with the big ears slip away. She brings joy to my life every single day. I love you, Rosie!

And some messages from Rosie's friends …

Tippy A:

I'll bet a common adjective from Rosie's two legged friends will be "sweet" and boy, is she ever! She loves to have visitors and plays until she runs out of steam. She allows us to rub her tummy as long as we want to and lies down close when we stop. What a love of a pup! My fondest recollections involve walking the beach with Rosie. We have a special beach where we are able to let her off-leash to run free. She wastes no time in rushing along the sand, scattering birds, circling, looking back to be sure her Mama is nearby. She smiles and frolics during her chance to be leash-less and brings us such joy to watch! Love this sweet girl.

Bogey: Is that a metronome at my front door? Or is it? Rosie? Yep, that's Rosie's wagging tail. Let me run to the door to greet her …

Quick mom, hide my dog food!!!! It's really a lot of fun when she and Donna show up for a visit (Donna is her domestic and manages her wardrobe). Rosie is always very polite and only barks on occasion. Donna seldom barks.

Our owners never take us to the beach so we have to find sunlight when and where it's available. Better than Coligny Beach!

P.S. Don't tell anyone but she's my best bud.

From one great rescue to another, Bogey and his staff, Lynn & Tom C.

(Photo: L.Cordy)

(All photos of Rosie: D.Morris)

Addendum:

What you need to know about our visits with Bogey, I never ring the doorbell. I let Rosie stand at the door and whine until Bogey comes to greet her and let his staff know that he has guests!

The first time Rosie visited Bogey she had the audacity to eat his food! Since then, whenever Rosie arrives, the first thing Bogey does is clear his meal-plate!

And Rosie's bark: If someone visits and Rosie is not getting enough attention/love, she does a funny little howl. The only other place she has done that is at Bogey's. That speaks to her comfort level with her best bud!

If you pick up a starving dog and make him prosperous, he will not bite you. This is the principal difference between a dog and a man.

Mark Twain, (30 Nov 1835–21 Apr 1910), American writer, humourist, entrepreneur

Stanley *(Photo: C.England)*

Dolly
Spain

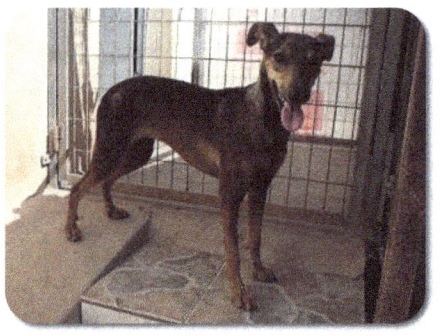

(Photo: PeaJayz)

This great little dog was brought into the shelter after being dumped, aged approximately 4 months. She was a sweet-natured, slightly timid girl, possibly with whippet somewhere in her background.

For some totally inexplicable reason, the charity found it impossible to get a home for this lovely little dog – goodness knows why as sweetness was written in her DNA.

So poor Dolly had to wait too many years in the shelter, which she hated as it was too noisy and frenetic for her, with too many more-assertive dogs around her. She particularly loved the volunteer visits when she danced up to them like a little ballerina on her hind legs, waving her fine forelegs to ask for some attention.

SECOND-HAND DOGS

When a lovely Spanish friend, Paco, expressed an interest in adopting a dog, Dolly immediately sprang to mind. She'd recently been attacked by one of the other dogs which had resulted in a large open wound on her rump so it was definitely time to get her out of there. Paco was thrilled to finally have such a sweet little dog and was as proud of her as any father would be of his first-born.

Her first few weeks in her new home were a bit worrying as Dolly retreated under the sofas and beds, reluctant to come out. Paco wondered if he'd made the right choice, and I worried in case this adoption wasn't going to work out for them.

And then, after 3 weeks, as if a light switch was flicked on and Dolly suddenly realised that she now had a great life, she came out from under the furniture to bond with Paco.

The two became inseparable, visiting the beach, going for walks in the campo when Dolly indulged in her favourite hobby of rabbit-hunting. She was quite partial to a game of footie too, and became a much-loved character in the local village. She couldn't have been happier and Paco loved his little girl to distraction.

(Photo: PeaJayz)
(Other Photos: F.Galindo)

But sadly this story doesn't have a good ending as Dolly's happy times in her home with her beloved master were tragically cut short to only a few years. She fell victim to a reckless householder dispensing rat poison without using a bait box, which killed not just poor Dolly but also 5 local cats including 3 kittens – leaving her adoring owner totally bereft without his little girl.

RIP, beautiful Dolly, deprived of that Happy Ever After life you deserved.

Amara's & Remi's Stories
By Marjon Tromp, Spain

We got our first dog, Kinny, as a puppy in August 2009 but because it was very quiet for him, we decided to get a pal to keep him company. We spotted Amara in the shelter where we used to volunteer; she was a sorry sight indeed – absolutely terrified and miserable, she was afraid to interact with people, and with very little coat on her thin body – you could see more skin than fur. We just had to adopt her and in October 2010, she joined our family.

Amara was very afraid of everything – the elevator, people, climbing stairs. The lot. She hated being driven anywhere – she threw up or peed in the car as soon as we drove away. That passed in one go when we drove to The Netherlands by car, a total of 2500 kilometres which was a baptism of fire for her. After that, riding in a car suddenly turned out to be no problem for her.

Kinny and Amara got on very well from the start and became close friends. She watched Kinny do everything she was afraid of and he taught her to overcome her fears. All those previous things – elevator, stairs and so many other things suddenly stopped frightening her. He was her example.

In June 2012, we found Remi. He was a sad outcast, roaming around our golf resort for a few weeks, being chased away from many homes where he tried to make friends with people, or get food. After failing to find him a home or a place in a shelter, we just had to take him in. Really thin, and riddled with worms and ticks, a visit to the local vet and good food quickly restored him to good health.

At first, he used to wag his tail whenever he saw a van, and we realised that he had probably been abandoned from the same type of vehicle by his previous owner. Unlike Amara, he really enjoyed riding in a car. Remi was immediately embraced and welcomed by Kinny and Amara, and he and Amara in particular have become firm hunting buddies. They enjoy hunting rabbits together and keep an eye out for each other.

I can hardly believe that Remi is now 11 years old, and Amara and Kinny are 14. Remi is super-sweet, he loves to cuddle and lie against you, and when the night temperatures get too cool for him, insists on burrowing under the bed-clothes! He does need his exercise and gets really bored when he doesn't get enough.

From Day 1, these 3 have always accepted each other, have never got ugly or had a fight, and are always very sweet towards each other. They eat from the same food and drinking bowls – often simultaneously. It is very special to see how they interact together, and how gentle they've always been with us.

Marjon with Amara, Kinny and Remi
(All photos: M. Tromp)

Nessie, The Patchwork Pup
By Nicola Solomon/Rabbi Jonathan Wittenberg, UK

(Photo: Nicola Solomon/Rabbi Jonathan Wittenberg)

Nessie was a tiny black puppy when we picked her up from All Dogs Matter. The family who had bought her from a puppy farm had realised their son was allergic to dogs and had responsibly given her up for rescue after a week. She had been sold to the family as a three-month-old Labrador but as she only weighed 3.5kg and her eyes were still blue she was clearly not.

She was gorgeous: playful and trusting and we spent a long time trying to guess her ancestry. There was clearly Labrador but what else? Collie, like our lovely 15-year-old, Mitzpah, whose original irritation with this lively new presence in the house was turning to interest and then affection? Something else? Why was she so thin? How big would she be eventually?

SECOND-HAND DOGS

People in the park with their designer puppies kept asking what breed she was and we didn't know. Eventually one of them suggested a DNA test. The process was cheap and easy. We took the swabs (a bit like a COVID test) sent them off and waited. The wait seemed interminable but was only three weeks. I opened them and excitedly sent the results to the kids: 37.5% Labrador, 12.5% spaniel, 25% greyhound, 25% saluki. Of course! That explained everything.

Are we glad we did the test? Yes. Do we love her any more or less now we know she's a patchwork pup? No.

In the immortal words of The Fiddler on the Roof: it doesn't change a thing but it's nice to know.

★

Author's note: I would highly recommend Jonathan's book "Things My Dog Taught Me", which is the most beautiful read with heart-warming stories about the family's previous two rescue dogs, Safi and Mitzpah, and the lessons that humans can learn from living with dogs.

Dogs and philosophers do the greatest good and get the fewest rewards.

Diogenes, Greek philosopher and one of the founders of Cynic philosophy

Ferdi *(Photo: PeaJayz)*

Ruby
By Angie Stone, UK

Found on a Spanish resort in terrible condition, her skin covered with sores and callouses, weakened by starvation to the point of exhaustion, this girl threw herself on the mercy of one of the residents in desperation, by sticking her head through

the metal grill of a gate, totally capturing the lady's heart. She couldn't have asked for help any more clearly than if she could have spoken. She was quickly named Ruby as she was found on a Tuesday … no prizes for guessing the lady's favourite pop-group!

A rescue campaign was then mounted in the community when so many people contributed to a fund to provide Ruby with food and the vet care needed to bring her back to health. She became a real favourite on the resort with her easy-going and gentle nature – a real noble lady, but sadly no one could offer her a permanent home. She then spent time in residential kennels where she was lavished with a lot of love and attention, while the search began to find her a home.

Finally, she found a lovely new home in the UK with Angie and Barry, where she's well and truly loved. Her very favourite people in the world are their grandchildren, who she adores and it's clear the feeling is reciprocated.

Ruby took a little time to truly settle – she appears more comfortable with Angie and is her shadow but is learning to love her dad ... with the help of those magic treats. She loves hugs more than anything, waits on command before crossing a road, has learned how to shake paws, wowed her vet who says that she's never had such a cooperative dog, and is very amenable to the "holiday" dogs who come to stay while their humans are away.

Ruby with her two favourite girls, Isla (l) and Amy (r) *(Photo: M.MacVean)*

She was awarded a very special nickname – Runaway Ruby, after visiting builders to the house accidently let her out and she was Gone-Girl ... with 5 burly builders following frantically in her wake! Fortunately, she took her usual walk route for her adventure and found her own way home 30 minutes later.

Ruby's journey through life has been full of twists and turns, she's got such a lovely nature she must have been loved in her previous life before being dumped. Her long road has led her to Angie, Barry and their extended family where she is very much loved and now has a real Forever Home.

Lucas
UK

Enjoying a spot of guy-time with best buddy, Ciarán

Things were not looking very good for poor Lucas in the shelter. His best friend had left for his new home, leaving him behind and while he loved seeing the volunteers coming in to help as they always gave him affection, it wasn't the same as a home of his own.

Then the charity received good news: a very discerning lady, Debbie, had finally noticed this boy's happy face and sweet demeanour, quickly made the decision to adopt him, and soon he was off to his new home. He stepped off the transporter and into their house as if he'd always lived there, immediately becoming a much-loved member of the family.

Debbie was amazed that he was so well-behaved from the moment he arrived; he's forever beguiling them with some of the cute things he does. She particularly loves his tenderness and his smile, the way he is so affectionate, and how mannerly he is – he waits patiently for his meals, never grabs food, and the sweet way he always says "please" with his eyes … and (both) paws! During the Covid-lockdown, he learned to lay down and roll over to a hand command, and is so intuitive, knowing just what to do. One of his favourite hobbies is to offer his unwavering moral support to mum Debbie by snoozing contentedly by her side while she studies. One of their sons has since left home to start out on his own life adventures, and the one thing he misses? Not mum's cooking (not that she isn't a good cook!) … but little Lucas!

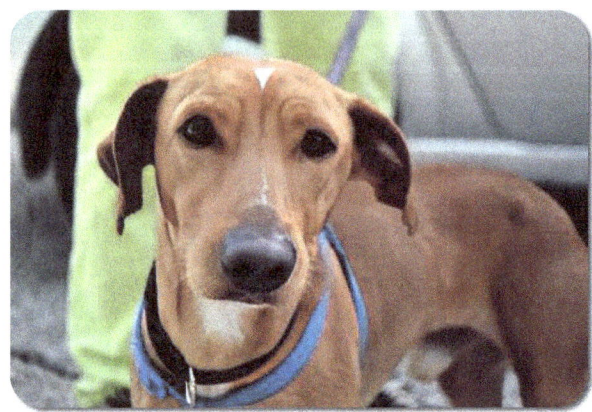

Lucas is quite the seasoned traveller and particularly enjoys going on his beach holidays in Dublin, happily taking car and ferry journeys in his stride – even one that entailed being tossed about in rough seas for over 8 hours while the ferry rode out a vicious storm before being able to dock … finally allowing him to have a much-needed pee!

Having been given the chance of a loving Forever home, Lucas has rewarded his family's kindness ten-fold with his very special brand of love.

The final word belongs to Debbie: "We still can't get over our astonishing good fortune to have Lucas with us. We've recently celebrated his third year since his arrival, he's about 6 years old now and we did give him extra treats on the day! Just an amazing little fella."

Life's a beach!

Neighbourhood Watch

Always the polite boy
(*All photos: D. Dunne*)

The dog was cold and in pain. But being only a dog, it did not occur to him to trot off home to the comfort of the library fire and leave his master to fend for himself.

Albert Payson Terhune (21 Dec 1872–18 Feb 1942), American author, dog breeder, and journalist.

Manzana *(Photo: K.Litfin)*

When Freja Joined Us ...
By Ramona Noack, Germany

I am a dog trainer and have been running my own dog school for 12 years. I have two – a Labrador, Bella, and a Border Collie bitch, Senta, that have been with me from the start.

In July 2019, the health of my trained therapy-dog, Bella, deteriorated and I had to make the decision that she was no longer allowed to work actively. The more I thought about it, the clearer the idea became that a "new" dog was needed. In the long term, I would need one that could work in the dog school again and that would take time, because the "new" dog would have to learn a lot, if possible from a still-fit Bella.

I was actually looking for a puppy here in Germany. Since Senta was already a souvenir from a house visit and I'd had to work with her for two years to help her overcome the trauma and abuse she had experienced, the new one should be a dewy, young dog, completely unencumbered and open to everything. A Labrador, if possible, no older than 8 weeks. There should be no mistakes from the start.

However, the "dog market" in Germany quickly made me sad. Completely exorbitant prices from breeders or dogs from senseless breeding farms, specifically set up to improve the state-paid livelihood. The more I looked through the appropriate media, the more it became clear that I didn't want to support either side at any cost.

So, I looked at sites where you can find dogs in need. Often enough, expectant canine mothers-to-be or small puppies come into the care of animal rescue charities. I looked at the pictures first because they generally appeared before I'd read the text, and saw a small, rather tousled young puppy with big, googly eyes. Somehow this picture touched me immediately. I started reading: "Border Collie/Labrador-cross, 4 months old". Ok, I thought, at four months not too much can have gone wrong … and somehow the breed suited us. I showed her to my husband: "Look, two-in-one would be perfect and Freja is her name too; what a great name". But we didn't make up our minds straight away as the idea first had to grow, before taking the step towards a third dog.

A few days later the subject came up again. I again searched the relevant puppy markets and came to the same conclusion again – there was nothing for us. My husband then said to me that he didn't want a puppy that way either. There is definitely an animal that needs us and is already out "there" somewhere. I remembered that sugar-sweet picture and told him that we had already found something there – our Border Collie-Labrador – all-in-one mix…

I found the ad again immediately and we looked at the other photos together: "Sweet young puppy …" I read through the whole text and realized that she was in Spain. I do want to mention that I take a very discerning view of animal welfare abroad, based on years of experience, which from my job, were not always good experiences.

Because of this, I looked for information about the association behind the ad, but within a short time it had me completely convinced.

After we had researched how the pup would come to us and my husband had looked at all the photos again, he suggested finally that I should write to them. With a pounding heart, I filled out the online form for initial contact. Hopefully the little mouse wasn't taken yet.

Some time later I got a very nice email that said that little Freja was still available, and they asked us to fill out a self-assessment form which seemed like an endless number of pages with very precise and profound questions. I was really amazed, but again thought it was great because this was the way suitable adopters can be identified.

I wrote like I was writing about my life – personal information about the family… what do you expect from a dog? Have you had experience? Have you already got a dog? What will you do with the dog in the future? Yes, I already have two dogs, we have a dog school and the dog will not only have a great and varied life, but can also experience and learn a lot.

Unfortunately, there wasn't a reply for a few days and the feeling was the same as if I'd applied for a dream job and had been left hanging in the air. What had happened? Why didn't they answer? Has she been taken or have they not liked our application?

Then finally came the long-awaited call. Yes, our application has been accepted and they couldn't ask for a better place for the mouse!

There were a lot of organizational issues to be clarified. How does she come to Germany? By car – and where and how can we meet the transport, and of course also the obligatory home-check. It was all so exciting, almost like the feeling when you know you are expecting a child.

The pre-inspection went without any problems, of course, but even at this point I was still a bit apprehensive. It was possible that our circumstances could be evaluated differently by the charity.

But we passed and with the positive result of the home-check, Freja was reserved for us. There it was – under her picture on the Internet – "Reserved for Germany". For us!

It had been hoped that Freja would be able to come to us in August but as the transport was already full, it wasn't possible to get a place for her at such short notice, so we had to wait another 4 weeks. The wait seemed like a never-ending time. So much anticipation and excitement.

But then finally, she was on the travel list. On the club's Facebook Page, it said that Freja was on the transport so now on our minds were with her on the journey. Hopefully everything would go well.

On September 22nd, 2019, a Sunday, a member of the charity's German Club met us as she'd arranged to get Freya from the transport half-way through her journey, and Freja was finally in our arms. Such an excited, very thin, tall,

sweet, black girl. She greeted us as if we had known each other forever. I had thought a lot about this – you only really get to know a rescue dog from abroad once he's arrived. Photos and videos are one thing but personally, as is usual here in animal shelters, going for a walk together and sniffing each other is another. Freja could not be stopped. On the drive home, she didn't think her stay in a travel box was all that great. It only increased her excitement and when we got home there was no stopping her. Run and jump was the motto!

First, after she had calmed down a bit, Freja met Bella. Bella is very gentle and calm and managed to get the little one to calm down even more, and relax. The two of them hit it off right away. My concern now was the introduction with my energetic border collie dog, Senta. But that wasn't a problem either. After an initially cautious approach, they both ran around the entire property with each other. It was like she had always been here.

Second big hurdle – we have 4 cats. What would Freja say to cats?

She hadn't met any in Spain. So – exposure therapy, everyone! Cats in the hallway, and super-generous treats to give to all dogs which seemed to work for now. The cats then withdrew to their usual observation posts, because they know when strange dogs are around as, occasionally, I care for dogs whose owners are on holiday.

But Freja had other thoughts – first she wanted to explore the house but there were the other two dogs as well and so she switched between investigating them and her unstoppable race through all the rooms – back and forth. I fully understood her situation. The long car trips and now other playmates – an energy that has got to come out; at some point she will be tired but much later, I found out that this dog never got tired.

Ok, she's completely over-the-top, I thought, that's okay too. Let her settle.

But it wasn't that simple, Freja didn't seem to settle. She was non-stop as if on high voltage. She knew NOTHING. No limits, no rules, no commands, no behaviour – just nothing.

Freja ran around with no brakes for anything in her way: the couch, the bed, the kitchen or living room table. If I corrected her to tell her that's not ok, she would watch you questioningly and did not understand what was required of her, even snapping at treats from the hand. This dog seemed tireless. She only really came to rest at night and only with physical contact in our bed. As soon as someone got up even to go to the toilet, she was in no time at 1000 volts, no matter what time.

She couldn't rest during the day. If she was nearby, you had to stay seated or woe betide you if you were to get up, as the dog stood up and followed you at your feet, or ran to the door. She looked downright rushed, restless, stressed, she had to be here, there, everywhere, and with everything she was in an extremely high level of arousal.

At first, I just ignored it all, thinking that if her actions didn't receive attention, they would decrease. But it wasn't like that. And the worst was yet to come.

For the first while, I stayed at home, I had moved all my appointments and didn't need to leave the house, but then came the day when I had to leave again. Not for long, only a quarter of an hour to bring one of my children to the nearby train station. I returned home to find bitten pens and headphones in the living room. My tattered slipper was in the kitchen. OK, I thought, it will only have been because she wasn't used to my going out.

Unfortunately, that was repeated and I bought myself a security camera, so I could see her body language, see what she did – how she moved and felt when she was alone. But she wasn't alone as the other two dogs were there too. But that didn't seem to help her as for some reason, she didn't get any comfort from having them with her.

The surveillance camera quickly revealed what was going on as soon as I had left the house. She propped her front paws onto the windowsill to confirm that we had really driven away, then she ran from room to room whimpering. She demanded again and again that the other dogs played, but when they wouldn't and had withdrawn to their favourite resting places, Freja began to look for a replacement – she stood on the coffee table and looked for things that were destructible, the glass pen-holder was neatly pulled down and she began to chew each pen, then books, documents, everything what was there. Apparently, she had to let out some invisible energy from within because she did not chew the object calmly and with relish, she tore it up and raged around with it.

When there was finally nothing more interesting to find there, she left the room. And then it was the shoes again and even something out of a bedroom: a watch strap, plush toys and more headphones.

At the beginning, I thought that this could possibly improve if she could only realize that everyone who leaves, does come back, but unfortunately that didn't

work either. On the contrary, every time Freja carried out her very best destructive work.

When I got home again, I found that my whole study had been reduced to rubble. Out of sight of the camera she had destroyed everything she could find. There were a few cardboard boxes in which flyers for our campaign and many other things we wanted to store. Everything was literally torn to pieces. Quite literally shredded.

And nothing else seemed to be getting any better. She could not regulate herself, or retain or execute any restraint;

on the leash, she completely freaked out so that serious work with her was not possible, she could not focus for a second.

But then, I looked in her eyes and she looked back lovingly, and I often had the impression that she was sorry, she seemed overwhelmed and disappointed with herself. I finally had to realize that this dog, even if she was only 5 months old, really had massive, serious problems.

But a switch came on in my head after she destroyed something really important to me and I had had to watch it on the camera. I sat in front of her and cried so much. I told her that I was so angry, she would have to go back to Spain.

Right now, of course, I knew in my heart that none of this was true and that wouldn't happen. It was like a burst of energy for me, because I was so sad and empty.

At that moment, professional ambition took over and the situation had become so urgent. I was convinced that there had to be reasons why this Freja was like this, so I started asking questions and researching. I wanted to know everything that all the Spanish animal welfare colleagues knew - EVERYTHING. Everyone should try to remember the smallest details in Freja's life so far.

Unfortunately, a lot of what they found out began to bring everything together.

It tore my heart out to hear that at 6 weeks of age she had already been taken from her mother, which explained a lot – that a lot of important elements of her early learning had already irretrievably been lost.

As such a small puppy, she went to a woman with a toddler – I didn't need much imagination to know what she would certainly have experienced there, and why.

She was then given away because things didn't go as the owners had hoped. At about 10 weeks, she already had her second new home. She was probably loved there, but through inexperience, various elements of her behaviour worsened and she also developed new ones. A vicious circle developed and even there, she couldn't stay alone.

Now everything was clear – this is not about a dog that just hasn't learned how to stay alone or follow rules. This is about a dog which is ripped apart emotionally when caregivers "leave" it. Such emotional as well as cognitive deficits in a dog can be alleviated or with difficulty, built up, but it's impossible to bring back what was never developed during the formative period of its life.

Freja is a highly intelligent dog, but she cannot sort her head out herself – with her, all fuses are constantly about to blow. This was the explanation for all her behaviour. It made me sad because Freja will have problems her whole life because she had to experience such traumas so early in her young life.

I now pulled out all the stops of my profession. First, I taught her the "clicker", which is a form of marker-training and so I was able to work with her in important situations and communicate with her in a positive way. I could tell her what she was doing right and she blossomed with it right away. She was finally able to learn rules and behaviours, memorize and execute them safely in the required situation, which gave her security and also a certain calm. It provided amazing relief for her.

We have worked out a ritual for staying alone; she was restricted to a limited area as everything else is secured. We installed a RelaxoDog and I take care that every departure always followed the same pattern. Naturally, she knows what to expect when I come down the stairs in a different pair of pants, but she also knows exactly what will happen.

All doors are closed, RelaxoDog turned on, the camera set up and switched on. Large chewy treats given out. She has chosen the place she wants to lie on for this moment, and I say goodbye to her every time with the words, "You're a great girl, you can do it", and walk out.

On the cam, I could see that she was still having trouble dealing with the situation, but she clung to her chewing stick and was able to control at least part of her emotions. In addition, she got Bach flowers and later, also CBD oil. In this way, she managed to stay alone for longer and longer, and was able to lie down even after her treat was finished, and be half-relaxed.

In the meantime, we found out that she wasn't a mixed-breed Border Collie-Labrador at all – as a young dog, she just didn't look like she was going to develop or behave like either of the two breeds. My tip was Setter ... and so we decided to do a genetic test. And indeed – Freja is a Setter/German Shepherd/Pointer.

The Setter shows in her behaviour and appearance but not completely though. I'm glad we decided to complete this test because it was possible to explain her behaviour in a way that is typical of the breed and apply this knowledge in further training and education. If one understands and can explain the behaviour of the breed of one's dog, it is possible to do the right thing for it.

Freja has been here now for exactly 11 months and has developed in a great way. She is an incredibly loving dog and will probably, in her mind, always remain a big baby. She has calmed down. She still jumps up immediately when you leave the room, but this has decreased. In the meantime, she can just lie down – it is no longer just 1000 volts all day.

She settled herself very well into our multi-dog household and has taken over a lot from Bella and Senta – just like I wanted her to. We are still miles away from working in the dog school, but she is a valuable family member that nobody would want to be without.

I remember that after a while the rescue association asked how things were going and I replied that if she hadn't landed here, they would have got Freja back after 14 days. I am convinced that there is a good reason that we found her.

I cannot yet say with certainty whether she can ever stay alone, because when Corona-virus switched off our lives, training in that regard was also on hold. She just didn't need to be alone anymore and for her safety, we designed everything around her during this time.

Now that a type of normality is slowly returning to the world, it has also returned into Freja's life and the first test runs make me feel confident. This standstill of time has served her very well. Peace, security, continuity, love and the certainty that this is now her home has allowed her to be a little more relaxed. Now her training can finally begin.

I would do it again, despite these nerve-wracking experiences. A dog like Freja would have been a huge challenge for other people and there are many such Freja's who just need love, a family, but also specialist knowledge.

Freya, with Bella and Senta

With human-dad Percy

Chillin' out
(All photos R. Noack)

One reason a dog can be such a comfort when you're feeling blue is that he doesn't try to find out why.

Unknown Author

Rondie *(Photo: L.Allen)*

Angel
Norway

It's difficult to understand why this adorable little fella was ever abandoned as a tiny puppy in the first place, and yet he found himself out on the roads, on his own.

A truly remarkable little puppy, Angel adapted to shelter life like the proverbial duck to water, unafraid of standing up for himself among all the bigger dogs (let's face it, he was so small, every dog towered over him), happily weaving his way through their legs to grab food, and holding his own in the general meleé of the shelter.

He was adopted by a lovely lady and flew to his new home in Norway where he became an adored member of his family, surrounded by love and comfort.

He was a really smart little dog, and his new mum spent many happy hours teaching him all kinds of tricks. Sadly, his Happy-Ever-After was short-lived as Angel was attacked by a large dog during one of his walks in the local park, tragically succumbing to his injuries, leaving his adoring owner absolutely bereft.

E.T. phone home

RIP Little Angel, you touched the hearts of many people in your all-too-brief life.
(All photos: N.E. Westerhus)

Jack and Cherry
UK

In Memory of Jack.
Life to him was his family, and a ball

Cherry and Jack, a sweet Mr and Mrs

Jack, always ready to play
(Photos: Ian and Clare Reed)

The Diva
Spain

Neva was found loitering around a bar in a small village, surviving by using her sweet charms to elicit food from the patrons. With long, gangling legs and a head too big for her body, her beautiful almost-white coat alive was with fleas, bony ribs and hips protruding through her skin from starvation. Eyes were dull through lack of hope, and with a terrible open wound on her rump where her skin had been ripped off, leaving raw flesh exposed, she cut a pathetic sight.

The first photo – those little black dots were fleas

With the local shelter now closed for the next two days, I found myself volunteering to foster her until it re-opened, but with a partner who had reluctantly allowed me to adopt one rescue dog, I really wasn't too sure how he'd view a second appearing on the doorstep. But home we went, this little sweet, scruffy, flea-ridden puppy and me. Surprisingly my partner didn't object too much to her arrival, convinced by my promise that she wasn't staying, and that I'd immediately start to advertise her through the charity dog rehoming pages on Facebook.

But the first problem were the hundreds of fleas. Three baths later, they had all resolutely hung on so Puppy wasn't allowed in to the house, much to her total irritation. She decided to work the guilt angle by lying close to the patio doors, mournfully gazing in with woe-be-me eyes, her breath casting a fog on the glass. Heart strings were definitely being strongly tugged.

Her reluctant little hitchhikers finally called for a trip to the vet, where they were quickly banished with magic spray. She was given her first vaccination, a tablet stuffed down her neck against worms and cream for her ripped rump, and to her utter delight she was finally allowed into the house.

By the following day, I'd received 2 firm offers of homes for this baby girl who I was determined not to name so I wouldn't bond with her. Puppy followed me wherever I went, a cold nose pressing against the back of my leg, her sweet little face gazing up at me. I couldn't weaken. Not to be deterred, she decided to turn her exceptional skills of persuasion on my partner.

When I told him the good news of the offers, I was told to "wait a day". Then the following day, I raised the subject again and was again told to "wait until the following day". I knew he was becoming totally smitten by this clumsy, awkward, leggy little puppy that fell up and down steps, miserably failed to clamber on to the bed, and ended up in the base of a hedge when trying to stand on it. By the 3rd day, the people who'd made the offers of homes were now virtually screaming at me as they were doubting if I was serious about re-homing her, so Partner was told that the decision was his: Keep Puppy, or she had to go to the other people.

"Let's keep her" was the reply and thus our second dog adopted us. (He never stood a chance and was basically putty in her paws!!) Her name changed from Puppy to Neva – Catalan for snow, although typical of this character who lives her life to her own rhythm, no sooner had I named her but her coat slowly began to turn to a light tan. Oh well! Blame the genetics!

Neva enthusiastically involved herself in all aspects of our household, she loved being where we were, she wanted everything that our other dog had just like a typical younger child, and she adored her walks chasing rabbits, or just … well …. running, jumping and having Neva-fun.

She then became the Team Leader on the walks, taking herself and her buddy on adventures all over the *campo*, as if deciding that life on the run was infinitely more exciting than staying with me. They even had a couple of overnight excursions (resulting in excruciating sleepless and worry-filled nights for us) returning happily early the following morning, to gobble a quick meal before she dived on to our bed where she stayed for 3 days while her aching paws and muscles recovered.

A few months after she joined our home, she began to vomit green bile and refused to eat, or even drink water. Weight quickly disappeared from her already thin frame, and she hardly had any energy even to raise her head off the sun-bed. Not knowing what the problem was, I really feared that we might lose her.

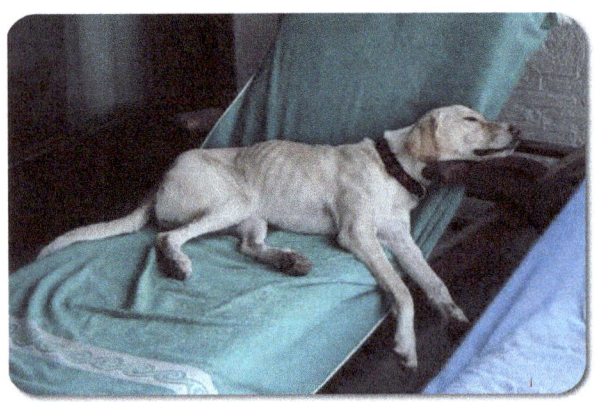

In the dark days of her illness, just a bag of skin and bones, with no interest in life

After blood tests, endoscopies and biopsies, it was discovered that she had Irritable Bowel Disease – something not limited to non-pedigree or shelter dogs.

Since then, the poor girl has had to put up with bi-monthly Vitamin B injections, all of which she suffered with such tolerance – the vet can more or less do anything to her and she never resists. She must be one of the few dogs that enjoys going to the clinic where she considers the staff all to be her friends, including the clinic cat.

Years of special and very expensive gastro food, expensive vitamins, B12 now taken orally, lots of patience and perseverance have taken her from a scrawny 17kgs to a mighty 22.200kgs (every gram matters!) over a period of 7 years. I have a running joke with my vet – the wonderful Susana – that one day she'll wag her finger at me, saying: "She's too fat, she has to lose some weight", the reasonably frequent general reproach that vets give to their clients with porky pooches!

Neva is definitely a dog with a mind of her own, she's wilful and funny – greeting us with a wrinkled nose over a toothy grin. She takes great pleasure from needling her very serious sister, glaring then loudly yelling at us with one very insistent bark when things are not to her liking or we aren't serving her quickly enough, fully living up to her nickname of The Diva.

She lives life to the beat of her own drum – if we're walking on one side of the lake, she'll be on the other. She disappears off for her own little adventures, and when we go in through the back gate to our garden at the end of our walk, she'll keep going in a different direction to visit the local cat hostelry. Her favourite trick is to wait until the other dogs have been fed and we've just started to prepare our own meal, when she will stroll in and "assume the position", as we've called it, for hers. Normally, I wouldn't give in to a dog in this way but I almost think she knows that in my enthusiasm to keep her weight up, I'm going to give in to her every time. And she's right!

Life is one long party to her; she loves to meet other dogs although can be a bit of a bossy-boots at times. She encourages affection by using her blonde paw to drag the hand back to her favourite tickle-spots, and every day, she sits high on the steps outside our house, from where she keeps an eye on her kingdom, venting her opinions on anything that's out of place, or any poor unfortunates who happen to venture past.

Is it a bird, is it Superman? NO! It's a flying Neva, living life to the full

Who knows why she was abandoned, had her previous owners realised that she was ill and weren't interested in trying to help her? It saddens me to think that if we hadn't rescued her, she might have died a long, painful death and we'd have missed out on the special brand of love she's brought into our home, with all the laughter at her antics on a daily basis – even when she's being a madam. Or is she our Free Spirit? Either way, we consider ourselves blessed to have been adopted by this great dog.

(All photos: PeaJayz)

Dobby And Cookie
Spain

Cookie (l) and Dobby

These two little rescues are blessed not just with Disney-star good looks, but intelligence too.

Multi-skilled Cookie has done detection training, agility, dog-tricks and appeared in obedience exhibitions in shows, including a dog-dance in the centre ring. He's slowed up a bit since reaching senior status but now participates in Hoopers – a great form of low-impact exercise for older dogs.

Dobby has been working his little metaphorical socks off with his agility activities, doing his best to make his mum proud. He's also become a dab paw at doing tricks and has an Advanced Dog Tricks certification, and picked up an additional skill of professional dish washer!

But aside from their many talents, more importantly, both boys are cherished family pets.

The smallest swimming pool in the world

Mummy's little helper

Cookie, defying the years

(All photos: C.Hall)

Sir Dougie

With or without rosettes, Sir Dougie is always a winner

(All Photos:D.Worth)

If you can resist treating a rich friend
better than a poor friend,
If you can face the world without lies and deceit,
If you can say honestly that deep in your heart you have no
prejudice against creed, colour, religion or politics,
Then, my friend, you are almost as good as your dog.

Unknown Author

Didi *(Photo: PeaJayz)*

Katla – A Very Special Dragon
By Raquel Carceles, Spain & UK

First of all, I need to explain that Katla is the name of a dragon of a Scandinavian fairytale. Someone at Casa del Sol Shelter gave her the name when we brought her to La Casa, before that we just called her Dragon. Her extraordinary split nose and her way of howling make her a very distinctive dragon, I might say, and there's no doubt she is a special creature.

When I first met Katla, my husband Robert and I were living in Murcia, in an urbanization on a golf course. Our neighbour had found her wandering down the motorway and had brought her into the urbanization, but he just left her outside his house.

We came back one day from work, and there she was, lying in the sun in front of our gate. When she saw us, she started howling in her weird manner (now we know that is the noise she makes when she is happy!). When we first saw her, we thought somebody had done something to her, as her nose is very peculiar and is split in two.

We could see she was a pointer, so I contacted a colleague of mine who is a hunter, who explained that there wasn't anything wrong with her, she was a pure Pachón Navarro – an Old Spanish Pointer, which are apparently quite rare nowadays. He was surprised she had been abandoned, especially being a young female who could be used for breeding, so we thought that maybe she had just got lost and were determined to find her owner.

Katla was very thin and covered in ticks and fleas, so we decided to take her to our vet, who washed her, had a look at her and took a few blood samples to test her for diseases. But no chip was found, so we didn't know who she belonged to. At that point we did not want to keep her because we had five cats at the time and thought a hunting dog was not ideal, but we kept her on the ground floor of the house, and facilitated the top floor for the cats.

I used all my social media to put up photos of her and asked if somebody had seen her. I received information from three different people pointing in the same direction, so I went to the place to find the owner. When I found him, of course he did not want to know anything about her, but his neighbours told me all the story: he was an old hunter who used to have her tied on a rope for two years in a neglected garden, feeding her human food only twice a week. He denied he had a dog – apparently, he had two but I never saw the other one – God knows what happened to it, but at least my Katla is now happy.

So she stayed with us for a few days, but again, the cats were not very happy. Our friend Tausha, who was a volunteer at Casa del Sol shelter, said she had asked the shelter manager and we could take her there, so that's how Katla ended up in La Casa Shelter.

After dropping her off, and although we knew she was going to be very well looked after, we felt really sad. The house was not the same without her, even though we had only had her for three days. She had been very good, and she had not even chased the cats.

The week after, it was Easter holidays and I went to La Casa to see her. She was so happy when she saw me, howling at me and wagging her tiny tail (which had been cut due to her being a hunting dog). I could see she was very happy there with the other dogs, so I left a bit happier this time. I asked if there was anything I could do to help, and as she had just been spayed, I went another day to pick her up and take her with me so she could recover from the operation, with the intention of bringing her back when the holiday finished.

She was (and still is!) a very special dog. The cats let her know who was boss, and she understood, so never chased them or tried to do anything to them. She never barked (she doesn't bark now either, she just makes that howling noise like Scooby Doo or like, of course, a dragon) and she loved going for long walks through the mountains.

So, when we asked Shelter Manager, Jose, if it was fine to keep her with us, he said that he knew we would!

That's how Katla ended up in our lives. That strange-looking dog we found is now to us the most loveable creature we could ever wish for. She has such a gentle nature, no malice runs through those veins, and she has all these funny habits every day that make us laugh every time. She adores our cat Rumpleteazer, and she still loves to go for very long walks in the countryside.

Raquel, with her beloved Dragon

We are now living in England and she loves it here, although you can tell she is Spanish as she is allergic to most of the vegetation and she doesn't particularly like the rain or the bad weather. That doesn't stop her from running around chasing rabbits and pheasants (which she never catches). She is extremely spoilt and she even has her own Instagram page: *thedogwithtwonoses*.

Our Katla might be a second-hand dog who once somebody did not love and decided to abandon on the motorway, but to us, Katla is our home, and nothing – neither our lives nor our hearts, would be the same without her. We adore her!

(All photos: R.Carceles)

Barney

Barney (*Photo: C. Okninski*)

Afflicted by the dreaded "Black Dog Syndrome", Barney had to wait a few months before being adopted but sadly he was returned due to the previous owner's "change of circumstances". He then had to wait quite some time before his new human mum, Charley, finally found him and whisked him off to his new home in the UK, where he's lived happily ever since. He's since been joined by three more *perritos* from Spain.

Scorrie's Story
By Richard & Heather Lorimer, Spain

After relocating to live in Spain, Heather and I decided to try to find a Border Collie through some of the many rescue groups operating here. In March 2016, we were contacted by a PAPS volunteer, asking if we were still looking for one as they were expecting a one-year-old pure-bred Collie, called Romeo, to be brought in to their shelter.

Romeo had been found on a property without food or water having been abandoned by his owner, and was rescued by keen dog-lovers in the area, who contacted the rescue charity to see if they could take him in to safety.

(Photo: PeaJayz)

After visiting "Romeo" at the kennels and quickly falling for this handsome boy, we confirmed with the charity that we'd love to have him as part of our family. The home-check had to be completed first, followed by a few alterations with trellising and mesh to our perimeter fencing and gates to ensure our home was escape-proof, and finally a letter from our landlord confirming it was acceptable to have a pet. Once all of this was done, we were invited to collect him from the shelter … when all the fun began.

On the same day we picked him up, we had to go straight to the charity's vet to change the owner-name on our boy's chip, when we realised that our first job was to change his name as his current moniker of Romeo really wasn't for us. We just couldn't imagine the scenario when calling him "Romeo, Romeo, wherefore art thou …!" So we chose a name after our favourite walk from where we used to live on the Isle of Skye – "Scorriebreac". And so, Romeo became … Scorrie.

Over the next few weeks, Heather struggled to settle with Scorrie as he was getting up at all hours wanting food and looking for a walk; sadly, at this point she even wondered if we had made the wrong decision in getting him. On the other hand, having had collies previously, I confidently stated (and hoped) that Scorrie would settle down and in time would fall into our routines, if we persevered – which he did shortly after this wobble.

We started home-training with the basics like, Sit, Stay, Down, Heel etc; at first, this was difficult for a dog who didn't even know what a ball was for. We continued this with some additional commands until around October 2016 when we enrolled him in the Costa Blanca Dog Training. This is when he started coming out of his shell, interacting with other dogs, and truly started to show his intel-

ligence and capabilities, and from then on he has been constantly top of his class. He progressed very quickly from Beginners to Intermediate, then on to Advanced within weeks.

He took part in his first dog show on the 25th March 2018 and also starred in the dog obedience show where his Training Club was demonstrating that day. Scorrie won a couple of categories in the competition, one being "The Dog The Judges Would Most Like To Take Home" which we were very proud of, but that wasn't where it ended as the best was yet to come. He then proceeded to win Best in Show!! A tremendous achievement by him, considering his start in life. He followed this up by

SECOND-HAND DOGS

winning Best in Show in another dog show in the San Javier area in November 2019 – as you can imagine we are very, very proud parents.

During his time with us, he has gone from strength to strength; with our love and determination he has shone through and we now couldn't imagine life without him, as he is one of the biggest parts of our lives, continuously showing his love and care for us both, also entertaining us and providing us with joy and laughter with his unique personality.

Scorrie – a true Champ

(All other photos: H & R Lorimer)

Gizmo

By Lili and Nick, UK

We had always wanted a dog, having both been brought up with dogs playing very large parts in our childhoods. It wasn't until we both became self-employed with flexibility in our working hours, that we decided the time was finally right.

There was never any question we would get a rescue dog; beyond that we were pretty flexible. The main criteria we had were: good with children (then aged 7 and 11); not a puppy; small to medium sized ie. not able to rest a head on the dining room table while standing on 4 legs; would be happy going on long walks. Our preferred breed would have been a Collie as Nick grew up with Collies and loved their loyalty, intelligence and fitness.

(Photo: PeaJayz)

After weeks of searching we were struggling to find a dog that fitted the bill; children seemed to be the main sticking point. When Nick saw a photo of Gizmo there was something about the slightly scruffy, bearded, big-eared dog looking back at us that appealed and, after many emails, photos, videos, family discussions and a home visit to check we had the appropriate space, we paid the adoption fee (for pet passport, immunisations, and transport costs). The arrangements to bring Gizmo over from PAPS were made. One throw away comment sticks in my mind when watching a video of Gizmo trotting around the pound: 'Isn't he quite big?' I asked, to which Nick said 'no, he can't be, he's a Collie'.

We waited for Gizmo late one chilly October evening, to meet the pet transport van *en route* from Spain to Cornwall. The delivery man slid open the door and went to fetch our new companion, unmistakably the scruffy faced dog from the photos. "My God, he's huge!" was our first reaction.

Gizmo is distinctively and undeniably big. We have a very small house and yes, he can rest his head on the table; although he doesn't have to stand, he can comfortably do it sitting down. He has the black and white markings of a Collie, the ears of a *Podenco*, the legs of a Greyhound and the huge deep chest of a Lurcher. People stop us constantly in the street with comments such as: 'He's the most beautiful/handsome/striking dog I've ever seen, what kind is he?' (often followed with musings as to his breed); 'He's so calm/well behaved' (he likes to sit and relax when we stop to talk to people – he's not always calm and well behaved!); "Mummy why is that dog so big?'; 'Is that a stick he's carrying or a small tree?' (Thanks to his 3-a-day stick habit, we have an enormous pile building up outside the front gate of our house, we did wonder if he was collecting enough to build an escape raft but once the sticks are home, he never looks at them again).

Gizmo is bright, anxious, nervous, loving and very excitable. He will chase anything and everything; there is nothing more beautiful than seeing him accelerating up to full speed as he runs alongside one of the many trains we encounter daily. With a fence between them, it's like athletes in their respective lanes for the Olympic 100 metre final. Unfortunately, he will also disregard our whereabouts and any boundaries when on the tail of a fast-moving deer, or even on the trail of a long-departed one. His senses of smell and hearing are acute, so letting him off the lead has to be done with caution and a check for any escape routes. He will prowl the length of any fence looking for a way through into the wider world beyond. Gizmo is a dichotomy of a dog – he desires independence, but panics if he loses sight of his people.

Gizmo is extraordinarily affectionate, his love for his family and supporters is absolute. A big lean and look of total adoration melts the heart and he never tires of cuddles, strokes or brushes. This wasn't always the case; initially he was incredibly fearful of anybody coming near or into the house apart from the 4 of us (although we were sometimes a little fearful of him; my son would jump behind the sofa when Gizmo got over-excited). Having an enormous dog barking at you in a confined space is terrifying. For a long time, Gizmo would allow visitors to sit very still on the sofa, but would then stand guard. If they so much as changed position it would set him off barking so loudly it once sent a friend's glass of red wine flying up to the ceiling and back down on to my Dad's head.

The first trainer we tried called him dangerous and refused to have anything to do with him, as did a dog sitter – both claimed "experience" and never having

"turned a dog down before". Luckily, we found a gentle and understanding dog trainer/behaviourist called Ryan (Oxfordshire Animal Behaviour and Training) who gave us the tools to work on positive reinforcement of desired behaviours and the confidence to believe Gizmo wasn't a lost cause, although we were now under no illusion that he'd be an easy case.

We also put in many hours of training with Martin (Headington Dog Training) who had absolute faith in him from the beginning and often used him as his demo dog (mainly because he didn't have to bend down to treat him!). Gizmo is now a proud Kennel Club Gold Award holder. We have an inkling he

may have used his looks to charm the assessor, as most training sessions ended sooner than expected when Gizmo would decide he'd had enough and lie down yawning or simply go and stand by the exit. None of this training has involved any quick fixes. Changing his environment so dramatically from the shelter to a domestic setting in a damp and cold country (he doesn't like the rain and will do anything to avoid getting his feet wet) was obviously very traumatic for him. It has taken 2 years and a lot of dedication from the whole family, and support from friends, to bring out the best in him.

Spanish boy to the core … tootsies MUST stay dry at all costs!

What we have learnt is that as much as we thought we knew about dogs; it doesn't add up to one iota of what we needed to know. We've also realised how complicated and unpredictable our rescue dog can be – why should fireworks be okay but the Thursday evening clapping for the NHS workers (during the lockdown for Covid-19) be impossible for him to handle? How can a fly buzzing around a room have him wide-eyed and panting, when he can fall asleep in a room full of overexcited 10-year-old boys?

Gizmo has transformed our lives and mostly for the better. The journey has been slow and difficult at times, we have had many supporters and made new friends but there have been detractors; some people still cross the street when they see us approaching with our huge wolf-dog, and his mortal enemy will always be the postman. Going on holiday requires a lot of forward planning. Luckily, we found a fantastic dog sitter who accepts Gizmo as part of the family despite his chicken-terrorising. Long walks in new places can be highly stressful, new sights and smells often prove far too stimulating and we may as well be trying to hold back a Ferrari. Fingers have been broken, shoulders damaged and Nick has even been dragged face down through a muddy field (to everyone's but his amusement!) – all thanks to the surprise appearance of a squirrel, cat, or sheep, although a leaf blowing across our path often has the same effect.

Gizmo, with his very proud family
(All other photos: N. Dunbar)

We wouldn't have it any other way though when Gizmo decides to join us on the sofa for a movie. That is until he inevitably, slowly, stretches out those long giraffe's legs, claims his rightful place as king of the cushions, and displaces half the family onto the floor.

Rondie

Isn't there something better you could be doing with me?

PAULA JONES

Abandoned by his previous owners, Rondie rescued himself by jumping, uninvited, into the car of the President of a local rehoming charity. And that was it, he was taken to the shelter where he became a much-loved resident, before he was spotted by Lizzie and whisked off to a new home to become a much-loved family member.

(All photos: L.Allen)

Stick around any place long enough and chances are you'll be taken for granted. Hang around for 20,000 years wagging your tail and being man's (and woman's) best friend, and you'll be taken for granted big time.

Lynn Van Matre (d.13 Dec 2012), Rock Critic, Chicago Tribune

Sam *(Photo: PeaJayz)*

Mia The Minx
Spain

I was just "knocking off" for the day from my volunteer work at the local dog shelter, when someone brought in a tiny little puppy that had been dumped outside the gate. The little mite was quaking with fear, her body shaking uncontrollably, eyes wide with fright. When she was put on the floor to meet the other puppies, she was absolutely petrified, particularly of one big fluff-ball that chased her all over the room, before she eventually crawled under a pallet of food, from where I had to retrieve her.

So I held her close to my shoulder, trying to calm and reassure her, in the hope that she would stop shuddering. And in that one moment, fell madly in love.

She was only 7 weeks old, had probably just been taken from her mum and discarded in the *campo* like a piece of rubbish. I think it was as much this thought of such a small baby being dumped on her own in a very large, frightening world, so scared of everything that made me decide that I'd have to foster her. My partner never particularly wanted a dog so I was worried about what he would say when I showed up with one. As it turned out, I think he had braced himself long ago for that moment when a dog crossed the threshold so reluctantly, he accepted that she was there until I found a home for her.

When she first arrived, Mia still had that bluish puppy-haze over her eyes but once this cleared, I was blown away with the clear intense eyes that literally bored into my mind. I quickly realised that she had a huge intelligence and eagerness to learn so we started immediately on her training. Within an hour she'd mastered Sit, and over the following days, this was quickly followed by the usual: Shake Paws, On Trust-Paid For, and her party-piece Dead Dog – when she indulged in shameless overacting.

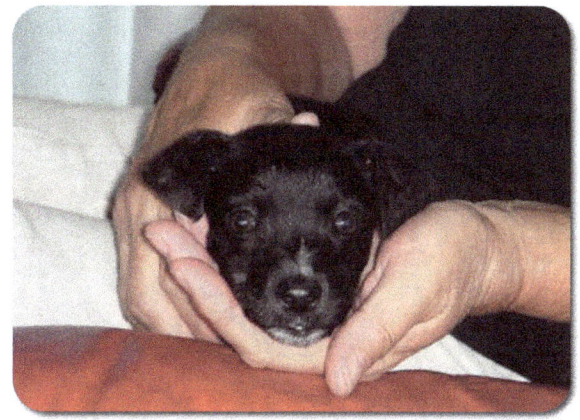

Amazingly for such a cute little pup, not one offer came in for her – the dreaded black-dog syndrome in action again? So, after 6 weeks, Mia was officially adopted and had found her Forever Home with us.

I brought her to Puppy Classes to help her to socialise – the first course was a disaster as the trainer was an ex-Police Dog Trainer with somewhat old-fashioned theories of "domination", and worse, forcing the dogs into the "down" position by pressing down and backwards on the shoulders.

One of the poor dogs on this course was a beautiful *podenca* that had been viciously cut along the length of her spine, leaving a terrible scar where you could still see the marks of the sutures. So pressing down on the back of a traumatised dog like this was little more than furthering the cruelty for this poor animal. I could see that Mia, too, wasn't happy as this man-handling was much too physical for this sensitive little girl, so the two of us very happily became class drop-outs.

Instead, we went to Michaela, a wonderful local trainer who believed in very much reward-based, non-physical methods – more or less persuading the dogs that they really wanted to do whatever they were being taught. Mia began to blossom in these calm, happy sessions as she was being exposed to a wide variety of differing activities which she loved.

During one class, Michaela sidled up beside me, and asked if I'd ever thought of doing Search & Rescue with Mia – which I hadn't, but we decided to work with her to see where it might take her. Apparently with a highly sensitive snozz with excellent scenting capability, together with her single-minded concentration, she had the basic requirements for a rescue dog.

And so Mia began her S&R training, first searching out treats and food in the house which – loving food as she did – she greatly enjoyed, then items of clothing outside, Find Object, before advancing to tracking people into abandoned buildings and learning how to Speak when she found them. She learned her Lefts and Rights on command but sadly her training became more sporadic as between the heat of the Spanish summers when it was too uncomfortable to work, and Michaela's regular production of children (currently at 6), the training rather fell to the wayside, which was such a shame.

Mia's definitely a Daddy's Girl as she ADORES my partner, following him around, snuggling up beside him in his chair (even though she's a little bit big to be a lap-dog at 45cms), resolutely refusing to leave his side when he had an accident on a walk. She loves me too but in a different way – I think my energy levels are too much for her whereas my partner is more tranquil, which she prefers.

But we have this wonderful, sweet, intelligent little dog that is a dream to train (it helps that she loves her treats) – it's almost as if she wants to win at everything, she's got to be the best – first getting to that ball before it stops rolling, getting it back as fast as she can, first to that rabbit disappearing into the scrub, first to the door to greet visitors – she always wants to be The Best. Which she is!

I feel quite bad that we weren't able to continue with her S&R training and in ways, I think that I've let her down as she had so much ability which I haven't nurtured enough, but we still have a great little companion that's so loyal and smart, of whom we're both so proud.

Over the past 2 years, I noticed that Mia began to act differently and out of her usual routine: stopping early on our walks, looking after us, then returning to the house on her own, asking to go outside at 8pm then standing on the terrace as if not understanding what she was meant to do – none of which she ever did before. Despite asking a few knowledgeable people who could offer no reasons for her change of behaviour, I just sensed that something wasn't right. And sadly, my fears were confirmed as she has recently been diagnosed with early canine-dementia.

It breaks my heart to think that that intelligent, bright, little mind is being destroyed by this insidious disease, but I try to console myself that at least she's not in any pain.

Trying to look on the bright side, she's now on a bucket-load of tablets – costing the proverbial arm and leg, that will hopefully stop further cerebral deterioration. These have to be stuffed twice daily into a little dog that defiantly locks her jaws together with a very determined look in her eyes that questions the wisdom of continuing with that particular course of action. But with the help of cream cheese, the tablets are disguised enough for her to deign to take them. And even more positive, she's forgotten that she really doesn't like Susana, her vet, greeting her like her long-lost friend and that treatments and injections can hurt, so visits to the clinic are not quite so traumatic now!

Dementia can cause a dog to become more clingy, which is the case with Mia; from being an independent little animal that only sought affection when she chose, she's now much more loving. She spends most of her day sleeping but constantly wants to be near me or my partner, and is my little shadow around the

house. She climbs up on the sofa between my partner and me in the evenings, and lies at the foot of the bed at night. When I wake in the morning, I find that she's migrated and is curled up by my shoulder, with her head on the pillow. What a lovely way to start each day!!

We have to remember that her little head isn't working the way it was before, and to have more patience and understanding of some of her behaviour, but the medical advice is that Mia could continue to live a reasonably good life for another 4-5 years, so we are blessed that we will continue to enjoy this wonderful little dog for more time to come.

(All photos: P. Jones)

Thank you for our wonderful journey together, Mia. This may have taken a change of direction but we'll be with you until the very end.

Chan
By Dorinda, Spain

It had been 4 heart-breaking years since my beautiful American Cocker Spaniel, Chloe, had died. I vowed that I would never have another, she had been the love of my life for 12 years and no other dog could ever take her place.

However, my circumstances changed and I had been living alone for 8 months, when after much deliberation, I decided to adopt a rescue dog.

I posted on Facebook that I was looking for a 4-5 year-old female, Yorkie/Shitzu type, but the replies that I got were all for large dogs – which was not something I was used to. I guess what I was hoping for was a small dog that urgently needed continuity of home comforts due no fault of their own, so as not to be faced with the trauma of being placed in a new home.

Then, about a month later, checking my Facebook posts on my birthday, my friend Nicola had sent me a photo of a dog called Chan, saying "What about this one?" It showed a small male dog, about 18 months old; my immediate reaction was "Oh, I wanted a bitch about 5 years old!"

However, I rang the owner and he asked me to come to view the dog, as he was desperate to rehome him in Spain (he also said that he was having to let him go as he was allergic to him). Arrangements had been made to send Chan to Germany but the home could not take him until the following month, when the transportation was scheduled.

That afternoon, I went to see Chan and after spending an hour with him, and in spite of him appearing to be a friendly little dog, he seemed to be a very excitable and boisterous puppy … I was unsure that he was right for me.

But the thought of his future bothered me and as I knew I could give him a good life, I agreed to take him.

(All photos: PeaJayz)

The first 6 months were not easy as he did not respond to anything I said, and he barked persistently (thankfully, I have a large garden!). I have to say that there were times when I regretted taking him, as I thought he seemed so naughty. I had continued to go to his previous vet, Susana, and she told me a little of his background and that "he is not naughty, it is that he does not know right from wrong".

With perseverance, things started to get better and he was finding a routine that he knew. Plus he also seemed to know what I was doing and saying. Within a few more months, he was a different dog.

I have had Chan for nearly 5 years now and to get to where we are today, I would say it has taken 12 months of TLC, but it has all been worth it as he has rewarded me tenfold, daily.

He is so affectionate and playful, we adore each other. I never thought I could love another dog after my Chloe but I was wrong, I now love 2 dogs … one in my heart and the one beside me.

Thank heavens I rescued him from the unknown.

MONGREL DOGS ARE TRULY UNIQUE

All different colours.

Different sizes.

Different shapes.

Different temperaments.

Different and multi-varied gene-pools.

But all with wonderful individual characters and abilities to make the most amazing pets.

Lady Edith *(Photo: C.England)*

Tasha – Thanks So Much

By Maya, Germany

I want to tell you about our new addition to the family.

I live with my daughter and mother, and have two small dogs (also from Spanish animal rescues) but I always wanted to have a bigger dog again.

I became aware through an acquaintance on Facebook when she posted about Tasha in her profile, and was very moved by her story. She was probably thrown as a puppy over a fence of an abandoned business premises and left to face her fate alone.

I was very excited when finally, after a couple of months, Tasha was ready and on her way to us. When she arrived, I was so pleased that I had chosen her, the introduction into her new home was no problem at all, and the other dogs completely welcomed and accepted her.

After a few days came the shock… Tasha had a seizure! I had no idea what was happening to her and couldn't help her at all. The second seizure came a couple of days later, and the diagnosis was made quickly… epilepsy! No one could explain it. Tasha had never shown any signs before. That's where I

am now. This has been confirmed to me by vets and clinics, it is an illness that is still inexplicable and complex with so many types.

She was given medication, and slowly the seizures ceased. And while it has got better, unfortunately the condition is incurable. I've learned from it and know at least how to be there for Tasha in these situations. Our love for this dog and her love for us have helped us to give her a fulfilling life.

My daughter and Tasha have over the course of time become a heart and soul, and I would even say that it is a friendship for life! I would always choose her again! Even if she has a potentially life-threatening illness!

We love you, Tasha!

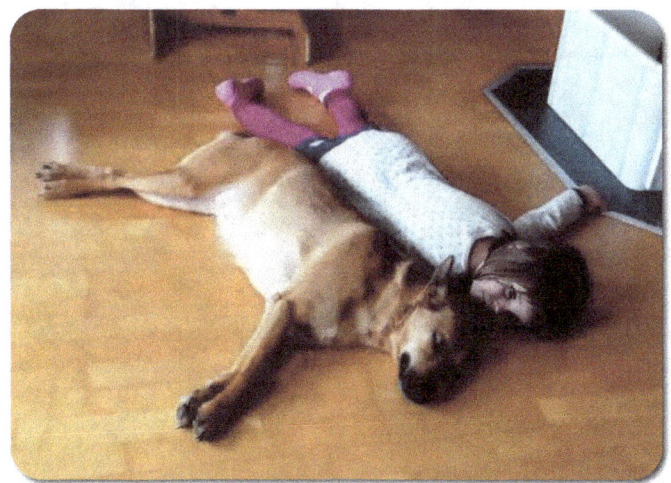

Sweet dreams for Tasha with her special friend, Lara

I always knew Tasha belonged to us

(All Photos: Maya)

If a dog will not come to you after having looked you in the face, you should go home and examine your conscience.

Woodrow Wilson, (28 Dec 1856–3 Feb 1924), American politician and academic who served as the 28th President of the United States from 1913 to 1921

Buddy and Bruce *(Photo: A.Davies)*

Puma

(Photo: PeaJayz)

Tragic Puma, left in a boarding kennels by his "loving" owners when they went on holiday, except … they never came back for him, or paid what was owed for his keep. Finally, the kennel owner lost patience and was going to have him put to sleep, before a charity saved him.

Puma never recovered from the trauma of losing his pet parents, was miserable every single day of his life in the shelter, and sadly never managed to find another home before dying approximately a year later.

IN MEMORY
Little Soldier, Tommy
By Kim & George Barker-Blakemore, UK

Tommy, through no fault of his own, was put into a rescue shelter in Spain by his elderly owner who, due to illness, could no longer care for him. Luckily for this little man it was a marvellous rescue run by volunteers who are real animal-lovers.

He had been in the shelter for 8 months when I saw him on Facebook. I explained my family situation to the charity, which then vetted us. We already had two Spanish rescue dogs, Bella and Olivia, and were approved to adopt him and so Tommy joined our family. And I volunteered with the rescue charity.

It was not plain sailing when Tommy first came as he wanted to be pack leader – which the girls were not happy about. But we persevered and it wasn't long before we were a united family.

Tommy was so popular with everyone. I soon realised that he had a way with people, especially the elderly. I was out with him one day, sitting on a bench at the local country park here in Kent, when an elderly lady started fussing over Tommy. I said, "He loves all that – keep going", when she remarked he would make a lovely therapy dog.

I looked into this and a few weeks later we were being assessed as to his suitability as a visiting therapy dog. He made the grade and we were off. Tommy loved it! After his first visit, they produced a newsletter about him and took photos, his picture was everywhere in the nursing home; it was pretty clear we would be making regular visits.

Being chauffeured to "work"

Tommy had motion-sickness in the car so I bought him a pushchair to ensure he was not worn out on his visits, which would have entailed a two-mile hike on foot each way from home.

His second site was a military retirement and injured personnel organisation. On his first visit, we were standing around talking and everyone started to laugh. I looked at Tommy to see him with his front paws on a small table, drinking an elderly man's tea! From then on, every time we went, a cup of tea was made especially for Tommy; they got him his own bowl and always had dog treats.

Tommy had an exceptional way with the sick and the elderly, he was adored by my father who passed away at 88, and my only surviving Aunt who is 99 – he always sat with her, usually on the next chair and would not get down until she went home; she always asked how he is.

SECOND-HAND DOGS

The paperwork stated that he was 3 years old when Tommy came to us, but we and our vets in England and Spain think he was older. He was a much-loved member of our family for 6 years, and was with the therapy group for several years.

Tommy sadly passed away in May 2020. He is missed terribly but what he gave to so many was joy and love and he will never be forgotten.

He will forever be in our hearts.

RIP, little soldier.

Tommy, with his beloved Aunt Nell

(All photos: K&G Barker-Blakemore)

Max (Photo: K. Schatz)

Poochie Princess – Part 2
By Julia Roberts, Spain

I've described my journey to becoming a first-time dog mummy to three-year-old Nita. My husband had been a dog owner, but not me. My thoughts were, *'I'm not really a dog sort of person'* and *'too time consuming and such a tie'*. Hah! What did I know?

A little over 12 months after adopting Nita I was again lying awake, thinking she needs a playmate. She loves people but has lost her social skills. She doesn't like other dogs, maybe a puppy? Yes, no, yes, no. How will Nita react? Too messy. Chewing. House training. No, no, no!

Milo (Photo: PeaJayz)

Someone must have heard my confused musings as a litter of 5 puppies were found abandoned under a hedge in our village by the wonderful Mailie Martin in the village of San Cayetano. It was arranged for Nita to meet the puppies here in her home to gauge her reaction. If she was at all unhappy or stressed it would go no further.

Turns out I was the stressed and anxious one. Nita was calm and very relaxed with the 5 jumping balls of fluff that had invaded her domain. I had done my research and knew we should choose a male which narrowed 5 down to 4. Then I remembered that black dogs are harder to home in Spain, so a black one was the choice. 4 down to 2. We then chose the less timid of the 2 left, which brought us to the one … Milo!

And two weeks later, he was here!

What can I tell you? In the space of 14 months I've gone from 'I'm not really a dog sort of person' to besotted mummy of two fur-babies. Yes, there is chewing, early wake-ups, scraps and so much poop. But there is also fun, mischief and so much love too.

The photos speak for themselves.

(Photo: J.Roberts)

Even if you can't have a dog, I would urge you to support your local rescue charity and help them with the work they do: walk a dog, donate some food, sponsor a dog, help to groom, have a coffee-morning to raise funds. Any rescue group would welcome anything that you could do to help them.

Twinkle
By Nicola Cherry, Spain

Ten years ago, we were leaving our house which is in a quiet gated golf resort, with our two dogs – one-year-old brother-and-sister Bischon-Maltese to take them for a walk when a little light-coloured dog appeared from underneath my car.

It was like she somehow had a hiding place in the engine. She followed us the whole way as we continued on our walk and then back to our house. She looked like a large-sized Chihuahua but was a very timid, quiet dog who already showed signs of being very loving.

It was a Sunday, so when we took her to the police station, they said that we would need to come back the following day as they do not deal with stray dogs on Sundays.

That night, we made her a cosy bed in the kitchen (our dogs sleep in their beds in our bedroom) and she was good as gold and just seemed so pleased to be cared for.

On the Monday morning, I decided I would take her to the vet to see if she had a chip. On the way there, she sat in the passenger seat – again, good as gold, with her head resting on the handbrake, just looking up at me.

The vet checked her over and told me that the little dog seemed healthy enough, that she was probably about one-year-old (so the same as our dogs), and any fleas on her were dead. There was also no chip.

Coming out of the clinic, I thought about taking her direct to the police station but there was no way I could leave this loving little dog at a police station –

from where she'd go to a dog pound. So I drove home wondering what my husband was going to say … three dogs??!!

However, when I parked outside our house, he came to the front door and the first question was: "Where is she?" When I told him that she was on the passenger seat, his reply was: "Oh thank goodness!"

So that was that, she was here to stay! We named her Twinkle – but there was still one obstacle – she had to be good with our new young baby grandson George.

Baby George came into our house, carried in his baby car seat and from the moment he was put on the floor Twinkle´s tail would not stop waggling and she was licking him like she had known him all his young life. In fact, we had to stop her as it was too much!

We now have four grandchildren and she is the same with all of them. The other two dogs greet the grandchildren but not like Twinkle – she just loves to try and attract their attention to be stroked and spoken to whilst the other two lose interest.

Twinkle loves to disappear into places where she can't be found; we think that she may have arrived hiding in the engine of our car and that's how she came to be in our resort, as the previous night we had been at a restaurant about a 10-minute drive away, just off a motorway.

She was, and still is, very timid and does not like even my husband putting on her collar and lead. She does not like going near bins so I cannot imagine what she maybe went through before coming to us. We never went back to the restaurant to ask if anyone had reported their dog missing, as I would not have felt comfortable giving her back. She certainly was not behaving like she was missing a loving owner.

I went to a spiritualist church not long after her arrival and the medium said that he believed that sometimes a pet can appear in someone's life as a gift.

I truly believe Twinkle was a gift to us. She follows me everywhere and looks at me when I go out as if asking: "Can I not come too?!"

(Photos: N.Cherry)

All our dogs are now 12 years old and they still love running around, playing with each other. The other two watch Twinkle going into the swimming pool, sitting on the top step splashing her face, then she gets out, shakes herself off and the three of them race off again like mad-caps!

Dave
By Daisy Merrell, UK

With rescue dogs, you are never 100% sure about the dog you are getting. They can come with "baggage" that you have to be willing to accept, and you need to learn how to cater for their needs, as you don't always know what they have been through.

Never in a million years would I have thought I would be getting my first dog from a rescue centre in Spain. But I won't lie to you, it is by far the best thing I have ever done.

With only being able to see what Dave was like through the pictures and videos that were sent to me, I was very nervous about getting him. As I live with my parents, my main concern was that they wouldn't like him and that he wouldn't get on with the family dog, Henry.

SECOND-HAND DOGS

However, as soon as Dave arrived at my front door, I knew I had nothing to worry about.

He's one of the loveliest dogs you will ever meet. He is very calm with a good temperament. He can be a bit clumsy at times but that's what makes him Dave!

It didn't take him very long to settle in and come out of his shell. Dave and Henry have got on so well together, and have become best friends. I think having Henry has helped Dave become more confident and settle in quicker as he has another dog to learn from.

Enjoying some guy-time with best bud, Henry

Dave has become my little shadow round the house, he follows me everywhere. I can't even go to the toilet without him sitting outside the door crying for me to come out! Some people might find that annoying but I quite like it.

So far, he has been very easy to train. Apart from the occasional digging of holes and chewing a few shoes, which any 1-year-old dog would do, I have had no issues with him at all.

He has fitted in so well, it is like he has always been a part of the family. With everything going on in the world, Dave could not have come at a better time as he has brought a lot of joy to me and my family. I could not have asked for a better dog. He really is such a bundle of fun to have around and he has made my life so much better.

Grrrgggghhh … gonna make this 'nake understand who's boss!

(All photos: D.Merrill)

Thank God I got the rejects. These animals are very, very affectionate.

Eartha Kitt, about her two poodles who weren't up to the breeder's "standards", (17 Jan 1927–25 Dec 2008), American singer, actress, dancer, comedian, activist, author, and songwriter

Pedro *(Photo: PeaJayz)*

Fleur

By Kelly Mander, UK

Having lost one of our dogs at the age of 9, our Hungarian Vizsla, Bodhi, had become depressed and withdrawn, so we decided to adopt another dog sooner than we had originally expected.

My partner had decided he would like a German Shorthaired Pointer, as they are similar in energy levels and characteristics of both our Viz, and his previous spaniel. We applied to go on the waiting lists for the GSP UK rescues and I began searching all of the dogs' homes in the country, to no avail.

During one of my searches, I came across a picture of a little puppy named Fleur following surgery to amputate a hind leg. I read her story, she was 8 weeks old and had been dumped in a shelter in Spain. Whilst in the shelter Fleur was attacked by a large dog, resulting in dreadful wounds to her hind leg including a fracture that were so severe, the leg couldn't be saved. Luckily a volunteer there got in touch with a rescue who offered to pay for her surgery and help rehome her.

I sent the picture of Fleur to my partner, not expecting he would be interested as we were both dubious of adopting from abroad at the time. However, he was,

so we contacted the rescue (Fairy Dog Fosterers) for some more information.

We are both veterinary nurses so were not at all phased by Fleur being tri-pawed. We felt that we would be the perfect family for her and in the best position to offer her a new life. Luckily for us, the Fairy Dog Fosterers agreed and after a home inspection and interview process, they allowed us to adopt Fleur.

After what felt like forever, she was finally on the van on her long journey to us from Spain. She arrived late at night, walked in to our home, had some food and then helped herself to the contents of Bodhi's toy box. Over the following weeks, her character began to show and she kept us on our toes. She is very mischievous and likes to steal everything she can – toys, shoes, food, basically anything she can get her mouth around.

The lack of a limb does not slow her down. She can hurtle around at top speed and still manages to sneak on our bed. When she is walking slowly, the hobble is noticeable but running is unaffected. She does lose her balance sometimes but is not discouraged when she stumbles.

Bodhi is very much in love with his new friend and they spend most of their day either playing or snuggling up together. He has definitely got his mojo back.

She understandably shows some signs of anxiety on the lead by barking and growling when other dogs approach. We are working with her with lots of treats to try and create a positive situation when meeting dogs and have enlisted the help of a dog behaviourist friend.

There is definitely a feelgood factor in rescuing an animal, even more so I think rescuing one with a disability. The only time she misses the leg is when she wants a good scratch on that side. But she's already learned how to tell us to get us to do it for her. We are looking forward to watching her living the happiest life she can as part of our family.

(All Photos: K.Mander)

Timmy – The Shortest Tale
Spain

Mailie and Timmy *(Photo: M.Martin)*

January 8: Little brown fella found by a roadside, scavenging for food. Was scooped up, taken to Petlovers Vet Clinic for a check-over and overnight stay to keep him safe. The lovely staff there want to call him Carlos.

January 9: Sent to super-fosterer, Mailie, for lots of TLC. We all think he looks like a Timmy. Petlovers staff are overruled.

January 10: Devilishly devious as she is, Mailie metaphorically dangles Timmy in front of a local lady, Patricia, who was "kind of looking" for a little dog, and suggests she "fosters" him.

January 11: Job done! Timmy has worked his magic; Patricia has fallen headlong in love with him. And it's official, the feeling is mutual – Timmy and Patricia belong together!

And Timmy's story continues to be happy; he and Patricia are a familiar sight in their village. In her words: "He's bright, happy, entertaining and very, very loving."

(Photo: PeaJayz)

Sweet dreams for Patricia and Timmy *(Photo: P.Foote)*

Lola *(Photo: L. Lovering)*

Dogs are not our whole life, but they make our lives whole.

Roger Andrew Caras (May 24 1928 – Feb 18 2001), American wildlife photographer, writer, wildlife preservationist and television personality

Maro *(Photo: J.Slater)*

Little Cuddle Monster, Ellie
By Lisa Dunlop, UK

When Ellie came into our lives, we had no intention of getting another dog! We had lost Jackson, our 15-year-old Lurcher Cross, two and a half years previously and were heartbroken, and just didn't feel like we could go through it again. But the house did always feel a bit more empty and less like a home, and the kids were pestering us to get another one.

It was during the height of the Covid lockdown here in the UK when I received a message in a Whatsapp Group from my friend Natalie, with a picture of the most beautiful Border Collie with the kindest expression I'd ever seen in a dog – you could just tell by looking at her that she was a sweetheart.

Well, Ellie's story was not a good one unfortunately. She had been found as a stray in Spain at six years old, and after the PAPS rescue group had found her a new home in Scotland, she was rejected after having only spent five days there. So Natalie was being asked to foster her as an emergency as there was nowhere else for her to go.

Something about it just kind of 'felt' right – here we were spending lots of time at home during lockdown, and here was this gorgeous wee dog just needing a chance at a loving family. So, after some discussion, my husband and I went to visit Ellie to take her for a walk and get to know her. And that was it! There was never any option of us not bringing her home to be part of our family.

We hadn't told the kids so when we brought Ellie home, it was a complete surprise. Our 12-year-old daughter Carrie burst into tears and our 15-year-old son, Adam, went immediately to get Jackson's bed for Ellie from his room which he'd kept all this time.

And it was like from that moment Ellie just 'hoovered' up all the affection she possibly could from us – I don't think I've ever seen a more petted or cuddled dog in my life, and she absolutely loves it! She's so affectionate and loving and likes nothing better than to cuddle up on the sofa with you.

It's definitely a challenge adopting a rescue dog – especially one from Spain where you don't speak each other's languages! We're having some issues with toy guarding, separation anxiety and reactivity towards other dogs which we're training with lots of treats, praise and other positive reinforcement. But she is slowly settling in and we're seeing little bits of improvement all the time, and you can't expect a dog who has gone through what Ellie has gone through to be completely well-adjusted straight away. To be honest, we love her as she is, with all her imperfections.

Adopting a rescue dog can be hard work but is one of the most satisfying and rewarding things you'll ever do in your life.

Her favourite place during the day now is in a bed underneath my desk as I work from home, and now that the kids are back at school, she loves to cuddle in with them as soon as they return home. She has bonded with each of us differently – I'm the mother figure she comes running to when she's scared (and I do the training with her as I'm home all day), she loves going on walks with my husband, and she loves the cuddles and attention (and sneaky treats!) she gets from the kids. We're all so happy to have her in our family and couldn't imagine life without her.

Ellie's favourite place when Adam gets back from school

(All photos: Lisa Dunlop)

Snow's Story
By Chris & Debs Wright, UK

It was about three years after we lost our beloved English bull terrier, Marley, that my wife, Debbie, started to notice more and more upsetting stories on Facebook about abandoned and ill-treated dogs that needing rescuing, and seeking safe and loving homes.

We had just moved to a new house and soon Debbie realised that something was missing. Of course! "A house is not a home without a dog". We decided that our next dog would be a rescue and one from abroad, because she had read of *perreras* in Spain which are basically killing stations for stray and abandoned dogs. They are "last chance" saloons for stray dogs and cats where they wait to be "put down" unless they are rescued. The *perreras* only keep these animals for a finite time before putting them to sleep. Although there are plenty of dogs needing rescuing in our own country, England, they have a much better chance here of survival than their foreign counterparts.

We discussed the pros and cons of doing this and decided to go for it! Debbie was determined to rescue a dog – even if she could save just one dog.

We didn't really research it in great depth and we didn't actively look at, or register with any particular rescue dog rescue organisation or charity. We weren't even looking for a particular type or breed of dog (although we had once said we would never have any dog apart from an English Bull Terrier!).

Then Debbie's sister, Maria, saw a Facebook post regarding a dog called Nora, which was an open appeal to raise money to pay the fee to save her from being put down at a *perrera*. Deadline was the end of the week ... two days' time!

We quickly sent the money to save her and also agreed to adopt her. We were told that Nora had been put into a privately-run kennels with many other dogs. We later heard that she had become ill and was taken to a vet who diagnosed her with Parvo virus and possible distemper. The charity told Maria that they were low on funds to pay Nora's vets bills. Again, we sent money to help. Later we found out that she had been taken out of the animal hospital against veterinary advice and placed back into the dog pound. She was fed normal food – again, against the vet's advice, and she suffered bad diarrhoea.

It was very upsetting and frustrating because we couldn't actively see what was going on and it wasn't easy to get any reliable information regarding poor Nora's health. After many requests, we were finally sent a photo which was terribly upsetting as she was so emaciated. Debbie was so concerned at the lack of accurate information and improvement to Nora's health that she said she was getting a flight out there to see exactly what was going on.

This trip didn't happen as sadly we received the devastating news that Nora had died, weighing the same as a Chihuahua and she was a Beagle-sized dog! It was so heartbreaking – she had been saved at the eleventh hour from being put down in the *perrera,* only to endure weeks of suffering and inadequate care. We felt terrible that we were in some way responsible for prolonging her suffering. We had tried to do the right thing but the poor dog had suffered more than if she had been put down at the *perrera*.

Still traumatised after this failed experience of trying to adopt Nora, Debbie was unsure whether we should try again and quite frankly, she didn't know if she could ever trust a dog rescue organisation again.

Whilst the adoption of Nora was ongoing, Maria had spotted a dog on Facebook called Snow, who had the most amazing blue eyes. She told Debbie about him and sent some pics over. Debbie thought he was beautiful.

He was in the care of a Spanish rescue centre called P.A.P.S (Protectora Animales Perros del Sol). They had taken him from another rescue centre who had looked after him for four months after he had been found living on the streets. We don't know the circumstances which led to Snow becoming homeless, but heard that he was often to be seen under a tree in the car park of a nightclub.

A couple of weeks after poor Nora's death we decided to try again with Snow.

His picture had again been posted on Facebook as a dog looking for a home; when we contacted the charity, we were told that a "home-check" would be required to ensure that our property, ourselves, and our lifestyle were suitable for a rescue dog from P.A.P.S. A lady called Lisa would be contacting us to arrange the home-check visit.

When Lisa phoned us, we discovered that she lived in the same village as us. Small world! She had herself adopted a couple of dogs from P.A.P.S and had even been to Spain to visit their rescue centre as a volunteer. She was immediately able to lay to rest any fears and worries we had. She was full of praise for the charity and could not speak more highly of them.

And so it was. We began the adoption process and it could not have gone any better or smoother. A definite five-star rating! P.A.P.S arranged Snow's passport and all the necessary health checks and vaccinations, and arranged the transport from Spain to the UK.

On the 23rd September 2016, we were to receive our rescue dog from Spain! We were able to track his progress via an app, which was a great as we could see our boy Snow getting nearer and nearer to his new home.

"He's in Southend now", "He's coming down Royal Artillery Way", "He's past Waitrose", "He'll be here in fifteen minutes!"

"He's coming down the road!!"

Mass excitement! Debbie, I, Maria, Bob and Sue went outside, phones switched to camera mode ready for Snow's imminent arrival. It was 8:30pm and dark. The transport van pulled up to a stop, the driver got out and walked to the back to open the rear doors. It was dark but a car's headlights provided a little light. The doors opened …

And the driver brought Snow out. Debbie and Maria were waiting just outside the back of the van and there he was, lit up by the camera flashes of all who were there to welcome him to his new forever home.

Debbie immediately hugged him. "Hello darling …."

She was so worried that Snow might try to escape and run off scared, she scooped him up in her arms and took him across the road and into our house where, after more cuddles and strokes from us all, he tucked into a chicken and rice dinner prepared by Debbie.

Looking back, it was probably a risky thing to do, to just grab him like that. He could have been scared and nervous. Who knows how he could have reacted? He could have bitten Debbie! But he didn't, instead he looked up at her as if to say, "Thank you for rescuing me". It was as though he knew he was safe.

But he was here. We had done it. We had rescued a dog.

When everyone had gone and after a meal, Snow followed Debbie into the lounge and sat down on the sofa. He laid his head on her shoulder and looked deeply into her eyes – "Thank you for rescuing me – I love you already … got any more of that chicken and rice?"

Debbie spent the first couple of nights sleeping downstairs with him. After that we left him downstairs on his own.

Everything was a mystery to Snow. He couldn't work out carpet and he was afraid of the stairs and the TV. To our amazement, he never chewed anything up, he never did a wee anywhere, he didn't howl or cry. So well behaved. He never showed any separation anxiety when we left him alone for a while. He is not a needy dog. I guess because he lived on the street he learnt to live and survive on his own. He was perfect!

However, in the first two or three weeks, there were a few times when he snapped at visitors in the house, but only when Debbie was also in the same room. We think he may have been protective of her as she was the first person he met from the van, who had been kind to him. Everything was so new, all these strangers approaching him, reaching out to him, touching him – it must have been all so overwhelming. P.A.P.S had said they would take him back but we said, "No way". This behaviour didn't last long. We knew he was a great dog but sought advice from an expert who told us that he just needed a bit of time to adjust to this new

SECOND-HAND DOGS

unfamiliar life. We were never going to give up on him. We had rescued him and it was our responsibility to make it work, and give him the best life we can.

After this initial period, he has never snapped or shown any aggression again, and absolutely loves everyone … except men in hoodies with sticks at whom he will bark. We are guessing that he may have been hit by a man or men with a stick when he was young. There have been two times when he started barking at women with walking sticks, one of them was Debbie's mother! He wouldn't let my mother-in-law in the house! Result! Good boy, Snow. Although I'm happy to say they are best of friends now.

Early on we took him to a dog training session where we were told that Snow didn't like people going on about his eyes and that he was a dominant dog. The group leader used her huge German Shepherd dog to play-fight with Snow to overpower him and put him in his place. Other dogs were aggressive towards Snow but he wasn't aggressive back in return. He just lowered his head and walked away from the training field with his tail between his legs – it was sad to see. He has never showed dominance as far as we can see.

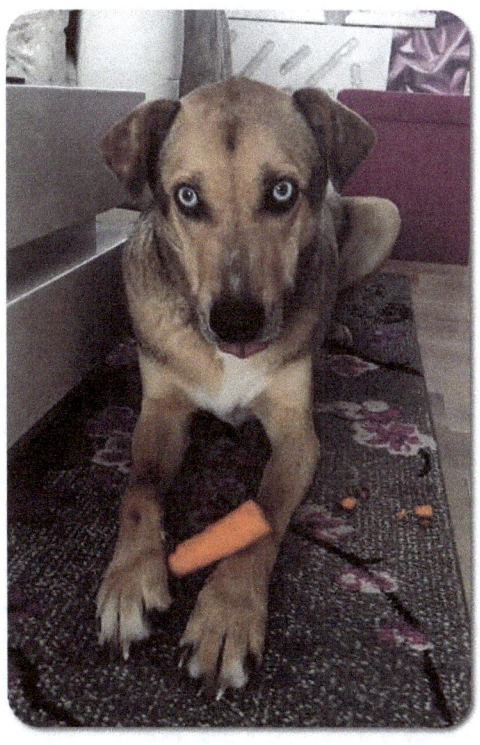

During one of these training sessions, about fifteen dogs crossed a dry ditch (normally full of water, acting as a boundary) and got off the training field on to a railway track, one of which was Snow. The trainer and other owners were shouting for the dogs to come back but to no avail. We called out to Snow and he came back straight away – the other dogs following him safely off the tracks. Two minutes later trains passed in each direction!

Needless to say, even though we picked up some useful information there, we didn't go back again. Snow didn't enjoy it and it seemed Debbie and I were the ones being trained!

Snow was soon elevated to the status of "Lord Snow" because he had his own human staff to attend to his every whim, and had free run of his manor. When Debbie and I went to visit P.A.P.S, we were met at the airport by one of the volunteers. As we passed through Arrivals, we saw her holding up a sign saying: "The Servants of Lord Snow"!

Snow has been a brilliant addition to our family. He is a great companion and friend, and is very loving. He is a very cheeky and intelligent boy who knows exactly how to play us!

After a few months of sleeping on his own downstairs, one night we let him upstairs to our bedroom. He has slept on our bed ever since with his Lordship in the middle, all stretched out and Debbie and I having to fit around him.

I'm not sure about his moniker of "Lord Snow", as recently he has been more like Lord of the Dance! If he wants more dinner, he'll stomp and tap his feet Riverdance-style on the wooden floor demanding another carrot! He loves carrots, apples and satsumas – perhaps he used to get food by digging up veg in fields and picking up fruit off the ground.

Snow absolutely loves running, and almost seems to be smiling as he bombs past us, looking up as if saying "look at me, yippee". He loves playing with other dogs too and generally leads them astray.

When we take him on group walks, he is the one who instigates the "catch me if you can" game, and leads the other dogs off across the fields chasing him, but never straying too far away, always keeping an eye on where we are. Rescuing Lord Snow has been one of the best things we have ever done. It has been so rewarding as he has enriched our lives and made our house a home.

We are just so glad we didn't give up after our first experience of trying to adopt a dog from Spain. We know of many smooth and successful adoptions and would definitely recommend it. I guess there will always be the odd case of adoptions not going to plan but these seem rare. I have met many people who have adopted their dogs from abroad Spain, Romania … they have never looked back and would always do it again.

We will definitely adopt a rescue dog again!

(All Photos: C & D Wright)

I know that I have had friends who would never have vexed or betrayed me, if they had walked on all fours.

Horace Walpole (24 Sept 1717–2 Mar 1797), 4th Earl of Orford, English writer, art historian, man of letters, antiquarian and Whig politician

(Photo: PeaJayz)

Lady
UK

Strange how things sometimes work out in life. There I was, minding my own business, when I received a text from the lovely lady, Cathy, who runs Fairy Dog Fosterers in the UK. She'd been asked by an acquaintance there if she knew of anyone in Spain who could help to find a dog. And immediately I popped into her mind.

A lady, Gill, and her husband, Rob, had been on holiday in Spain in their motorhome a few weeks previously and at one campsite, they came across a very beautiful young Mastin pup that had been abandoned. Despite the site-owner's rules, the pup used to sneak in to scrounge food, and Gill lost her heart to her, completely and utterly. But as they were due to travel back to the UK, there wasn't time to make the relevant arrangements to adopt her, and they'd had to set off on their journey leaving the young dog behind. Totally breaking Gill's heart.

Arriving back in the UK, Gill couldn't lose the images of the beauty she'd left behind, and decided that she just had to have her. Which was where I came in.

Apparently, the campsite was near Calnegre, close to the ancient town of Lorca in a beautiful natural region of Murcia – just over an hour from where I live. So, one day, armed with satellite coordinates, off I set – with more than a bit of trepidation as I have the navigational abilities of a gnat. But I had Ms SatNav to keep me on the correct path. Right?

The drive there was lovely, the sun beamed down as it tends to do here, traffic was light and I enjoyed passing through some of the stunning wild national parks in the area. The roads became narrower, I could see the sparkling sea in the distance so felt I was at least going in the right direction. Ms SatNav, who I sometimes suspect has even worse navigational ability than me, seemed to be on top of her game and quite alert that morning, and was very conscientious in instructing me where to turn. With each turn the roads became even more narrow but my excitement was mounting as I could see the chequered finish flag on the satnav. I was getting closer.

"Turn right", Ms SatNav ordered. Really? I asked dubiously. "Yep, turn right" (she can be unreasonably bossy at times). Turning right brought me on to a narrow, gravelled track that wound up a **very** steep hill. Well, I suppose campsites can be anywhere, so up I went, my little car's engine growling with the strain of 1st gear, the wheels scrabbling for traction on the loose stones. The track narrowed drastically as I climbed, with steep drops on both sides when my stomach began to tighten with fear, until we reached the top at the finish flag.

We were there … outside a small ramshackle hut. Not a campervan in sight. Hmmm! Definitely not a campsite. Not to mention the postage stamp on which I now had to turn to retrace my steps, sheer drops on all sides. Definitely squeaky-bum time! Ms SatNav had suddenly gone very quiet, as well the stupid woman might, while I contemplated my options. Home? Or dog? Home was the easy option, but guilt made me think of that poor Mastin puppy on her tod in a campsite with a not-too-bright future, so a very technical 25-point turn on the stamp was completed, before carefully inching down the little gravel path.

Ms SatNav suddenly awoke from her slumbers to remind me to do a U-turn to go back to my finish flag. For not the first time in our very tetchy relationship,

I told her to pipe down in no uncertain terms while I went back up the road to where I'd seen a small campsite. Perhaps someone there could tell me where Gill's site was.

There were only a few vans there, a couple of people reclined on chairs soaking up the Spanish sun, staring at my little car with something akin to horror. Obviously only motorhomes are to be trusted.

Undaunted, out I got to ask a couple – who turned out to be from Denmark, explaining why I'd had the bare-faced audacity to enter the site. The lady, Susanna, turned and pointed through the wire fence behind their motorhome, from where a sad white and grey face peered. Unbelievably, I'd found the pup despite Ms SatNav's best efforts at sabotage.

The young Mastin girlie nervously came in to the campsite – Susanna told me that they'd been feeding her despite the site manager's directives, and had been thinking of taking her back with them to Denmark but, like Gill and Rob, were hindered by the length of time required to sort out the health and passport requirements. But they happily agreed to help me to catch the pup, from where she'd go to our shelter.

Easier said than done, as the poor girl was very timid and scared, and try as we might, we couldn't get close enough to get a lead on her. She used to fall on her side submissively, going totally limp, and then scarper as soon as the lead appeared. Half an hour later, I was really wondering if we were going to be successful until we came up with a crazy strategy whereby we'd try to corner her, in the hope that she'd hit the deck on a blanket we'd lay out, with which we'd try to net her and then we could get a lead on her. Easy-peasy, eh?

But sometimes, crazy plans do work – even this one, and we finally had her leashed, and between the three of us, carried her over to my car, then man-handled her into the back – the inside of which suddenly seemed to shrink significantly with this very large pup!

Waving a very grateful goodbye to the lovely Danish couple, we were on our way. To say I was chuffed was a tiny understatement – I was over the moon. The pup refused to sit or lie down so every time I checked the rear-view mirror, all I could see was her sweet face staring back at me. I was pleased to see that she was relaxing a bit, as if she knew she was finally safe.

Stopping in a lay-by, I called Cathy in the UK, to let her know the good news to pass on to Gill, who was beside herself with joy to hear that her girl was safe and now in the safety of the shelter. She'd already decided on her name … the poor scared Mastin stray was now Lady.

Lady was immediately microchipped, and began her course of vaccinations; she now had a bed to sleep in, and good food so began to put on weight. Her nervousness was becoming less as she met more people who didn't chase her away, and was turning into a really sweet, gentle girl.

Finally safe in the shelter *(Photo: PeaJayz)*

Gill and Rob couldn't wait for Lady to come to them, so revved up the motorhome and immediately hit the road back to Spain, to pick up their girl! They were so thrilled to see her although their dog Sam didn't look to enamoured to have to share his life with another pooch. We all held our breaths when they met but he was a total gent, and Lady was … well … a lady! And off they all went. I was so sad to say goodbye to this lovely girl but it always makes it somewhat easier when one knows the dog has gone to a loving home, and will have a good life.

Many might have been nervous about just picking up a dog off the campo (or street) but everything has gone so well – Rob had to carry Lady … all 30+ kilos – into the campervan the first few times as she may never have been in a home, let alone one on wheels. She very quickly found "her" place in the vehicle and is now a seasoned traveller, happily going wherever the road takes her and her family. They have now bought a better motorhome with more interior space with Sam and Lady in mind.

Lady had to accustom herself to the new strange things that came into her life – bicycles, large trucks or buses, and now doesn't blink an eye when she comes across any of these. Sam soon discovered how nice it was to have a doggy companion and the two of them are best buddies.

Lady loves her new life, particularly fishing for trout in the local stream, walks on the beach, fun dips in the sea with Sam, with rolling in stinky things a particular favourite. Rob and Gill adore every inch of their big Mastin Lady – now nicknamed Ladybird, who has turned into a beautiful companion and a much-loved member of the family.

OK! I'm ready! Where are we off to now?! *(All other photos: G.Collins)*

Joselito *(Photo: PeaJayz)*

Claudia & Eddie

By C. Lessander, Germany

On one of our first visits to the Casa del Sol refuge, our plan was to help other shelters by taking a few of their dogs and as there was spare capacity in the Casa at that time, keeping them there until we found them good permanent homes.

We needed to take a few puppies and young dogs, so at one shelter, we took a look at a puppy run to see which dogs we liked and thought could be easily trained. My eyes immediately fell on a cute brown girl, and so we were allowed to take her and 2 more young dogs with us. We each had one of the little ones in our arms and fell completely in love with them. When they arrived at the Casa, the dogs were christened and we were each allowed to choose a name. We came up with the idea of naming the little ones after us, so the little brown dog with the short legs became "Claudia".

We soon returned home and I often thought of little Claudia. I thought that such a sweet dog would certainly be rehomed quickly. Unfortunately, that isn't what happened and it turned out that Claudia had a serious heart condition. She couldn't run fast, would often cough and wasn't doing well. She was also unable to play with the other dogs in the shelter and mostly hid under a wooden pallet. She was examined in a Spanish clinic and later operated on, followed by rehab in a foster home, but quickly it became apparent that her condition had not changed.

The following year, we visited the Casa again, and Claudia was still there. I finally lost my heart to her this time and thought about whether we could bring her to Germany. It upset me to see how ill she was but we already had two dogs, I worked while my father took care of our two dogs during the day. How could he do that with a third dog? It seemed impossible to adopt Claudia. Again, we went home without her, but we couldn't get the poorly little dog out of our heads. And then we just said: 'Let's try, we'll manage it some way or other'.

Claudia was immediately taken back to the foster home and there, she received the necessary training to live in a house. I contacted my vet in Spain, and she passed on the findings so that Claudia could be treated again in Germany. We hoped that she would survive the transport, and a few weeks later she came to us. She immediately adapted well and got along fine with our two dogs. She also walked well on a lead, so my father was able to walk three dogs without any problem. But it was also clear how ill she was. When I would return home from the office, Claudia was happy but after 3 seconds she was exhausted. It broke my heart! However, we already had an appointment at one of the best veterinary clinics in Germany.

In autumn we set off with Claudia on a four-hour drive in the direction – hopefully – of health. Claudia had to stay in the clinic for a week. She underwent surgery when another problem was diagnosed, and that too was fixed. The doctor called me and said that the operation was complicated, but successful. Claudia was practically a healthy dog.

When we were allowed to pick her up again after a week, we noticed the difference immediately. She was able to run around much longer, had more stamina and was much happier than before. It was as if she had been swapped with another dog. We were just speechless! Now, nothing stood in the way of her having an almost normal dog life – she still has to have a check-up once a year and has to take a tablet every day for the rest of her life, but she has the life expectancy of a healthy dog.

It has certainly been worthwhile adopting little Claudia. We are very happy that we were able to help her and she thanks us every day with her cheerful manner. She is popular with everyone and is the best watchdog imaginable!

(Photo Courtesy of Just Moments Photography)

(Photo Courtesy of Peggy Rodrigues)

(All other photos: C.Lessander)

PAULA JONES

Eddie

Eddie is a dog that used to live on the streets, but he'd been injured in an accident. While under the name of the rescue charity, he was very lucky to be able to live in various foster homes but could not find a Forever home for a long time and became their "problem child". Even today, I still don't know why he had to wait

so long for a Forever family, but it's certainly not that easy to rehome a disabled dog.

At first, I only saw Eddie in photos. After he'd been taken to the vet and his paw X-rayed, I saw the pictures and thought: *Oh dear, the poor dog, so young and already such bad osteoarthritis*. I was already very familiar with osteoarthritis, as one of my deceased dogs had this disease and I knew all about vets, physiotherapists, and about food additives and treatment options. I had become somewhat of an osteoarthritis specialist, so to speak. We wanted to get a third dog anyway, of course from the Casa del Sol, and as I always felt the need to adopt a dog that wasn't very easy to place, we chose Eddie.

With Eddie it wasn't necessarily love at first sight and we had quite a bumpy start. When I picked him up from the transport, I was surprised … he was very lively, given his physical condition. You could see how badly he was walking but he wanted to move and somehow he managed to do it. He jumped around and straight away wanted to jog with me on a lead. He was so sweet and jumped straight into the car, so he could begin the final part of his journey to a new life.

On arriving at home, he immediately targeted our cat. He saw him and the hunt was … ON. I always thought that Spanish dogs are fond of cats, as I had experienced with my previous dogs but Eddie, as a real hunting dog, was different from the others. And so, we taught him over many months not to do anything to the cat. I really feared that it would never work, as there were always moments when Eddie lost his control, and just *had* to chase the cat through the garden again, so I was close to despair. But after 8 months, we finally did it and this hurdle was overcome – our poor cat regained confidence in the dogs, and everyone was finally happy.

Eddie's health deteriorated greatly from one day to the next. Suddenly he couldn't walk anymore and, if I wanted to touch him, he snapped at me. He had to be muzzled and I took him to the emergency vets. They gave him strong painkillers, and I was only allowed to keep him in the garden. There was no more we could do. We ran small, slow laps which Eddie didn't like, but he was also happy that he could lay down again at the end of the laps. After 4 weeks of running practice, he was again quite mobile and we were able to start with the actual treatment.

Eddie received gold implants. I had heard that this was a very good way to take away the pain permanently. At the same time, during the anesthetic, a claw on his crippled paw was also amputated. It had pointed upwards at a 90-degree angle which always got caught on things. The operation was a complete success. Eddie was able to move well again and obviously had no more pain. He's still going to get a new hip in the future, but we can afford to wait a little while for that. Even though you can clearly see that his hip is broken, his quality of life is good.

After all these experiences with Eddie when we were often close to despair, he has secured a firm place in our hearts. I can almost never let him off the lead, but I accept that. He always remains a hunter but instead of our cat, he is now looking for deer. We train every day and have found a way to deal with his passion for hunting. Eddie is a big clown, who has adapted very well to our lives.

He has also fitted well into our small pack and, despite his occasionally odd behaviour (he sometimes growls when you stroke his head, but still visibly enjoys it), he has made many friends from dogs and people alike. We would never give him back because he enriches our family and our pack so much.

Even if the road is sometimes a rocky one, if you really want something and consistently pursue your goal, you can do anything. You just have to get involved, accept the help and advice of others and be patient. Sometimes it just takes time until things come good.

(Photo Courtesy of Just Moments Photography)

(All other photos: C.Lessander)

Shirley & Gracie
By Shirley McGillivray, UK

It had been a long time since I'd had dogs as with long working hours as a nurse it simply wasn't feasible, so for the past 20 or so years I'd had a succession of cats.

Then came retirement and for the first time I knew I would be spending more time at home and that it was probably a perfect time to think about getting a dog again. Never a keen walker, I hoped – and I was right, that a dog would encourage me to get out and about. And now living right on the seafront in Sussex there is no better place in which to do it.

To adopt was never a question and the plight of dogs in the rest of Europe seemed far more serious than in the UK. Here you don't see packs of stray dogs roaming around and if one is seen, it is usually picked up fairly quickly and taken to a place of safety.

It was a relative of ours who lives in Murcia and volunteers at PAP's rescue who brought my attention to Gracie soon after she arrived at the Casa with a seven-month-old puppy (eventually adopted by an English family living in the area). After seeing photos and videos of her and hearing about her placid nature I decided she was the one for me. Arrangements soon began for her to be spayed and have the necessary vaccinations, before being transported overland to the UK.

Gracie settled in quickly and has proved to be a near-perfect dog; sweet, kind, gentle, she loves everyone she meets. She walks well both on and off the lead although more often than not is off-lead around here. She likes to play with a few special friends and especially likes the company of a neighbour's dog, Florrie, who we sometimes take out with us.

Beachcombing is a favourite pastime especially since she found a large slice of cake there one day which she managed to eat before I could reach her!

Gracie's only downfall, if you can call it that, is that she is rather nervous of big and/or bouncy dogs. If they come running towards her, she will have a little 'snap' just to warn them to stay out of her space. Then it's forgotten and she'll wander off. Usually if they ignore her she's alright, never going towards them and causing trouble. With Florrie, although she is big and black she is very sweet and doesn't pester Gracie so they've become quite good friends.

Gracie has also fallen in love with 2 neighbourhood cats and always has to go and say 'hello' if they're in the garden when we go out.

Deciding to adopt Gracie was the best thing I ever did; she is the sweetest, loveliest dog I've ever known and I'll never regret my decision.

A comment from a family friend: "Honestly, this doggie is

loved so much and not just by her family. She is loving life! (Although not totally keen on the windy wet cold English weather!) xx

(All photos: S.McGillivray)

Josh
Spain

At 5 months of age, this exuberant puppy went off happily to his new home in France where, for the first few months, everything appeared fine. The shelter had believed that the couple who adopted him were experienced owners but despite the obligatory home-check, after a while it became apparent that something wasn't right. The couple claimed that he'd turned "dominant" and was "terrorising" their other two dogs, he had laid claim to the sofa and had snapped at the male owner, breaking skin.

This wasn't the Josh that the shelter knew and loved.

Despite advice to contact a trainer or a behaviourist, the couple did nothing with him and in an angry, abuse-laden rant to the charity's president, she was told to take him back immediately or they'd leave him at the local shelter where he'd be put to sleep.

Within 24 hours the charity managed to get Josh back to their shelter but they were shocked to find that every time someone raised a hand to scratch an ear or whatever, he would duck. The message was clear to all who saw him.

When the President made a comment to this effect on the charity's Facebook page, the female ex-owner took umbrage, and a friend wrote a long and strong message in support of the couple. However, unwittingly, she had also revealed the problem that had resulted in Josh's adoption failure:

"He was allowed to do anything he wanted."

"He was treated like a king."

"He could go wherever he wanted."

And therein lay the problem. The friend had inadvertently told the charity exactly what had gone wrong – something the so-called experienced owners were unable to recognise.

The couple had never introduced any boundaries for Josh and pretty much allowed him to do what he wanted; just because their other dogs seemed to live happily with this system, there was no guarantee that Josh would adapt as well, as every dog is different.

He was undoubtedly a strong-willed lad, but little had been done in the way of training – he sat beautifully but beyond that, pulled like a train on the lead. The owner had previously admitted that they used to open the door in the morning and out he charged to hunt rabbits, sometimes for hours on end.

He jumped up at people which – at approximately 45+kg in weight and 70cms at the shoulder – was not something for the faint-hearted. Josh was fun, affectionate and good-hearted but he was pretty much like the proverbial mad March hare. So one can picture the situation: a large, strong-willed, poorly-trained dog that hadn't been shown any boundaries as to what he could and couldn't do, and never given any training that could have helped his overall behaviour.

A real recipe for disaster. And one that could have cost Josh his life.

So, he underwent some training, and being a smart lad, he soon learned how to go into the down position, he wasn't allowed to jump, and was taught manners on the lead, and thankfully there was a happy ending as he was adopted again by a local couple.

And guess what? Josh has settled very well with his new family and is proving to be a wonderful pet.

Whether a dog is adopted from a breeder or a shelter, it is so important that owners ensure that boundaries are set, consistent rules made and followed, and the dogs receive at least basic training to help them to understand how to live with humans, and behave as a well-behaved member of the household.

If there's a leadership-vacuum at the top of the team, a determined or assertive dog will quite happily step in to fill it.

(Photos: PeaJayz)

Money will buy a pretty good dog, but it won't buy the wag of his tail.

Josh Billings (21 Apr 1818–14 Oct 1885) was the pen name of 19th-century American humourist, Henry Wheeler Shaw

Unnamed puppy *(Photo: PeaJayz)*

THE MALAGA FOUR

These puppies are quite famous in the history of the Casa del Sol shelter, as this was probably the first time that I'd seen such stressed and unsocialised puppies up close.

They were born to a mum that had been abandoned a few years before in the Malaga area of Spain; she'd probably had one or two other litters before this latest one. A kind lady, Kath Morris, found them roaming in the *campo* and was desperate to try to get them to safety. Having contacted all the rescue agencies in that area, it was a matter of "no room at the inn", a common complaint of the majority of shelters in this country. Undaunted, Kath then cast her net to rescue charities further afield and finally made contact with PAPS which, having a few spaces free in their kennels at that time, agreed to take them.

However, catching these wild little fugitives was quite a different thing! The mum had had 6 puppies in this litter which were by then approximately 2 months old – fast approaching the limit by when puppies are most open to socialising and accepting new experiences. It took the rescuers the best part of 2 weeks to catch 5 of the little rascals – they found a home for one of the puppies in that area, but sadly, it proved impossible to catch the remaining pup and mum, so only 4 would go to Murcia.

Kath and husband Dave made the journey of over 5 hours each way from Malaga to Murcia with 4 petrified little puppies, and thus Dylan, Becky, Jenni and Daniel arrived in Casa del Sol to start their adventures. Upon their release into the puppy pen, they showed how terrified they were of people; mainly they just ran in circles around the run, absolutely panicked, looking for an escape route. It was almost impossible to get near them, even for the vet to vaccinate them. They were as close to feral as I've ever seen in a shelter, and I despaired that these poor young animals would ever experience loving homes.

Scared little puppies, Becky & Jenni *(Photo: PeaJayz)*

But luckily for them, there are some absolutely amazing people out there in dog-rescue-land with the biggest hearts imaginable and one by one, the puppies were adopted – Daniel to the UK, Becky and Dylan to Germany, and Jenni found a loving home here in Spain. The following are the amazing stories of these scared little puppies and the phenomenal people who were prepared to do their utmost to help them, from Yvonne Schallamach, former President of PAPS, who first fostered these puppies in an effort to familiarise them with living with humans, to those who opened up their homes and hearts by adopting them. Without everyone's commitment and effort, goodness knows what would have happened to these beautiful dogs.

Dylan
By J. Pastewsky, Germany

Dylan is a wonderful dog!

In the time from June 2017 when he arrived with us, up to today, he has really learned so much. At the beginning, he was very distant – we made sure to avoid looking directly in his eyes so he wouldn't feel threatened. Then one week after his arrival, he bravely came up to us and sniffed at our hands – perhaps this might seem like such a small thing, but it was a huge step for a dog like Dylan, but following this tiny step he then became very "clingy". Then, that September, we brought him to dog classes so he could learn dog-rules and importantly so he'd learn that other people wouldn't do anything to him, since when he's made great progress.

However, Dylan has two big problems: the first is that he isn't comfortable with men; this takes a few forms, one of which is when my boyfriend comes home, Dylan barks very loudly at him, something that continues to this day. The second problem is around strangers, but I  don't think that's such a bad thing as it means that they will not try to stroke him.

Up to a few months ago, he used to go to classes two days each week – where he did "Trickility" because Dylan has amazing talents and this activity provides great mind-exercises for him.

At home, he's a playful dog that enjoys testing the limits! He still has his scared moments but he knows that we'll protect him.

(All Photos:J. Pastewsky)

Barnaby
By Jenifer Andrews, UK

The second member of the Malaga Four is Daniel, another little scared baby that arrived in to the shelter with his siblings. And yet another that we feared may never find a Forever Home, but out of the blue, a lady in the UK asked to adopt him. All his fears and problems were explained to her in detail, and she was asked several times: "Are you really sure?" but the lady was adamant: they wanted Daniel, and his name was going to be changed to Barnaby, after a well-known British TV detective.

So, in October 2017, he went off to his new family who had to work hard to get him on a lead, and socialise him. While Barnaby wasn't too crazy on adults, especially men, he adored children and was very good with the family cat. He seemed to have settled into a life where he was happy and content, and his family accepted his limitations, loving him regardless of his issues.

However, out of the blue in the autumn of 2019, PAPS was contacted by a shelter in the UK to where Barnaby had been surrendered by his adoptive family –

contrary to the clause in the adoption contract that the Spanish charity should be notified first, to give them a chance to bring him back to their shelter. No particular reason for his surrender except for the well-hackneyed one of "change of circumstances". As the UK shelter reported that he was "uncontrollable" and they couldn't cope with him, poor Barnaby once more found himself back in Casa del Sol, homeless yet again.

However, in June 2020, he captured the eye of a lovely English couple, Jennifer and Bernard, who were here on holiday. They took him out of the shelter as a foster – it brought tears to Jennifer's eyes when he hid behind the sofa in their home, but despite all, they totally lost their hearts to this scared lad, so much so,

Learning to play with Daddy

flights home were changed to a dog-friendly cabin on the ferry as they couldn't bear the thought of being separated from him, and Barnaby went home as a fully-adopted member of their family.

Now, from hiding behind the sofa, he gets on it. He still has his quiet moments but is so different to the Barnaby that first arrived in their home. He interacts when he wants to. He sits on his cushion in the lounge, if that's what he wants, and he's never made do anything he doesn't want.

Since joining his new family, Barnaby has thrived and become such a happy dog. From once not being able to get near him, he now loves attention from family and friends, and particularly the joys of a kiss and cuddles, and visits from the grandchildren. He didn't even know what a toy was before but now realises that the toys are his and carries his favourites around like a puppy. When his family return from trips out of the house, they can see he's been playing, and always has one of their slippers in his bed.

He's a social lad and has plenty of doggy-friends to play with and even though he's still a bit shy, he'll even allow people to stroke him, once he gets used to them. What a turn-around!!

Walks are the highlight of his day when a good roll in the grass is enjoyed to the full and, best of all, going to the woods. He enjoys being chauffeured in the car, watching the scenery passing by, he's even had a trip to the beach where he was finally allowed off-lead, when he was so well-behaved. To his delight, he has grandchildren to play with, he loves to chase cats but only to get them to play … but they misinterpret his intentions and escape up the nearest tree, much to his confusion.

In Jennifer's words, "He is just so cute, all the family love him. We couldn't imagine life without him now – Barnaby has completely taken over! He's given us a new lease of life and is here to stay".

(All photos: J & B. Andrews)

Daisy's Journey
By Debbie Pryke, Spain

In 2016, myself and hubby Russ, packed everything up and moved to live near Orihuela in the south-east of Spain, not forgetting our beloved Poppy the Beagle, who was then 4 years old. After a year, we decided that Poppy needed a friend and, having a villa in the *campo* with 5,000 sq. metres of garden, we certainly had the room.

I started to trawl through the multitude of rescue sites until finally, on the PAPS Facebook page, I saw a cute little puppy, Becky – who looked a bit like a beagle. I enquired about her but was told that she had been reserved but that her sister, Jenni, was still awaiting a home. I was also informed that she was very nervous and was currently living with the President of PAPS, Yvonne, with 3 other dogs. We arranged to go and meet Jenni with our Poppy. Jenni was terrified and it must have taken Yvonne at least 30 minutes to get her on the lead.

We took her and Poppy for a walk and totally fell in love.

Approximately a week later, home-check, paperwork and vets all done, Jenni finally came home. And became Daisy.

Now the fun began!! Daisy was by now 11 months old.

On the lead she was very timid but off it – WOW! The first day and night she spent hours running around our perimeter fence, never stopping. We tried everything to get her in, we left food and a cosy bed on our *naya* until eventually, well past midnight, she came into the house. She was stressed, exhausted, and terrified.

Over the next few days, she found a spot on the sofa which is known by all our friends as "Daisy's place" with a snuggly blanket, she wouldn't go in a dog-bed, only on the sofa. Poppy wasn't too bothered about all her antics, they just get on together as dogs do.

As Daisy wouldn't let us touch her or even take a treat from us, this was going to be a long road. Even though she'd stay close in the garden, she wouldn't come up to us. To take her for a walk, we had to wait until she jumped up on her end of the sofa so I could put her harness on her when she would shake like she was about to be beaten.

We had adopted her in November 2017 but a few months on, she was still the same. I tried everything to get her to come to us or let us touch her, but No Way seemed to be her motto.

She would only drink water from an outside bowl, and ate outside on her own – which hasn't changed to this day. She always runs off if I open a door or disturb her, and that's it – no more eating! Sometimes at night we hear her drinking from the indoor dog bowl when we are in bed.

She never knew what to do with toys, she doesn't play even now, she will run off with one but always drops it a long way off.

After about 7 months, I took her to a couple of dog-training sessions; she was so terrified, she clung to me like a leech even with the lead off. It made my heart melt because it was the first time we realised that she had some love and trust for us, and I was her safe zone that day. Unfortunately, the classes shut down which was such a shame for her.

One pretty girl, Daisy *(Photo: D.Pryke)*

Daisy loves other dogs and playing with them, her problem is people. She eventually found her voice and – boy! – does she bark!! And she has a brilliant howl as well!

We found a dog trainer to do one-to-one sessions with me and Daisy, when we found one of our problems is having a very large garden, as she can always run away from us; in a confined space it was a bit easier to get control of her.

SECOND-HAND DOGS

The training progressed to a class out in the open, the trainer was pleased with our progress – I even got brave and let her off her lead with the other dogs. When she was on the lead she would cower, but the other owners could gently touch her.

She is strange – on the lead I could do anything with her but off-lead it was so different. Again, those lessons stopped sadly, but I'm continuing to work with her.

Anyway, Daisy is our adorable odd-ball! If we talk to our neighbours over our fence, after barking at them furiously, she comes and jumps up at us letting us tickle her belly, and pawing at us for attention. Any other time or place, she runs away from us, we can't touch her.

We are surrounded by beautiful orange and lemon groves, and farm land, so there's an abundance of rabbits, hares, partridges, rats and birds – lucky for her as she enjoys a good hunt and is a fantastic rat catcher, and if a poor rabbit should be daft enough as to appear in our garden, she's off! Sadly for her, this means we can't let her off-lead in the *campo* but despite this she adores her walks and gets so excited but still has to go to the sofa for me to put her harness on.

As for cuddles, both dogs come into our bedroom in the mornings, but Daisy is the quicker and always gets the prime spot in between us and allows us to cuddle her. I share the couch with her in the evenings when sometimes she stares at me, nudging me with her paw. Sometimes I'm really lucky and she'll snuggle into me which truly makes my day. She loves Russ in the morning, and I get some love in the evening, but if you make eye contact, she often runs off!

She is one crazy Daisy, she has her weird ways but we know she loves us in her own funny little way, and we absolutely love her to bits ... even though she barks too much! We

Daisy, in "her" place on the sofa, being photobombed by Poppy

211

wouldn't be without her, we're approaching our 6th year with her and she's still an ongoing project, but hopefully one day, she will trust us 100%.

Update!!! I received the following message from Debbie:

Well, what can I say? Recently, at last, Daisy is now loving a cuddle! She runs up to us in the garden for a stroke and belly tickle, and wiggles her bum so hard when she comes into the house, before rolling over on her back in the lounge for her daddy to play! We can't believe it – it's taken 6 years for the brave girl to get to this point! What a proud mummy I am!

She's a special girl … well worth the wait.

And finally, Daisy appreciates snuggles with her human-mum
(All Photos: D.Pryke)

Becky
By Bärbel Wehmeier, Germany

In 2017, we found our dog, Becky, on the internet and immediately fell in love with the little sparrow. What did those beautiful, sad eyes have to endure?! It was clearly communicated to us by the rescue charity that she was particularly fearful and shy. We already knew about scared dogs back then and it was clear to us that we still wanted to offer Becky a beautiful and loving home. We also knew that such special dogs need a lot of training, time, consistency and love.

After we contacted the association, we were thoroughly checked – every dog should come to the best and most suitable home, which reassured us too. There are still prejudices about dogs from abroad but these were all thrown overboard by P.A.P.S Casa del Sol and we always felt that we were in very good hands.

On December 2nd 2017, the time had come! Finally, after what had seemed like endless weeks, we were able to pick up our princess. After a 4-hour drive and 2 hours waiting on site, the time had finally come. The van drove up and I already had tears of joy on my face.

The doors opened and from a distance we looked for Becky in the cages. Where is she? Will she like us? Will she feel comfortable with us? Is she finally going to enjoy life?

So many thoughts whirled around in our heads. Armed with my documents, I went to the van and waited longingly for Becky to be given to me. The first dog came out and jumped into the arms of its new owner. The second got out of the van, relaxed, and greeted his people shyly. After a few more dogs, it was Becky's turn. What a moment!

The driver lifted her out of the box, put on her leash but Becky was full of panic – she jumped from his arms and immediately fled under the car. Thank goodness she had the leash on!

Getting her from under the car was a struggle but we gave her time. Treats and voice were not going to work, only with the leash could we get her in the direction of our car. Fortunately for us, she immediately jumped into the back of the car, retreating to the furthest corner. I sat beside her and put on the safety harness in very small steps over the entire four-hour journey. At first, she snapped, but little by little, I was allowed to get my hand closer to her.

Many might have been sad in such a situation … we were not! We were full of happiness and love! To be honest, I was crying with joy the whole time. We were just so happy to have Becky with us.

Two hours into our drive home, I was getting hunger-pangs so my husband got me chicken nuggets. I quickly realized that I wasn't the only one who was hungry! A little furry nose came very carefully and slowly from the side and tried to sniff the food out of my hand. So I removed the breaded coating from a small piece of nugget and handed it to her. Which she accepted! As soon as she had it in her mouth, I began to cry again with joy. From that moment on, I was allowed to touch her lightly and she was already hesitantly looking to get close to me. My husband had absolutely no chance – he was growled at directly and she tried to get away from him!

Back at home, Becky immediately took to her self-made dog bed and took shelter in it. We left her alone and totally ignored her which was good for her and she slept a little. To our surprise, she was already looking for us on the first evening and jumped onto the couch with us and even into bed with us at night. So, our feelings hadn't deceived us. We just belonged together! Becky developed a very strong bond with me in the first few weeks. My husband, on the other hand, had a much harder time. Only after he took a 2-week vacation, could he stroke her and put her on a leash. Before that, she had always fled, and snapped at him.

(Photo courtesy of Peggy Rodrigues)

Going for a walk was a challenge for the three of us as they were marked by panic attacks at the sight of people and endless attempts to escape. For Becky, however, meeting other dogs was like taking a vacation from fear. Only then could you see how she really was as she just loves to be with other dogs and really blooms in their company.

After plenty of training and patience, Becky no longer panics in front of people, has self-confidence and enjoys her life to the full. But one thing was still missing for Becky and us. But what was it? (Becky's story doesn't end here … more to come!)

(All other photos: B.Wehmeier)

Happiness is a warm puppy

Charles M. "*Sparky*" Schulz (Nov 26 1922 – Feb 12 2000), American cartoonist

Ciara, with unnamed pup *(Photo: PeaJayz)*

Cassie
Spain

(Photo: T.Johnson)

Cassie's story is a bit hazy with various rumours abounding, one of which was that she was found hanging – it might just have been that she'd been tied to a tree. The extent of her extreme fears leads her family to believe that she'd certainly been badly abused, before being rescued, aged 2 or 3.

An expatriate woman adopted Cassie from a rescue group but when she repatriated to her home country, she left the poor dog alone at the rental house in the mountains, leaving her to fend for herself for over a year. It could have been that the woman couldn't catch her to get a lead on her, but most people would have tried everything in their power to bring their rescue dog with them … if they really wanted to. Basically, Cassie had been abandoned again.

When Tausha moved in to this mountain house as a tenant, unbeknownst to her Cassie came with it as a non-optional extra. By hunting rabbits or whatever she could find to sustain her in the mountains, and drinking fresh water from a local stream, somehow, she'd managed to survive the long months of her solitary abandonment in the wild, through the torrid heat of a Spanish summer, and the inhospitable winter when cold winds and heavy rain can sweep across the countryside, drenching everything in its path.

Thinking back, Tausha remembers going hiking in that area 6 months previously (far from where the house was located), when she saw Cassie standing high on a mountain, watching her – her wild kingdom must have stretched far and wide. Tausha tried to call her to her but Cassie's trust in humans was understandably rock-bottom by then so there was no way she was going to go near anyone.

Now contentedly resident in her mountain retreat with her "guest", Tausha quickly learned that Cassie was ecstatic to be taken for walks every day, and would literally dance with joy for her food! But there was still no way that she would either go close to her or enter the house, preferring to sleep outside on her own. After a week, the other resident 6-month-old rescue, Kiwi, persistent little dog that she is, refused to take "no" for an answer and soon she and Cassie were firm friends, enjoying a good romp and play together.

Move forward 3 months, and Cassie would at last allow Tausha to stroke her but at a time of her choosing, and only for a few minutes. A year later, yet another rescue dog joined the household; this time, it was only when Cassie saw this dog enter the house that she finally plucked up the courage to go inside as well.

When Tausha decided to move house, she worried about how she'd catch Cassie so she could come too. The vet gave her a little "something" in a syringe to calm her down. Perhaps there was some divine intervention as fortunately she chose to come into the house that night, and incredibly even allowed Tausha to give her the injection – to her total amazement, which enabled her to attach the lead to take Cassie to her new home.

Seven years later and Cassie would, by now, let Tausha pet her more often and even allowed her to put on a lead, although strangers were still too much for her to deal with.

Tausha believes that Cassie is approximately 14 now, she's had her just over 11 years and after all that time, it's only recently that she really seems happy to be with her, actually *wanting* to be close. She sleeps in the bedroom on Tausha's side, and will accept little pats from familiar neighbours and friends.

Even after all this time, she's still learning and gaining more confidence, sleeping by Tausha's feet at dinnertime – something she never did before. She surprised everyone recently by voluntarily going up to a young visitor to lick his hand – for the first time ever, a small but very huge thing for her. Cassie appears content in the knowledge that she's finally in her Forever home, and is allowing herself to get close to people.

Despite all her ordeals, Cassie is a really happy dog, her eyes smile and her tail never stops wagging. She's been a member of this loving home for such a long time, but it was never about what they could get from her, but rather how they could provide a safe and good life for her. She knows she's part of the family and will never be abandoned again, and to see her happy and finally opening up after such a long journey has been totally worth it.

The final word belongs to Tausha, who says, "I do think Cassie is heaven-sent – she's my angel, and is such a wonder dog. And I'm so in love with her!"

Merlin Magic
By Peter Schier, Germany

My biggest wish after my 7th cancer-free year was to have a dog. Through my job in the security industry, I had seen many Malinois and had always been impressed with the breed. Their nature and character are very special, they notice immediately if you are not focused, but they are not for everyone.

This robust working dog is extremely intelligent and resourceful, they are strong guard dogs but are never aggressive without reason. The character of these proud animals is solid, they know no fear, are full of energy and always ready for action, but their strong will to work should not be confused with nervousness.

It is with good reason that Malinois are considered to make excellent service dogs. A typical representative of the breed is lively and spirited, yet people-friendly and sensitive. They bond strongly with their family and are considered to be loyal and affectionate. With appropriate early socialisation, the Mali gets along with other pets.

I was positive that I wanted to have a Maligator★ as a companion and was willing to accept the responsibility that would come with this special breed. And so I began the search.

On social media I came across the page of PAPS Sonnenhunde and as soon as I saw the picture of Merlin, I knew that this would be MY dog as he captivated me immediately. I was shockingly in love with the golden boy! After a lot of writing back and forth with the rescue group, it was clear that he was my soul-mate, I didn't want any other but Merlin. From the moment my fiancée and I picked him up, it was clear he was OUR dog. We opened the car door and so quickly, before we could even look and react, Merlin had already jumped in with a look of relief that said, *Now I can go home*. We have so much in common, one look is enough and I know how he feels.

At first everything was new to Merlin – he didn't know the language, in fact, he didn't know much about anything. He was so afraid of chickens and cows, along with everything that was different for him. We taught him bit by bit about life in Germany and the countryside. He also got to know German food – our gourmet, who prefers supermarket food to branded dog food and will do absolutely anything for ham, the sweet guy!

For the first 2 weeks in his new home, Merlin was very cautious but then he became very comfortable with us. He

SECOND-HAND DOGS

suffers very much from fear of loss, even up to the present day, but this has been improving over time. You have to train and practise a lot with Malis. He loves being driven around and would like to be in the car all the time. At first, he was a bit crazy as he jumped against the locked boot-door when he heard it unlocking. We managed to modify the car so it would be comfortable for our golden boy, I even bought an extra ramp for him and he looked at me like, *Are you serious?*

But that is not Merlin's only quirk. He likes lying crooked on his back when he sleeps, making faces (he sometimes has facial expressions), he growls like a bear which is why he is our Growler, and sometimes purrs when his coat is being brushed.

When we go out for a walk, Merlin always has to take one of his toys with him, be it a squeaking duck of which we have already bought at least 25, because after about 3 days it no longer squeaks. There is no such thing as a Maliga-

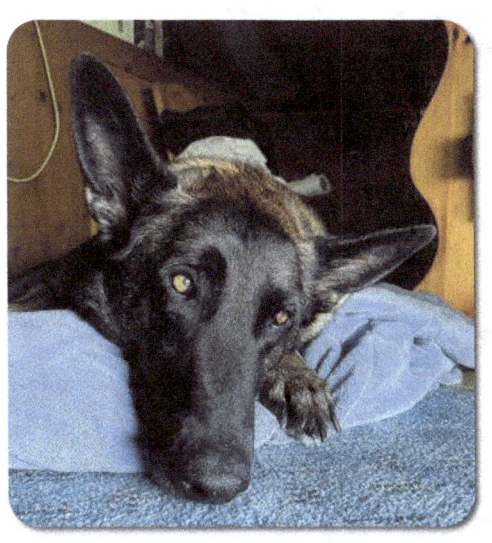

tor-safe chew toy! He also likes to take his grunting pig with him or above all, his favourite pillow. And if Merlin doesn't feel like running about and just sits, the only thing that helps is a ball.

Merlin is a bit of a bully if he sees other males, as he starts to whine ... but if they are females ... then he plays the Spanish *macho*. A few treats in the bag and you can calm down even the craziest half-breed a bit!

Merlin brings so much joy into our lives, and he is so grateful to have found such a beautiful home. No matter how bad the day has been, when you get home and he greets you, your mood immediately improves. No money in the world would make us give up our golden boy. He has totally changed during this past year, and we look forward to sharing the future with him.

★"Maligator" is Peter's affectionate term for a member of the Malinois breed

(All photos: P. Schier)

Honey *(Photo:B.Stafford)*

Kiki - Part II of Becky's Story
By Bärbel Wehmeier, Germany

(Photo courtesy of Peggy Rodrigues)

In 2019, we drove with our friend who had helped us to adopt Becky to the shelter from where we adopted her. We just wanted to know where she'd come from and were so excited about getting to know this loving animal shelter.

On the very first day there, a young female dog stole my husband's heart. Kiki! She was the first one who ran to him, not leaving his side for a second. Each departure from the shelter became harder and harder.

Since Casa-Papa José (Manager of Casa del Sol Shelter) knows his babies the best, I talked to him about whether Becky and Kiki would fit together. Since Becky is a rather dominant lady, any second dog had to be a submissive one. Ok,

SECOND-HAND DOGS

I admit that the second dog topic is always just incidental but Kiki just snuck into our hearts.

At first, I was a bit hesitant because I wasn't sure if it was the right thing for our single princess. But what can I say? We had an amazing vacation in the Casa, learned a lot of new things about Becky … and lost our hearts to Kiki.

In May 2020, the time had finally come. We made our way to the pick-up point and collected our little treasure from the transport. The contrast couldn't have been greater. From a completely panicked Becky on pick-up day to a happy and cuddly Kiki. When we saw her in the cage, it almost seemed as if she recognized us. And again, I was really walking on air! Immediately there were kisses from Kiki and everything was so exciting.

We were with the other adopters at Kerstin's place (Chairperson of the board of the German P.A.P.S association) to relax a bit, where the dogs were able to get to know their new owners in peace. Finally, we had our Kiki and we immediately had the feeling that she knew exactly that she was finally going home.

The first meeting with Becky was so relaxed that I was totally dubious. We brought them together on neutral ground and from the first second it was as if the two had known and loved each other for years. The two had no bitching, jealousy or food envy. Kiki is the sister Becky always wanted. The two of them prefer to run around and cuddle together but also the joint training, walks and cuddling with masters and mistresses are a top priority.

Kiki watches Becky a lot and is so easy to deal with – the two together are the absolute dream for us, and now the four of us feel complete as a family. Both Becky and Kiki have become family dogs. Funny how the tide turns!

What would masters and mistresses not do for their princesses?

Everything for them, and everything for their happiness.

(Photo courtesy of Peggy Rodrigues)

Bärbel, with her two princesses *(Photo courtesy of Peggy Rodrigues)*

(All other photos: Bärbel Wehmeier)

"Hi," I said. She came over, licked my hand discreetly, allowed herself to be scratched for a time, chased her tail in a dignified circle, lay down again. I remember thinking: "There are times God puts a choice in front of you." I often had such thoughts back then.

We took the dog.

Gil Schwartz (20 May 1951–2 May 2020), known by his pen name *Stanley Bing*, American business humourist and novelist

Bella *(Photo: PeaJayz)*

The Collectors

There are many special people who open up their hearts – and homes, to more than one rescue dog; however, while this can lead to much fun to share their lives with a pack, this is perhaps something better left to more experienced owners.

Rosemary's Fur-Babies
By Rosemary Pockett, UK

We have always had at least two rescue dogs at a time, and when we went to our new holiday home near Murcia in May 2008 with our then 14-year-old daughter, we certainly weren't looking for another dog.

However, upon arriving at Sierra Golf for a long Bank Holiday weekend, as we unlocked our front gate a young, skinny *Podenca* ran in and started to drink out of our swimming pool. She was obviously very hungry too but all we had in the house were frozen burgers, which we quickly defrosted, and some tins of tuna. All were wolfed down quickly, followed by some bottled water!

She then ran off over the golf course and we thought we wouldn't see her again. The next morning, I was up first and there she was, lying outside the front gate. Again, I fed and watered her and she settled down on the patio and went to sleep.

In 2008 there weren't many animal charities in the area that I was aware of, so we phoned round further afield but no one was willing to take her. So, with Plan A out of the way, we went on to Plan B, which was to find kennels which could keep Lucy, as we had now named her, for 6 months quarantine and then get her over to the UK.

SECOND-HAND DOGS

With the help of Google, we found an excellent kennels near Benidorm, Shieldaig Kennels, run by the lovely Denise and Steve. They looked after her for 6 months, during which time she came to live with us when we visited Spain. They then arranged for her to have all her jabs and a flight back to Gatwick in February 2009. When we collected her from the airport, she was completely unfazed and seemed pleased to see us again.

Lovely Lucy

We took her home and had to introduce her to our two old-timers, Scruffy and Dipsy who were both around 11 years old. They both found her a bit too lively and a bit of a pain. She was also very food-orientated which was completely understandable, but that caused problems with the 3 of them. She had a dominant character and needed some firm training, so was booked into a 3-week residential boot camp, as we'd been unable to train her ourselves. It seemed to work so all 3 could live together, as long as Lucy was fed separately.

We then heard of another dog being looked after by the bar staff on our estate. In October 2009 we visited over half-term break, and while at the bar met 'John', a small brown and white dog, who was extremely submissive. He was so passive he wouldn't walk and had to be carried everywhere. Other people on the estate assumed he had health problems with either his back or legs but when he was on a lead, we could persuade him to walk 2 or 3 steps, so we knew it wasn't health-related.

One day we saw some young boys throwing stones at him so we went over to get him, keeping him at our house for a few days. So, it was off to Benidorm once again for 6 months quarantine. During his stay at the kennels the staff worked really hard with him, building up his confidence, enabling him to act like a proper dog.

Six months later, he was on a plane to Gatwick and settled in straight away to life in his new home. Even today he and Lucy are still best friends, with Lucy often using John as a pillow. However, he still has confidence issues and is bottom of the pecking order!

By now, Facebook was becoming more popular, meaning easy access to lots of dog charities across Europe. Around the middle of 2010 I saw a photo of a large smiling *Podenco Canario*. He and his sisters had been transported from Gran Canaria to a greyhound charity in Wales, as they thought it'd be easier to rehome them from there. His sisters had already been rehomed but 'Scooby' was still available. As he looked just like Scooby Doo, I was smitten and arranged to collect him at a service station in Bristol. I drove over one morning and met Scooby in the car-park. He promptly jumped into the car, and slept on the back seat for the 100-mile journey home.

Best buddies, Lucy and John

He's the largest dog we have but is also a gentle giant, his best friend being Gabby, our mini *Podenco*. He's also the fastest, having caught squirrels and rabbits in the back garden (we live on a farm, so not your normal back garden!). He does have one habit I haven't come across before – even though he's been neutered, he does like a bit of self-pleasuring first thing in the morning, after playing with his partner in crime, Gabby!!

Gabby was also found on Facebook the following year.

The very handsome Scooby

SECOND-HAND DOGS

She's a miniature *Podenca* and looks identical to Lucy after going through a hot wash! Gabby's a little live-wire but after we'd had her a couple of years, we noticed she was occasionally limping on a back leg. Over the next few years, she had multiple examinations by vets and referral specialists, and eventually our local vet suggested she was tested for Leishmaniasis which is a common disease in Spain, caused by sand flies. After owning her for 7 years she was finally diagnosed with this, but with a single tablet a day (costing next to nothing in Spain) and a good squirt of Metacam, her leg – and Gabby – are now as good as new, living her life to the full.

Again, on Facebook I saw another charity which normally only takes in *Galgos* and *Podencos*, were feeding a plain black mum and pup in a local village, but were worried they would stray onto the road. I asked the charity if they could get them to the kennels in Benidorm, in which case we'd have them. This they did and Yazmin, the mum, and Lola arrived at Gatwick in early 2012, to join our family.

Yazmin loves everyone she meets while Lola, who was about a year old, was quite nervous and excitable. As Yazmin was so good-natured, she was enrolled to be a therapy dog, visiting 2 different care homes each week, where all the residents loved her.

Unfortunately, she had eye problems and firstly had one eye removed, and then a couple of years later had to have the other one removed, so her visits stopped. She's done remarkably well since and can find her way round the house and out into the garden on her own.

Next dog to be seen on Facebook was Maisie, a Peke/Tibbie type of dog at PAPS, where we have done some dog walking in the past.

Hubby and I had arranged to visit during June 2015 to help out but when he was called back

Hitching a ride

to the UK for work reasons, I went on my own, saw Maisie, paid a reservation fee, and arranged for her to come back to the UK on the next available transport, which just happened to be the following week.

When hubby got home that evening his first reaction was, '*WHAT* is that?'!

Maisie is the smallest of them all, but doesn't realise it and is the boss of them all. We've since had her DNA done and she's half-Pekingese, quarter-Chihuahua and quarter-Yorkie! With the attitude of a Rottweiler.

We had a caravan for a couple of years and she was our caravan dog, and loved going away with us and going for long walks.

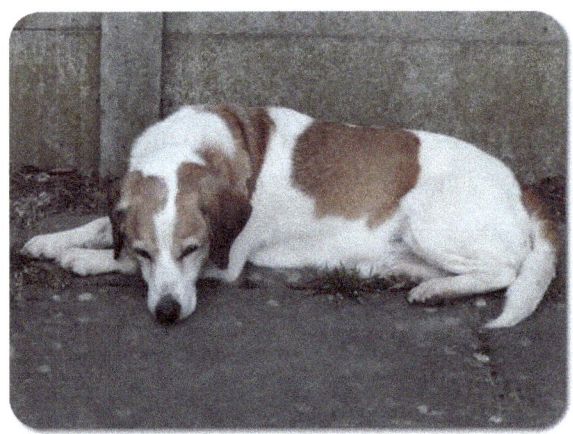

While we were at PAPS, I had also noticed a small chunky brown and white dog who was keeping himself to himself. He was still on Facebook around Christmas time as, at ten years of age, he was harder to rehome. Anyway after a few drinks over Christmas lunch it was agreed that we should have Hercules, now Herman, and he joined us early 2016. He's a big cuddle monster and the only one who's allowed to sleep on our bed!

However, with multiple dogs, things don't always go as planned.

Lucy has always been our dominant female and when Yazmin joined, she also saw herself as No 1 female. They tended to stalk each other, but nothing more than that, until one day I heard a bit of commotion in the garden and Lucy and Yazmin were just starting a punch-up. No one was hurt but Maisie, who always wants to be the centre of everything and is far too confident for her size, had launched herself at them and had an eye scratched for her troubles. Off to the vets and a referral to a specialist, who confirmed she'd lost 50% sight in one eye, but this doesn't bother her in the least.

Another more serious incident happened last year. Yazmin and Lola had always interacted every day, but now as Yazmin had had both eyes removed, she just sleeps and wanders round the garden on her own, completely ignoring Lola, who doesn't understand why.

With Lucy getting older and slower, the dynamics between the dogs had changed. One day, I heard a lot of barking in the garden and found Lola seriously attacking Lucy, who was trying her hardest to get away, but wasn't fast enough and didn't fight back. She'd been bitten all over, including near her throat. I hadn't seen what had set it off so hoped it was a one-off, but unfortunately the same thing happened about a month later. Both times involved a lot of stitches, antibiotics and of course, cost.

It was unfair on Lucy to be in this situation, and we couldn't risk it happening again, so rang round local charities to see if anyone could take Lola. Unfortunately, they were all overflowing but Battersea Dogs Home agreed to take her, but had a 3-month waiting list. As we couldn't take any chances at home, we booked her into a local kennels for 3 months, where the owner took a liking to her and let her have the freedom of the kennels. She'd follow him around all day and got on well with all the other dogs, so obviously it was only Lucy she'd turned against.

Eventually we took her to Battersea Dogs Home, where I thought it'd take a while to rehome her as she was 7 years old and plain black, but Lola had a happy ending, quickly finding a new home as the only dog, with an adult-only family.

In Spain, *Podencos* and *Galgos* are viewed as not being an ideal pet dog, but once you've owned one you will see they are easy, laid-back animals that like to sleep a lot! They can be very energetic between sleeps but don't require an exceptional amount of exercise and can be very entertaining in their antics. They can have a strong prey instinct, but while both Lucy and Gabby ignore our cats, I wouldn't trust Scooby around them!

It can be hard work having so many dogs but it is also very rewarding. We have been lucky that on the whole,

Winter-time in the Pockett household

they've all got on, even though we hadn't met some of them before they came to the UK. Feeding time can be complicated if some have food issues but you soon get into a routine. Also, it's imperative to find a reliable house-sitter if you want to go on holiday, as many don't want to look after so many dogs.

We are lucky living on a farm, and as the dogs are now getting older, they are quite happy to exercise in our grounds, so we don't have to walk 7 dogs at a time! Maisie, Herman and Gabby still get taken out for an hour a day but that's more for our benefit!

I'd recommend anyone who is looking for another dog to go to rescue centres instead of breeders.

Exciting Addendum!! Rosemary and Glen have fallen for another little lad … meet Joselito! When he was found he had a very infected eye which sadly had to be removed, but what a future he's got ahead of him.

(Photo: PeaJayz)

Herman and his Spanish Señora Maisie, on deer-watch duties

(All Other Photos: R.Pockett)

Berry, Sansa & Allegra
By Jill Williams, UK

We have been adopting ex-racing greyhounds for 12 years and have had many different characters, but none quite like Berry!

Greyhounds are amazing creatures – and sadly, totally misunderstood. They require just 2 walks a day for about 20 minutes each, they don't have to be let off-lead for a good run, although some do like to stretch their legs. In fact, they'd much prefer to lie on the sofa with their legs in the air! They are not, generally, aggressive but like any other breed, there is always the exception to the rule. Not all greyhounds have a dislike for small fluffies – we have 2 cats, chickens and have had rabbits in the past, all of which got on fine with the dogs.

We adopted Berry 9 years ago following 4 previous failed re-homings. She had been a non-racer so was retired at 18 months, she came into the rehoming kennels and was adopted by a family who had a young autistic son.

Berry couldn't cope in the home so was returned, she then went to 3 other homes, in each one she couldn't settle, eventually we "fostered" her, we had 6 other greys at that point. She fitted in like a glove as it turned out that she liked a "pack". She very soon became the boss of that pack – the others were pushovers!

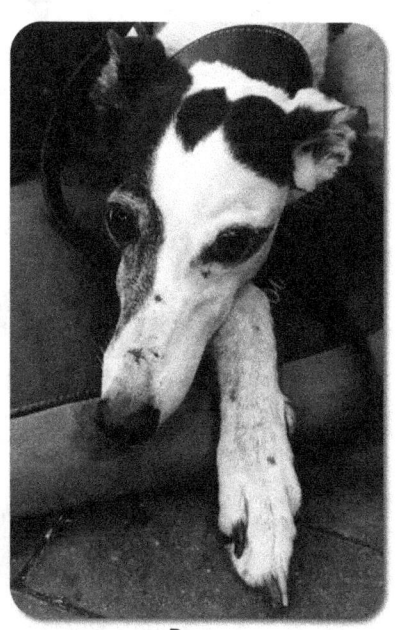

Berry

Her character is very different to any of the other greyhounds we have had. She enjoys sitting upside-down on your lap, with her paw under your chin! She also speaks to you, not by barks but just with an odd sound whenever she wants to go out, have dinner, or if she's getting ignored. She certainly knows how to let us know what she wants!

Five years ago, she escaped from our home during a storm when she actually opened the front door; all our door handles are now fitted backwards so she can't do it again! She is a true Houdini! We searched for her for 11 hours, walking the streets, parks, fields etc, we live in quite a rural area so there were lots of fields to cover, but … nothing.

At 11pm, we had to stop as it was so dark, I put a bed, water and food at our front door. At 11.30pm, I checked to see if she was back and there she was, like butter wouldn't melt, turned out she had probably been hiding under a neighbour's pine tree the whole time!!

Berry is 12 years old now but still has a spring in her step. We can't help but love her!

The entire "Grey" gang (Photo: Hartstone Photography)

OK …so whose bright idea were the ears?

(Photos: J.Williams)

SANSA AND ALLEGRA

We adopted Sansa, AKA Maria, and her pup Allegra 6 years ago. We fell in love with Sansa as soon as we saw her photograph and, as Allegra was the last remaining pup and also quite reliant on her mum, we decided to adopt her too. How could we have left her behind?!

We have been adopting ex-racing Greyhounds for the past 12 years and when Sansa and Allegra arrived we had 5 Greyhounds in the house, so they joined a large family.

I'm not going to lie, it hasn't been easy, I think we were so used to our laid-back, very easy-to-look-after, gentle Greys that the "terrible twosome" was quite a shock, it's probably easier to list the problems we experienced:

1. They pulled like a train on walks, something that we definitely were not used to, but with perseverance and many different leads etc, we discovered that harnesses worked and now they are very well behaved on walk – unless someone gives them any attention and then they just can't get enough fuss!
2. They chewed everything – books, furniture, shoes, clothes, anything they could sink their teeth into! As Allegra was only 6 months old, she was a little happier being crated when we left them at home, in fact that was where she took her treats and went there when she wanted to be alone. Sansa was a different story, she hated the crate so we didn't push the issue; whenever we went out, we moved everything out of chewing range and put barriers at the bottom of the stairs to prevent her going up. Nylabones were our saviour, and the chewing eventually stopped.
3. Sansa was very dominant when she arrived, and so wanted to be top of the pack but we were top of the pack, then our Greyhound, Berry! Sadly, we

had a fair few fights between Sansa and Berry and many trips to the vets, mainly with Berry, as a greyhound's skin is very thin. We became extra vigilant around them and any sign of potential aggression, they were separated; over time it has got better and, although I would never totally 100% trust them both, life is a lot happier!

4. Barking! Oh my, can they bark! Again, not something Greyhounds do very often. We had to deal with complaints from the neighbours, mainly because it was them that were getting barked at. We're not sure whether Sansa was used as a guard dog previously, but she certainly likes to guard! Patience and lots of treats has sorted this, although we still have the occasional "Don't come near my garden" bark.

There were many occasions when I wanted to return them, as I said, this hasn't been an easy journey, but I'm so pleased that we gave them the time to "find their feet" and settle in.

Would I do it again? YES, because I now know how to deal with any problems that may arise. We love them both dearly and all memories of past problems disappear when they cuddle up to us on the sofa.

Sansa (l), not just beautiful but a bit of a brain-box too as she finished 2nd in her very first obedience class just a matter of months after arriving in her new home

Sansa (All photos: J.Williams)

The Creation of Team Litfin

By Kerstin Litfin, Germany

My rescue journey began with the dog my cousin adopted from Spain. We already had our poodle, Moritz – an inheritance from my mother, who had always lived life to his own rules but was now getting on in years, and our big dog, Zora. When my cousin's dog arrived, I was absolutely thrilled with him and decided that I wanted to adopt a companion for Zora.

After some thought, I looked on a rehoming website, which showed that there were 3,870 dogs up for adoption in Spain. After a long night, five females had been shortlisted – a second cup of coffee helped me to narrow it down to three. Since I couldn't make up my mind, my husband, Andreas, and daughter, Celina, were invited to give their opinion and the decision weighed heavily in favour of a dog called Maggie, a Husky-Shepherd hybrid, who wasn't handling the stress of the shelter at all.

Since Maggie's departure for Germany was still a few weeks away, the idea that a second rescue dog should also be given a chance of a home grew on me. That way, you only have to do the work once and can raise both dogs at the same time. Right? BAD decision, as it later turned out!

I was looking for another female, up to 5 years old, about 55cm and black to become a member of our family. In the pictures we received of Branca, she looked a bit confused and scruffy but we immediately liked what we saw! Her pictures suggested character – exactly my thing. So, she was reserved as well, to travel to our family four weeks after Maggie – who was soon to be called Bailey.

Within a very short period of time, we had two dogs that had very strong hunting instincts, but also were very competitive with each other, with cats being favourite victims. When they met a cat in town (usually early in the morning or in the evening), my two *señoras* barked so loud that all the window-shutters shot up in the whole neighborhood. We quickly became the No.1 topic of conversation in town.

Since both dogs could not be unleashed, we bought Flexi lines.

Pah! Only beginners are that stupid!

Handy as Flexi-leads may be, the dogs pulling at the end of the long lead gave us no control while we literally sweated blood and tears – so this mistake was corrected very quickly. The two dogs were a disaster going for a simple walk, which felt like we were running a gauntlet. Then I started to find out more: anti-hunting training was the magic solution! Training lines and implements along with other aids were found, and we learned to become consistent, and stubbornly followed our chosen course of action. It was a long journey and as our "parenting" improved, it was no longer so stressful when walking them.

In the evenings, while browsing the homepage of my Spanish animal shelter, I came across an emergency call! A female that I'd always liked was to be put to sleep because the people who found her were no longer paying sponsorship money to the animal shelter. Her name was Sol, and of course she was black. I didn't even look at other dogs. I immediately showed her to Andreas, suggesting that we should foster her until she found a home. "As if you would let her go after she set foot in our house!" was his reply. OK! So, I phoned the Protectora, and Sol was reserved for us. This vixen was going to be part of our team. End of!

SECOND-HAND DOGS

Six weeks later, shy, scared and reserved, Sol arrived in Germany and was renamed Sunny. She found petting absolutely gruesome – so we left her alone. Our dogs, especially Zora as the leader, helped her and Sunny slowly learned to trust us. It took her nearly two years before she'd voluntarily approach us, asking for pets. Elementary school or kindergarten children would scare her when she would run for her life!

Sunny wants to be the first for everything, patience is not her strong point, so waiting is definitely not her thing! She's a very active dog who wants to be busy. Bored, she looks to entertain herself, which means … hunting everything that moves. So, yet more blood and tears were shed but it was fun meeting her needs – riding a bike, search games, fishing line …. we became very inventive in keeping our dogs entertained.

Unfortunately, our big Zora became very sick – it turned out she had pancreatic cancer and as we couldn't help her anymore, we had to let her go. Even with 3 other dogs, Zora's loss left a huge gap in our lives. We wondered which of the remaining dogs would take on the role of leader and were amazed that Branca, our scared girl, took over this position. It soon became clear to me that the recently vacated basket would have a new resident.

Sunny

Who wouldn't love to be adopted by Team Litfin, it's Dogneyland?!

Since I am on many different rescue websites on the Internet, I soon spotted our little Hungarian, Sparky, who was being kept in a place that was like hell on earth. He immediately charmed me but I had to act quickly. An e-mail was promptly sent, stating that I would like to adopt him. Transport was arranged and Andreas was informed by phone that a little Hungarian was coming the following week. I must say that my husband's enthusiasm really left a lot to be desired.

Well, the only way to describe Sparky is a "little big man". He came, he saw, and he conquered. Sparky was a total charmer and had a lot to say for himself. A LOT. Sparky never shut up for a second. He barked, he howled, he whined around the clock. His description said: "Doesn't bark"! Probably a translation mistake from Hungarian. Sparky loved us, his home and his girls. He was the protector of the female pack members, his courage was enormous, fear unknown.

Since Sparky wasn't exactly the biggest dog, I decided to get little Ina from Casa del Sol for my husband. Two little dogs as a replacement for our big Zora seemed like an AWESOME idea. Ina had just been brought to Casa del Sol with her mother and siblings (the same shelter from where my other girls came).

Ina had beautiful markings, she was brindle and had such great ears. Well, once again, I made a reservation and brought Baby Ina into our team.

What can I say…? My cute bonsai puppy became a bonsai on stilts. She is really no longer small, growing a little bigger than expected.

SECOND-HAND DOGS

Ina and Sunny soon became close buddies. Excellent! Great team! But together, they had double the mischief on their minds. I had holes and ditches in the garden that would have drained many large rivers. However, we had been warned right from the start: Ina likes to dig – it was just that nobody told us how much!

Ina was actually the first dog we adopted that was relaxed, calm, reserved, and not a hooligan. Oh, how nice life had become, you hardly noticed when out for a walk that a new one had joined the pack ... so I was already browsing the site of my animal shelter again.

Well ... what did I see there?

My sister had fallen in love with a young female in Casa del Sol shelter. Her name was Pata and she was with her black sister, Gara, in the puppy enclosure. Both were extremely attached to each other. If her sister was to leave, Gara would be alone and she would mourn intensely afterwards. Gara's chances of a quick adoption were very slim as she was black, very temperamental, and she was going to be very tall.

Even Andreas thought Gara would be a good fit for us – powerful dogs are much more our thing. After a day's deliberation, Gara was reserved. We called Pata and Gara our Christmas elves, especially since Gara had a white star on the chest and both arrived in Germany just before Christmas. Gara soon lost this nickname, becoming the Grinch instead. She guards everything I leave around from bags, shoes, jackets, socks ... no matter what. As soon as someone approaches, she squeezes her eyes shut and growls fiercely, so Grinch seemed a very appropriate name for her. Since Gara is a *Podenca-Pastor*, we now had a strong hunting watchdog on hand.

All of a sudden "something" was happening again during the walks. At the start, Gara was usually pulling on 2 legs on our walks, which is more than a bit tiring. We were very consistent and strict in her upbringing because if she got out of hand, there would be huge problems due to her size and strength. There was a lot to do in the coming weeks! Dog encounters were back to being disastrous as each one of the dogs forgot its training.

Puberty in dogs is exhausting ... very exhausting. Based on experience I knew by now that it would pass and calm would return. Knowing this, the following months were survived.

In the meantime, I was learning more online about pack posture and pack dynamics, and was noticing a change both in handling, and among the dogs themselves. The pack developed its own dynamic. It no longer had to do with a normal "multi-dog husbandry" of 2-3 dogs.

I found a handful of groups and trainers (even pack owners) who explained the dynamics and rules within the pack to me. Most important though, was the interpretation and understanding of their body language. So, by watching the dogs – sleeping, eating, playing, going for a walk – it was enough for one ear to move for me to know exactly what its owner was up to.

The rowdy phases in the pack improved and walks were slowly becoming fun again and dog encounters were also more relaxed. It was now possible to meet other dog owners without running the risk of the pack making minced meat of their dogs.

At about this time, a new home for a young, very spirited Dutch Shepherd/Bardino cross was being sought in Murcia, Spain. She lived with older people who had rescued her from beside a street-bin. However, she became too large and spirited for them and they found that they couldn't manage her. I wrote an email to my Spanish friends, asked if the dog could go to the Casa and I would take over her sponsorship. About two weeks later, Suerte moved into Casa de Sol. She was just what I wanted. Young, full of power and ... huge ears (people may notice that I have a "thing" for ears!!).

Meanwhile, another brindle Bardino bitch was up for adoption in another shelter where she had been taken by her family – to be put down. This poor dog cried, mourned, and screamed in desperation. The people in charge asked the Casa for help. In Casa del Sol, she would have more freedom (the dogs are not locked in kennels during the day) and would be better looked after ... and so Gordie moved into the Casa a few days later. Both dogs immediately touched my heart. I wanted to get one of them into my team, but which one should it be? Suerte, who was full of power and would mightily stir things up again, or the calmer Gordie?

We had had enough stress and wanted our pack to return to calm again, so it was Gordie who moved in one week before our summer vacation and came with us to our favourite home in the Bavarian Forest.

She chose her mistress on the first day – but that wasn't me! No! My daughter Celina and Gordie struck up a very close bond from the very first second. Gordie adores my daughter and does everything to please her. As Bardino dogs bond very closely to one person, I hadn't adopted a dog at all as Gordi was hardly aware of me, she had become Celina's shadow. She integrated into the pack without any problems and was able to run free after a short time. No need to pay attention to her after our vacation, she was just there, totally easy to care for!

So, my friends in Spain were informed that Suerte was allowed to move to her new home. Before she came, I made a little visit to Spain which was great as it allowed me to get to know my Suerte, falling in love with her straightaway. Of course, all the other dogs were great too, but they couldn't match up to MY girl.

However, one male caught my eye ... Freddy was his name. He was white ... Oh God! What was wrong with me? I just liked black or brindle. But there was something very special about Freddy. Most of all, he was calm – very calm! I need about a quarter of an hour to walk ten meters. A snail is definitely faster ... I thought perfect – just the dog for my husband. I sent Andreas a picture of Freddy, raving about him in the highest terms – this dog would be perfect for him. Andreas thought he was fantastic, especially the idea that the dog would be for him, so he quickly agreed to his adoption. The "white man" was immediately reserved too.

Other people may have black sheep in their families ... well, I now had a white one! However, Freddy had to stay in Spain for a while, because we'd learned our lesson about bringing two new dogs into the pack at the same time. Suerte arrived in Germany that week, and as soon as she was picked up from the transport, she jumped into my arms and was so happy.

At home, Suerte integrated quickly, only it didn't work that way with the Grinch Gara. Both were the same age, which was probably the problem so they had to be watched. Two days later, when I was walking alone with the dogs, a deer crossed our path, Sparky and Ina shot forward, the tow lines slipped out of my hands and they were gone. With the excitement of the others in the hustle and bustle, Gara attacked Suerte. The others immediately followed suit. Separation was impossible, I threw myself on Suerte to protect her from the bites – it felt like hours later that I finally had them apart; brought the brawlers to the car, where they were separated into crates and then I trudged off to collect Sparky and Ina, eventually catching up with them in a freshly plowed field. Of course, I looked like someone who'd been through hand-to-hand combat.

From then on, Gara and Suerte were walked separately – better double the walks than experience something like that again; they were kept constantly in my sights over the following days with immediate intervention at the slightest movement, and calm slowly returned.

When things finally got back to normal, a friend needed some help. She had adopted two sibling bitches from my Casa. One dog worked out well but the other, Sally, had problems dealing with children; she'd snapped at the little daughter and generally reacted differently to the family. She was totally overwhelmed and afraid in the presence of children.

Before it got worse, we decided that Sally should come to us immediately so we could look for another childless home for her. The family blamed themselves, feeling they had failed – even though that wasn't the case at all as sometimes a dog just doesn't fit.

Sally immediately felt at home in our team, however, she chewed everything that was lying around or within her reach. Holes and ditches in the garden were very generously expanded and house training was completely alien. No matter how often or how long we were outside, Sally only did her "business" indoors and I got to do major cleaning every morning.

Walking on a leash was a catastrophe. Zig-zag, forwards, backwards, back and forth, which made me even more anxious which, of course, made things worse. How could this carry on? After all, our Freddy (Baxter) would be joining the team in two weeks. For the first time, I doubted that I could handle it.

Andreas and Celina went on a trip two weeks later, bringing donations to the Casa del Sol and Freddy/Baxter would travel with them on the way back. Baxter was so proud and loved going on the trip very, very much. I don't know who shone more: Baxter or Andreas. At home, the integration went as usual, after all, we now knew the routine. Baxter and Sally hit it off right away and became close friends but together, they just had devilment on their minds and things were destroyed even more than before which encouraged me to accelerate the search for a family for Sally.

The White Sheep, Baxter

After 11 weeks, I found the home I was looking for – above all, there were four other dogs in the family so Sally would not be alone. Saying goodbye to her was very difficult for me ... I howled crying on the way back. I howled for the next 3 days, feeling like such a traitor. At home it was really quiet, no more cleaning orgies in the morning, no torn objects on the floor. It was just quiet – too quiet.

Meanwhile, Baxter discovered his legs. Because I can only walk ten meters in 15 minutes ... he ran and jumped non-stop and was a real rascal, and kept teasing the girls. He was really fast, swerving like a rabbit. He was also very docile. He also ignored Andreas. That was the worst! Baxter looked through him as if he didn't exist at all, even though he was supposed to be The Dog for my husband. When he saw me again as soon as he arrived, Baxter must have thought: *O Divine One, I will rule behind you* ... and that is the case to this day. Andreas was very disappointed.

Remember Moritz, our inherited poodle? Throughout all the arrivals and changes to the pack, he always remained a full member and was always treated with respect by the others. However, at the age of 15 we had to put him down because his little body was no longer strong enough. It was peculiar, even though he never stood out or made special demands, he still left a big void in our family.

His empty basket was still there when we were asked to help a young woman from Austria with the upbringing of her aggressive bitch that had also come from our animal shelter in Spain. We felt it was a matter of honour for us to try to help. Chici was now 5 years' old, having come to her family at 4 months of age, but was now biting everything and everyone.

It was difficult to get a picture by remote diagnosis and I invited the young woman and dog to join us. The date was postponed several times and the situation worsened as time went on. The dog couldn't get out at all, instead she was locked up and destroyed the entire facility out of sheer frustration. She opened doors of any kind with her left paw.

The woman was desperate and didn't know what to do next. So I suggested they gave Chici up and she would come to us as a foster. If she was ready at some point – I would look for a suitable family for her. That was the plan. It took a while before the young woman decided to take this step, despite everything she loved her Chici.

The woman came to us on a Saturday with a friend, and a very sullen and grumpy Chici. It took less than 5 minutes and Chici had bitten Andreas's arm and hand several times. However, he stayed cool and calm, after all, we had been warned. She had a very strange body language and sound. You couldn't classify – was it joy or attack? Even my dogs hid behind me fortunately, otherwise it would have escalated.

Celina was forbidden to go near her, and told to ignore her completely. Later in the evening it was already clear that we could get Chici's problems under control, but it would be a lengthy affair. Since she was smaller than expected, looked very similar to our Sparky, and Moritz's basket was without a resident, we decided to keep her. We also feared that this would become a true challenge – one tiny mistake and the old battle-mouse would come through again.

Chici had been messed up by many different dog trainers who thought they had to suppress the dog in her. Unfortunately, the latest mistress was young and inexperienced and believed that dogs had to be treated like that. The more insecure the mistress became, the more beastly Chici became – a very vicious circle. She no longer warned by growling either. She shot straight out and bored her teeth into the meat. She had learned that after a growl – punishment follows .... so sad, that sort of thing. She also had to lose weight urgently, she had almost 10 kg too much on her ribs and could no longer move properly.

I researched the topic of aggression in dogs – how it can be diverted, which directions one should take and so on. I also found out about muzzles and ordered one for Chici. From then on, her food bowl was well-filled, but low in calories. With a muzzle, she was able go for a walk again, although I shielded her from strangers and dogs, and she began to enjoy it more and more, and the sullen facial expression gradually disappeared. I was able to do everything with Chici from the start. She would never bite me – but that didn't apply to Andreas who became her favorite victim. As soon as he got careless, she shot forward and bit.

Chici has been with us for five years now, we have achieved more than we could ever have imagined in the beginning. She rarely needs the muzzle now, but it is always at hand as she is still a "jackass" dog. She stalks her favorite victims in the pack, starts mock attacks and puts on a show of being strong.

Almost three months after Chici's arrival, I was asked to look out for a dog that came from the Casa. I even knew him and had met Babieca on one of my visits to Spain. He was thought to have bitten a dachshund and had to leave his new home immediately. A friend, Annett, who wanted to step in as an emergency carer, was packed into the car and together we drove down to Spain. I was horrified when I saw Babieca as he was completely dejected, and totally stressed out. I didn't argue with the owner for long, but packed up the dog and drove off – I would never have left a dog there.

On my morning walks I often saw my friend Annett with Babieca and her dog Hero. I learned that Babieca had a broken leg, which needed straightening by means of an operation, which the rescue association wanted to pay for.

After a time, Babieca and Hero were no longer getting on together and the two of them fought more and more – to this day, I don't know what the reason for this was. In any case, I brought the big black guy to my home on a trial basis and he worked out wonderfully with my team.

Babieca's operation was carried out, after which led to the hardest time we had in all our years of dog ownership. The splint needed to support the operated knee-joint caused a multitude of pressure points on his leg, which in turn meant Babieca's body shed skin and flesh. There were huge and deep wounds. Bones and tendons were exposed. We had many vets and clinics on hand but none could help. We changed the bandages every hour. Babieca trusted us, and despite the terrible pain, he tolerated it over and over again. How many times did tears roll from my black man's eyes because it was so painful, despite the strong medication?

We often cried with him and wondered if it was worth it. Many thousands of euros were spent just for the care of the wounds and we worked day and night to pay the bills. The operation had been performed at the beginning of September and at one point our goal was just to get Babieca without a bandage and with well-healed wounds in time for Jose's visit (Manager of Casa del Sol), that was planned for the end of January. Exactly one day before Jose's arrival, the bandage was removed. Goal achieved!!

During Jose's visit, I got a WhatsApp message in the morning. Sally was to be brought back. There was a fight and she was deemed to be the guilty one. So, Jose and I went to get her. I was horrified to see the poor dog, as she was just a skeleton and very nervous. While still in the car, I told Jose that Sally had now arrived home and would not be going anywhere. I really regretted giving her up. Andreas could say whatever he wanted, but I wouldn't give in. When we got home, you could tell the pack was reunited. She also took up her place in the pack as if the intervening year had never happened. Since Gara was calmer now, I was able to concentrate on Sally's upbringing and was no longer distracted by the others.

Weeks later, Sparky fell very seriously ill and within a few hours he had to be put to sleep. It was a such a terrible shock!!! Life without our Sparkely … our product tester, the boss in the ring – unimaginable. After his death, I posted the Dog's Last Will which I wanted to fulfill on his behalf.

Meanwhile back in Spain, a young Bardino bitch, Bailey, was brought back from her adopted home as it was discovered that she had only been kept on a balcony. After she'd been found as a puppy with her siblings in a bag and lovingly raised by hand, it was thought she had found a nice home. I wanted to see Bailey during my upcoming visit to the Casa, but one week before arriving, I was happy to hear that she'd been adopted with her sister. Anyway, my head told me that she'd have been way too big, and wouldn't have fitted in the car either.

Then Princessa caught my eye. I wanted to take a closer look at her. She was so pretty, small, petite, a flea … she also looked delicate and simply cute. While at the shelter, I always had Princessa by my side like a dream … and then I saw her in action. After a visit to the seaside, we entered the Casa and Jose's dogs came towards us. In the blink of an eyelid, the "flea" was hanging onto Perdita's throat. I was totally perplexed. As she didn't let go either, we had to help out a bit. I found out later that something like this is not unusual with Pinschers. Sweet and golden, the little girl still completely overflowed with charm and despite all … I wanted her. We'd be able to handle them but I didn't tell my husband about her megalomania. Had I done so, he would have been better prepared.

Hopefully the pack unification would work out well, even though Princessa was probably tired and a little intimidated by the number of dogs in our gang, she behaved in an exemplary manner and I breathed a sigh of relief.

Unfortunately, the mood changed two days later, when everything degenerated into a huge fight in which our pack-leader, Branca, was almost bitten to death – which hit me hard, in more ways than one. In trying to protect Branca, I was bitten all over.

The problem with a pack of this size is the momentum – if there is a fight between two dogs, all the others join in and gang up on the weakest, and will only stop when that one is dead. That I would not just stand by should be clear to all, so I had to try to protect my dog as best as I could.

My screaming alerted Andreas and Celina, who jumped in to the fray and after a huge struggle assisted with a dollop of water, the dogs were finally separated and Branca was brought to safety. I wrapped a towel around my ripped arm, wrapped poor Branca in a blanket and drove quickly to the vet. It looked bad for her as she had many serious injuries. We really didn't know if she would survive – the operation and treatments took almost 9 hours.

After I knew Branca was well-taken care of, I had to get my own wounds stitched or stapled, which was unusual as normally bite wounds are left open to heal. I had already swallowed antibiotics at home as they are now a regular part of my medicine cabinet, but my entire body ached. Despite all her terrible injuries, I was amazed at how well Branca was two days later. Our grandma-dog is pretty tough.

Fortunately, we were going on vacation the following week, where we would have time to relax. Branca's wounds would also have to be rinsed daily and I was shown how to pull my stitches out by myself after ten days – otherwise I would have to visit a doctor on vacation which I didn't want, the vet visits would be enough.

After ten days I solemnly pulled out my sutures and was glad that it was over … but one day later everything popped open again. This time the situation was at the swimming pool of our hotel. As Suerte didn't want to give the ball to Andreas, I took it from her instead. Princessa immediately attacked Suerte and the crowd was there right away, luckily Branca and Ina were still in our suite.

Andreas and I rushed down the embankment with chairs and dogs. I grabbed Suerte and he grabbed Princessa, fortunately the other dogs couldn't get through the bushes properly and could be kept at a distance with our feet and the chairs. Celina arrived with Chici's muzzle and before Princessa knew it, she had it over her mouth. Once again, we were a topic of conversation.

Number One and I had to be sewn up again ... after that, I no longer take any chances with Princessa. Outside the home, along with her collar she wears her muzzle – that goes without saying and she's not even bothered at all. But thanks to this, she no longer jumps on anyone or has mood changes.

After this big fight I'd finally had enough. It was now over! Definitely no more dogs! That was my strong opinion ... but everyone else was skeptical.

Of course, very soon I got mail. The family of the Bardino, Bailey, asked if I wanted to have her as they'd heard that I'd previously wanted to adopt her. They wanted to rehome her because they were finding two pubescent dogs difficult to deal with, especially when the two were left to their own devices during the day. But I said no. This time sound reasoning had kicked in. My wounds hadn't healed properly and I would just have more stress and more work. No need for that!

Weeks later, we noticed that Branca had finally given up her position as boss and was holding back more and more. She no longer reprimanded the youngsters and came to me more quickly to seek protection which I found good and comforting. But who would succeed her? We watched our pack and were astonished to see that Sunny took over the top position, and she does her job very well. The pack has now become relaxed. Only Princessa will argue but thanks to the muzzle these arguments are harmless. Barriers and privacy fences have been installed at entrances so that there are no external stimuli that could trigger attacks.

At some point, I went on the Facebook page of our animal shelter and discovered that the Bardino siblings were both brought back to the Casa. I was angry and disappointed … my brain rattled. Bardinos are great, no hunting instinct and in my opinion, are very easy to care for. They can run freely and are totally loyal once they have established a relationship with humans. I knew this because we already have two in the pack. Dare I do it again?

I corresponded back and forth with Jose. He sent me pictures and videos … the mind said no, but my heart screamed: YES. Since I am an emotional person, she was reserved. However, another name had to be found as we already had a Bailey, so she was named Kylie as it sounded similar. I hid the reservation from my husband, as he would be hopping mad … but it didn't matter. During the transport I took Princessa with me to be on the safe side so that she could get up close to Kylie in her own way. Fortunately, she loved Kylie and even asked her to play. There were no problems with the rest of the pack as they were old hands with newcomers by now, and knew how things went.

In the garden I noticed Kylie's strange way of moving, and she kept tipping over at the back. She ran completely out of kilter – I suspected something bad so it was off to the vet again. I stood with Kylie in the clinic during her examination, which showed that both kneecaps were loose and could be pushed back and forth. One could feel a thickening in one leg – an old, badly healed fracture was suspected. In order to be sure however, Kylie had to be X-rayed; no sooner said than done, but the result was devastating.

Kylie had neither hip sockets nor knee joints on either hind leg. Her bones were almost loose, only held in place by ligaments, tendons, and skin. We were all shocked because the young dog ran and jumped around as if everything was in perfect working order, but she had become used to the pain and didn't know it any other way. The next step was to build muscle, mix pain-relievers and joint-building additives into the feed with a specific regime to build up the hind-quarter muscles. Finally, the kneecaps sat firmly, and Kylie was allowed to run again. We still held our breath as she only knows one pace and that's full throttle. She and

Princessa had become real friends and played, ran and fought with each other.

But tragically, poor Kylie's general health began to fail and we lost her in September 2020.

My dogs are not just my hobby, they are my great passion and are an illustration of my approach to life. Problem dogs have become very exciting and fascinating, which is why I want to further educate myself in this area.

Author's note: Since this story was written, Team Litfin has welcomed Mona, yet another Casa girl!!

ARRIVALS & RAINBOW BRIDGE DEPARTURES:

Moritz: September 2002–March 2017
Zora: May 2008–May 2013
Bailey: January 2012–June 2023
Branca: March 2012
Sunny: January 2013
Sparky: June 2013–February 2018
Ina: December 2013
Gara: December 2014
Gordie: July 2015
Suerte: April 2016
Baxter: September 2016
Chici: April 2017
Babieca: August 2017
Sally: January 2018
Princessa: July 2018
Kylie: September 2019–September 2020
Mona: June 2021

Back (l-r): Bailey, Baxter, Ina, Sunny, Branca, Sally;
Front: (l-r) Suerte, Princessa, Gordie, Chici, Gara (the Grinch!), Babieca

Andreas and Kerstin, with members of Team Litfin
(*All photos: The Litfin Family*)

Dexter, with a smile to melt hearts *(Photo: A.Jones)*

Art and science aren't enough, patience is the basic stuff.

Konrad Lorenz, on training animals

Zeta *(Photo: PeaJayz)*

Lorenz (7 Nov 1903-27 Feb 1989) was an Austrian zoologist, ethologist, and ornithologist who shared the 1973 Nobel Prize in Physiology or Medicine with Nikolaas Tinbergen and Karl von Frisch. He is often regarded as one of the founders of modern ethology, the study of animal behaviour.

HOUSE RULES …

I've carried out many, many home-checks on prospective adopters and one of my questions is "What rules might you put on your new dog?" – to which the answer is primarily, "not on the furniture". Hmmmm… let's see …

Rule 1: No dogs on the furniture

Huh? There's a *rule*? (Photo: L.Lovering)

But seriously, this is the warmest place – THIS is summer????!!! *(Photo: G.Collins)*

Oh, pretty pleeaase, can you just bring me a treat? *(Photo: J.Williams)*

This sofa's terribly lumpy (*Photo: L.Lovering*)

Just dawg-tired (*Photo: J.Williams*)

Whadyya mean ... "I didn't buy this sofa for you"? *(Photo: P.Jones)*

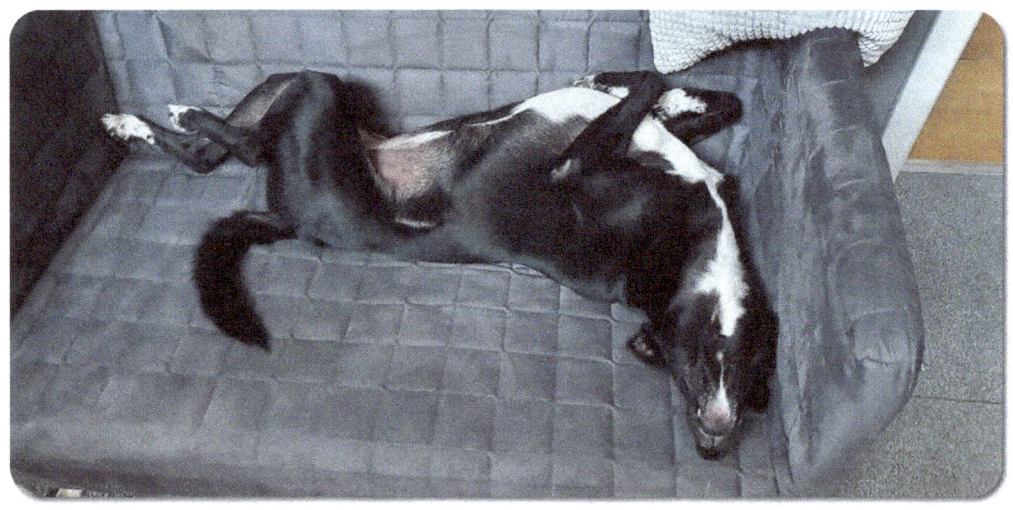
"Go to my own bed? Thanks, but I'm very happy here!" (Emma: *Photo: S. Eichler)*

Rule 2: No sleeping on human beds

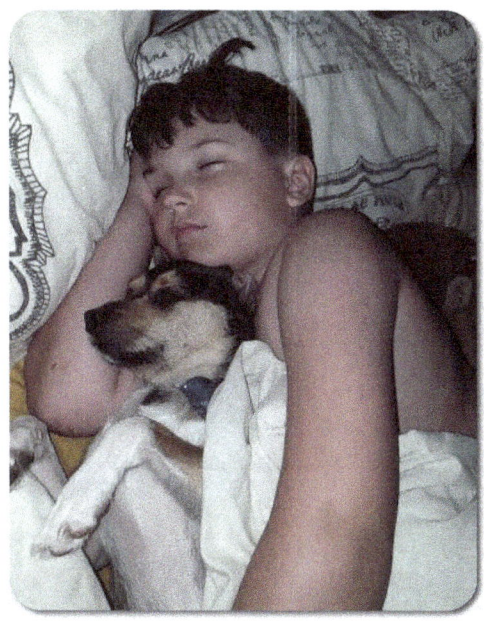

And Noodle nestles in for the night *(Photo: C.Okninski)*

They made me do it. Honest! *(Photo: L.Lovering)*

As I still have a paw on the floor, technically I don't consider this ON the bed
(Photo: P.Jones)

We can share, if you like …? *(Photo: P.Jones)*

Well, *hellllo* *(Photo: C&D Wright)*

Rule 3: No feeding at the table

But it's MY birthday you're celebrating
(Photo: I.Horn)

Do you need any help with that ...?
(Photo: R.Pockett)

... but it's okay for you ...? *(Photo: M.Davies)*

A DOG'S LAST WILL

Before humans die, they write their last will and testament, giving their home and all they have to those they leave behind. If, with my paws, I could do the same, this is what I'd ask…

To a poor and lonely stray, I'd give my happy home; my bowl and cosy be, soft pillow and all my toys; the lap, which I loved so much; the hand that stroked my fur; and the sweet voice that spoke my name.

I'd will to the sad, scared, shelter dog the place I had in my human's loving heart, of which there seemed no bounds.

So, when I die, please do not say, "I will never have a pet again, for the loss and the pain is more than I can stand."

Instead, go find an unloved dog, one whose life has held no joy or hope, and give my place to him.

This is the only thing I can give…

The love I left behind.

— Author Unknown

PART II

Adoption Advice

Snow (Photo: C & D.Wright)

CHAPTER 1

So You Think You Want A Dog?

It's comparatively easy to get a dog these days, but while owning one can be the most pleasurable and rewarding experience, sadly not enough people actually sit down to think seriously about whether having a dog would suit their home and life-style. Nor do they think about the long-term commitment and responsibility involved. A dog should be FOR LIFE.

The very first question you should ask yourself is why do you want a dog in your life? And what are you looking for from the partnership – protection? companionship? a dog to participate in competitions?

Anyone contemplating adding a puppy or dog to their home **should take their time** to consider what is involved with dog-ownership, before adopting. Thoroughly research everything from the possible cost involved, general commitments, and the amount of time required to adequately care for the dog's emotional and physical needs. As important is the decision as to which breed, size or type of dog that would suit you or your family's lifestyle.

Having a dog in the family could be regarded a little like a marriage – are you ready to commit to this living creature for richer, for poorer, in sickness and in health, until-death-one-of-you-do-you-part? Consider that this fluffy new addition to your home will become **part of your family** – almost like an extra child. You wouldn't throw your child out for making a mess or taking up too much of your time, would you? Would you discard your parents because they've become old and/or ill? Or just because you've tired of them (even though your children may sometimes have this effect on you)?

Depending on the breed, size and general health, a dog's average life-expectancy can range anywhere between 12-15 years although some can live to as much as 20 in exceptional cases. Larger breeds like Great Danes or Irish Wolfhounds, etc. tend to live between 6-10 years. Are you prepared to look after your dog for so many years, especially when it becomes an OAP with all the health issues and expense that that may entail?

Prospective owners should always keep the thought foremost to their mind that the rescue dog they're interested in adopting may have previously had an unsettled life which has caused him insecurities and worries. He will need stability and security; the last thing he needs is a new home that may not be committed enough to look after him for the rest of his days.

If there is already a resident dog in your home, you may want to consider if he or she would accept another in what is – to them – their den, their patch, especially if your current dog has a history of fighting. You may want to consider their happiness ahead of your own desire to add another pet to the household. If you are dead-set on adopting a new dog, please speak with an expert behaviourist beforehand to discuss what behaviour modifications may be required with your present dog (if he's a scrapper) **before** a new one arrives.

Adopters should be very honest with themselves in considering these questions, because if they aren't, it will be the poor dog that will suffer by being surrendered back to a shelter, or worse still, destroyed. They should minutely examine their own lives and future plans to see if a dog will fit into their home. Owning a dog should be for the duration of its natural life, not just as long as it suits the owner.

Think carefully about adopting a rescue dog if you're not willing to commit to this length of time.

Life-style

Like your lie-ins? Well, kiss them goodbye as your dog will want his morning walk.

Don't like going out in inclement weather? Sorry! Tired from your day's work, and just want to put your feet up? Sorry again! Most dogs enjoy their daily constitutionals regardless of the weather or your state of fatigue, and they need exercise to stay healthy, stimulated and content.

Deprived of sufficient exercise, dogs – and especially puppies – will use that abundance of energy in other, less-acceptable ways to its owner, by being destructive or badly behaved in the house. Owners should be prepared to give up a part of their lives, no matter the circumstance, to provide their dogs with what they need.

Contrary to the mistaken belief of a certain percentage of owners that puppies and dogs learn good behaviour by osmosis, all canines need at least elementary training by its owner, or with the help of the local dog training classes. Too many dogs are abandoned or surrendered to shelters because of *their* "bad behaviour", when sadly the truth is down to a rarely-acknowledged failure on the part of the owners who have not provided even basic discipline to the poor animal. Will you be willing to spend time teaching your furry friend good manners, which may include trips to your local training centre?

Do you fancy the idea of being a canine hair-dresser, happy to groom its long tresses until the coat gleams, or perhaps having to pay a groomer to coif your fur-baby's coat into fashionable styles? Or is a grooming glove on a short-coated pooch about as much time as you're prepared to put in?

Too posh to scoop poop? It is the responsibility of the owner to pick up their dog's excrement, or be prepared for large fines. It's the polite, socially-accepted thing for every dog-owner to do in their community. On occasions, you may even have to remove poop from around the nether regions of a long-coated dog (yes, I know, eeew … clothes-peg-on-nose time and shallow breaths!).

Home

Are you particularly house-proud and enjoy a neat and pristine environment, with fluff-free floors, sofas that you wouldn't be embarrassed to ask your in-laws to sit on, with that beautiful cream carpet in the lounge free of muddy paw prints during wet winter months, and no squeaky toys to trip over?

As most dogs shed their coat to a greater or lesser extent during the year on to floors, furniture and clothes, can you lower your ambitions to have a show-home suitable for Homes & Gardens, to a more relaxed one that a dog can call its home?

If you're not the kind that's able to live with or ignore that fur decoration all over your house, and paw prints traipsing over the lounge carpet, are you prepared for the additional housework involved in returning it to its pristine condition?

Can you provide the appropriate environment and is your property big enough for the type of dog you'd like?

Are you living in a rental property? Will your landlord/lady give permission for you to have a dog in their property? Bear in mind that having a pet will also make moving to a new rental home more difficult, and possibly more expensive. Sadly, too many dogs are surrendered to shelters because pets are not permitted in a new rental property. Consideration should also be given to the neighbours – not all will appreciate a dog that may be barking or howling, or they may just not like animals.

Career

Consider your own personal situation. Are you a career-minded person who has plans to advance in your job which may mean longer hours in the office, perhaps weekend working, or business trips away from home?

Have you considered how you'd manage financially with a dog if you lost your job or your income isn't covering your existing expenses?

What if your career takes you overseas? In all cases, what will happen to your dog?

You've been a hard-working stay-at-home parent, caring for your children, but they've become more independent and don't need you so much, or have finally flown the nest. So you've decided that the time is right to re-join the workforce and find a job? Have you thought about what will happen to your pet that's been a much-loved part of your family, a best friend to the children while they were growing up? This is especially pertinent to a rescue dog that may be somewhat insecure and timid – how will he deal with such upheaval in his life?

What kind of life is it for a poor animal left on its own for perhaps 10-12 hours with only a dog-walker popping in during the day to take it out for an hour, or to spend its days in doggy-day care? While the dog may at least be having fun with its friends at the day-care, surely the general idea of getting a dog is to have the joy of their company, to be able to benefit from having a good reason to get out and exercise, and to enjoy their characters and personalities that can bring so much laughter and fun into your life.

I repeat, dogs like to spend time with us. Potential owners should think of what is best for the dog, rather than what is good for them.

Social-life

You may have to prepare to spend more time at home with your furry family member. If you're a bit of a social butterfly and like impromptu get-aways or late nights out with your friends, provisions will have to be made to ensure he's well-cared for in your absence.

Your dog will still need your time, enjoy personal interaction with you through play-time, training or generally just having fun, and particularly he will need exercise to lead a happy life. So if you don't want to give up some time from your busy social life, perhaps a dog isn't for you.

If you fancy the idea of visiting the shopping mall or to the High Street for a mooch around with your furry friend, you'll have to check beforehand to ensure that dogs will be welcome. And no one should have to be reminded that **they should never be left in a parked car for any length of time.**

Partners/Children

What about your own personal circumstances? Does your partner willingly agree to having a dog (rather than doing it just to please you)? Are you in a relationship where you want to have children in the future?

Consider carefully if you'll have the energy and time to provide adequately for the needs of both a baby and the dog. The dog should be considered an integral part of your family and it should not be an immediate impulse to surrender him to a shelter upon the arrival of a baby. Would you hand your child over if it becomes "too much trouble to care for"? Could your partner step up to take more of a rule in your dog's life, taking him for walks, etc? These are very important questions to be discussed and decided before ever adopting a dog.

While of course there should be strict monitoring when children and dogs are in the same house and they should NEVER be left together unattended, it is possible to socialise a dog with the new baby, and when the baby grows older, to teach the child how to treat dogs with respect.

Are your children pestering you to get a dog? To justify his ban on having a dog, my dad used to say that "it would be a 9-day wonder". Children can quickly bore of new "toys", of clearing the garden of poop, or dog-training, when the duties will invariably fall on the parents' shoulders.

While some children may be mature enough to take on the responsibility of a dog, others will be less so. Unless the parents are prepared and have the time to take over the dog-care duties, bringing a dog into the family may not be such a good idea.

Do not be afraid to say "NO" to your beloved offspring if you are not prepared to look after the animal.

Think about the "What if's", unpalatable as they may be. What if your relationship breaks down? What will happen to your dog? Will you or your ex- be able and prepared to adequately care for your pet? As uncomfortable and unthinkable as this topic may be, unfortunately all shelters will have experienced lovely dogs being handed in as "unwanted" because of a relationship breakdown.

What if you meet a new partner who doesn't like animals? And trust me, this is another regular "excuse" for surrendering a pet that shelters encounter. Most dog-lovers will scream: "Find another partner", if your new beloved doesn't like your dog but unfortunately not all share this view.

What if there is a serious illness in the family? What will happen to your dog? Or if one partner passes away? Will there be someone who can care for the pet?

And then the ultimate "What if" … if you're on your own, what will happen to your beloved fur-friend if you fall seriously ill, or worse, pass away? Could you make provisions with family members, friends or a local rescue charity to look after him or her if you're no longer in a position to do so?

Company For An Existing Resident Dog

Even though dogs can enjoy being in a small pack, not every dog will be amenable to having a buddy, especially one living in the same house. If the resident dog is badly socialised or is prone to fighting, think very carefully about adding a new one – it might be better to be content with the dog you have.

Cost

Without doubt, dogs can be an expensive pet. The UK charity, PDSA, estimates that it could cost between £25,000-30,800 over the potential lifetime of the dog, depending on size, breed, longevity and general health. You should be prepared to budget for:

1) Fee to the shelter or charity for the adoption of the dog (most shelters will include the cost of microchip in this fee).
2) Initial health check, and required health vaccinations, plus the subsequent yearly booster shots for the life of the dog.
3) Dog-license, depending on the country in which you live.
4) Pet insurance, don't forget to factor in the insurance "excess".
5) Vet care that involves uninsured treatment costs, plus the cost of medications required to treat the ailments. Note that these costs may increase as your pet gets older.
6) Regular worming, plus flea/tick treatments.
7) Grooming (if you've decided on a dog with a coat that needs professional care).
8) Spaying or neutering (most rescue charities do this before adoption of adult dogs).
9) Best-quality kibble/wet food that you can afford, and treats: cost will depend on the size and type of dog you choose, ie. couch potato, K9 Olympic athlete or anything in between. (Note that sometimes dogs can develop medical issues that may require special "prescription" dog foods, which don't come cheap.)
10) Equipment: bed, crate (if you choose to use this), collar, dog tag, lead/harness, car restraints, and toys.
11) Residential kennels or pet sitters for when you go on that exotic holiday.
12) Training classes.
13) Dog-walkers, or doggy day-care, if you work full-time.

> If the answer to any of these is "No", think carefully about bringing any dog into your home, especially one adopted from a shelter. Rescue dogs need STABLE, SECURE FOREVER HOMES.

Many owners get dogs because of their own needs and desires – they like to have a wagging tail meet them at the door on their return. They want the company or they like the kudos of owning a particular breed of dog. Sadly, not all people consider the needs of the dog concerned, and the commitments entailed in keeping that animal happy and healthy over the entirety of its life.

Few owners who surrender their pets to a shelter ever see the devastation that it causes to their pets, how the animals retreat into themselves, not eating, not interacting with other dogs or their new carers, often withdrawing totally from life. Some poor animals literally sob with the emotional pain and fear in their new "home". Ask anyone who works in a shelter what it's like to see a dog suffer in such a way and you'll see the pain of those memories written on their faces.

Please don't only think of yourself. Think of the dog, and what he or she needs.

CHAPTER 2

The Search Begins …

So you've made the decision to give a rescue dog the chance of a good life, but care should be taken as to where to find him. There are many different sources through which to find a dog but some should be avoided at all costs.

Resist the urge to adopt a puppy or adult dog from **private** Facebook Pages, flea-markets or sites like Craig's List, Gumtree or similar online advertising sites which are basically set up for people to flog their unwanted items. Sadly, pets that have become surplus to requirements in their owners' lives will also be offered for sale or sometimes free-of-charge.

It's an absolute crime that it is still permitted to rehome domestic animals in such a way. These sites provide an unregulated outlet for owners to off-load their unwanted pets as easily as possible, with little care as to where the animal is going, and to whom.

With no security or background checks carried out on the new owner, there is no way of ensuring that the animals will go to people who genuinely want to give that dog or cat a good home. Tragically these advertising mediums provide easy access to animals by evil individuals involved in hideous activities such as dog fighting – where unfortunate ex-family pets will either participate directly in the fights or be used to bait the protagonists, or for badger-baiting. In any case, the poor creature will have its life snuffed out in the most miserable, excruciatingly painful and fear-filled way – nothing that anyone with a beating humane heart would ever want their dog to suffer.

Equally, by obtaining a pet through these channels, a potential owner has no way of knowing just what kind of dog they may be taking on, as people will invariably lie. The new owners will have no idea as to the dog's past, how it has been raised or trained, whether it will make a suitable pet, or if it's an animal with aggression issues. Lastly, there is no come-back on the previous owner if the dog is found to be unsuitable for the new home.

How often is the hackneyed phrase "dog being rehomed due to a change in circumstances" used? This is one of the most familiar excuses given when a pet is being surrendered to a shelter. Online sites make it all too easy to get rid of a dangerous dog that would be highly unsuitable to a home.

Unregulated internet sites also make for easy advertising of the products of the infamous puppy-farms, be they from organised enterprises, pet shops, or a back-street breeder.

While the following refers more to so-called "pedigree puppies" and the purpose of this book is to persuade people to adopt from reputable rescue organisations, it is important to raise awareness of puppy-farms or -mills.

This business mass-produces "pedigree" puppies like goods off a product line. Bitches are forced to continually produce off-spring – generally in dark, dirty, unhygienic conditions. The breeding mums lead miserable, unstimulating and unrewarding lives for years, devoid of affection, only to be discarded once their usefulness is over, leaving them in poor physical and mental condition. Many of these unfortunate canine breeding machines end up in shelters, from where the charity will attempt to find them genuine, loving homes.

Unfortunately, some countries still allow the sale of puppies through pet stores which may obtain their stock from puppy-farms whose primary interest is to churn out puppies as fast as possible for profit, with little or no concern for the welfare of the animals. There is no way for the buyer to know the circumstances of either the pup's breeding, general health or upbringing until too late.

The health of both mums and pups is often poor as any medical or disease control costs will eat into profits of backstreet breeders. In all likelihood the parent dogs will not have been vaccinated, and even more likely that neither will the puppies. Even if the breeders have bothered to inoculate their "stock", often because of the number of pups and poor record keeping, some pups may be vaccinated twice which will not allow their little bodies sufficient time to respond properly to the serum. Raised in unsanitary conditions, combined with a lack of preventive vet care, the pups will frequently suffer from a myriad of health issues that only come to light down the road.

Many of the puppy "farms" remove the pups too early from their mums, offering them for sale before 8 weeks. This deprives the poor little babies of vital emotional, social contact with their mums when they'll learn how to establish the accepted boundaries with other dogs. They are unlikely to have received much in the way of human affection, leaving future owners with severe problems of dogs that have been poorly socialised in every way.

There are of course responsible breeders around who do their best to ensure the puppies in their care are socialised appropriately. However, if purchasing from a breeder who will not or cannot show you the pup's parents, or if they don't want to show you the kennel where the puppies are, in both cases walk away quickly. It is possible that these people are purely dealers who obtain their puppies from puppy-mills.

If a "breeder" is advertising many different breeds, including crosses, it is more than likely to be a front for puppy-farming as reputable breeders will generally only raise one, or perhaps two breeds – no more. If they tell you that they have a few available litters with perhaps more "coming in", run a mile.

The good rescue re-homing organisations or independent shelters have reputations to protect and genuinely care for their animals. They will do their best to make sure an adopter chooses the right dog for them and their circumstances. They will have observed the dog in their facility and evaluated it on its behaviour, activity levels and personality – as far as is possible, and may offer back-up support if the dog doesn't adjust to the new home.

It is important to bear in mind that not all rescue dogs come with problems, many will have been surrendered due to a death or serious illness in the family, a new baby, or change in circumstances of the previous owner. Many adopters find their rescue dog to be very affectionate and quick to bond with them. Even elderly rescues and those who experienced trauma from their abandonment can make loving companions.

Unless the dog has been surrendered to the shelter by its previous owner who can provide a lot of background information, the shelters may not know **all** of the dog's behavioural history. Sadly, as said previously, people will lie – which is not always helpful to potential new owners, and by default to their former pet.

It is difficult to be 100% accurate to be able to advise people regarding the behaviour of dogs in a shelter environment, because this behaviour can be vastly different to that shown by the dog in a home.

While many shelters receive small puppies without knowledge of their background or history, at least these organisations will have the animals' interests at heart, rather than profit. They will take the time to give these little babies love, care and attention. As they grow, the development of their characters and behaviour will be monitored. The down-side is that not all rehoming agencies will have the wherewithal to properly expose the young puppies to the myriad of sights, sounds and experiences that they need to enable them to be fully socialised.

There are many very good rehoming organisations around – many, like Dogs' Trust, Battersea Dogs Home, RSPCA, American Humane Society, etc. need little introduction. It would be worth looking at some of the smaller independent shelters as well, as they will also have plenty of lovely dogs for adoption, all in need of good homes.

Take your time to research and identify a reputable shelter or rescue charity. Preferably it should be legally registered in the country where it's located, be run efficiently and humanely, with good canine healthcare programmes including vaccination, neutering and parasite control.

Its representatives should be professional and knowledgeable about the animals in their care, and honest and forthcoming in their responses to your queries. It is also a huge bonus if the charity does good behaviour assessments, and has qualified staff that can train, or retrain those dogs with behavioural problems.

The shelter personnel should be able to provide as much information as they know about the dog's temperament and state of health – with the proviso that it may not be possible to evaluate every aspect if the dog was abandoned. Sadly, animals with no obvious previous medical history can develop illnesses. Sometimes, bad things happen through no one's fault.

Good shelters will provide a back-up rehoming service in the event that an adoption is unsuccessful with the dog chosen, although every shelter absolutely hates to see dogs returning. So again, consider very carefully if adoption is right for you.

Prospective adopters should remember that each dog is different and to be fair to the poor animal after all the stress and trauma he's experienced in his life, the adopted dog should be given at least 3 months or more to be allowed to settle into their new life.

Adopters should check out the independent rescue groups carefully, look at their Facebook Page and/or website, check any reviews, and see how much information they provide on both their adoption process and the dogs in their care. Look carefully at the background of the photos for cleanliness – do the dogs seem happy and well-cared for, do they provide good healthcare for them?

Also watch the interaction the rehoming group has with their social media followers. Are the comments generally supportive of the charity, and does it treat their contributors with respect? In other words, is this a nice group that has decency and honesty in how it treats both the animals, and people?

If you live close to the shelter, why not offer to volunteer as all organisations need willing helping hands? It will give you a chance to see the charity in action, and better still, get to know the dogs. It could well be that one furry will look at you one day and grab you by the heartstrings, and that will be it – you'll have found The One. Sometimes I feel it's the dogs that adopt us, not the other way around.

The decision to adopt dogs from overseas is often quite a contentious one eliciting many negative comments and criticism from certain quarters. But when it comes down to it, that should be the personal choice of the adopters, many of whom want to help animals that they feel live miserable existences in countries with poor or non-existent animal welfare laws. That being said, great care must be taken to ensure that the rescue shelter is trustworthy and honest in all regards about the dog you're considering to adopt. Word of mouth from friends who may have adopted from a particular shelter might help to narrow down the search.

One of the arguments put forward by people in certain parts of the animal world is that dogs from the European continent can harbour canine diseases. While undeniably these diseases exist in a small percentage of rescue dogs, it has to be remembered that dogs **cannot** transmit these diseases directly to humans. With proper preventative care, which all dogs should have in any case, there is no reason why any of these diseases should be spread to other animals in their new country.

Many dogs infected with some of these diseases are adopted every year in Spain and elsewhere across the continent, go on to live happy, fulfilled lives – many to a good age.

Let's run through the main "offenders":

a) *Ehrlichiosis* is a tickborne bacteria which affects platelet cells. This can be cured if treated promptly, although antibodies may remain in the blood for years.

b) *Babesia (Babesiosis)* is also found in the UK, and is a parasite spread by ticks that have fed on rodents, infected cattle, and roe deer. The most common type of the disease in Europe is *Babesia Canis* which can be treated by injections with other treatments also available.

c) *Filariasis (Dirofilaria Immitis)*, a heart worm spread by mosquito or sandfly which introduce larvae of the parasite into the bloodstream. This disease can be successfully treated in dogs presenting no or mild signs of infection. More severe infection can also be treated effectively although the likelihood of complications is greater.

d) While treatment for *Leishmaniasis* (a parasite spread by small biting sand flies) will not cure the disease, a dog can still live a long and active life with the help of medication. However, as the infection remains in the system, relapses are common after treatment is stopped.

e) *Anaplasma (Anaplasmosis)* is a bacterial tickborne disease, also found in the UK. Some dogs with *anaplasmosis* may never show signs of illness or require treatment. Those that do normally get a fever which can be quickly treated with a course of antibiotics. Providing tick prevention throughout the year is the best way to avoid infection.

Most shelters will have tested for these diseases if and when the dog showed symptoms and the animals will have received the appropriate veterinary treatment.

It is possible to get lovely rescue dogs from some Eastern European countries and many adopters enjoy their beautiful pets from that part of the continent. Some behaviourists believe that a percentage of rescue dogs from these countries will have been fending for themselves quite successfully in their previous lives on the streets, and that transferring them to a domestic situation in another country can cause them increased stress and anxiety, leading to behavioural problems.

If a dog has only known a life on the streets it is important to understand that it is incredibly difficult for them to find themselves living in a family home with the rules and restrictions that will be placed on them. They very often find this very stressful and you should only take on a former street dog if you have a lot of experience working with dogs and have the back up of a reputable rescue organisation.

As already said, adopters should think very carefully **prior** to adopting – especially from abroad, to ensure the dog you choose is right for you and your family, and that you can provide the home, emotional and physical care, and security that he needs for the rest of his life. Not only will you be paying an adoption fee and perhaps transportation costs, but you'll be uprooting the dog to travel hundreds of miles with the inevitable stress that that will cause to him, only to decide after his arrival that he isn't right for you. Sadly, many rescue charities have experienced this and it is a great cause of frustration to them, not to mention the additional trauma it causes to the poor dog.

Whichever shelter you chose, take your time, think over the information you need to know about the dog you're interested in and don't be afraid to ask as many questions as you want. The honest organisations will be patient and happy to answer all queries to the best of their ability and knowledge, and will tell you of any problems, ie. temperament, illness or physical infirmity the dog might have. Most will know how the dog interacts with others, and will also carry out cat or children tests upon request.

Ask if any blood tests have been carried out especially in respect to dogs from abroad; if not, some shelters will agree to have a blood test done (due to financial constraints of most charities, some will only do this if the dog has been reserved by the adopter, or the adopter offers to pay).

Many overseas charities will also assist in processing the correct import documentation, and arrange transport to the adopter's home.

If the charity appears reticent about certain aspects or details, ensure that you get adequate answers to your queries.

Or walk away.

Some charities have a special FB Page or website section dedicated to rehoming stories featuring dogs in their new homes, which can help to give a good idea of how happy adopters are with their dogs, and if any report issues.

You will more than likely be asked by the rescue agency to complete an Adoption Application – please be very honest in your replies on this form.

Do not:

- pretend you are an experienced dog-owner, if your "experience" has only been the dog your family had when you were a child (but which your parents actually looked after), or you've dog-sat for friends or family;
- go for a dog that might be too demanding for your level of experience or require more expert handling than you possess. Accept and take the shelter's advice on this;
- choose a dog that is bigger than you can handle, or needs more exercise or work than you are prepared to give (which would include puppies). Research what the breed of dog you are looking at was originally bred for and what traits that breed may have. For example, a border collie bred to work daily and require high levels of mental stimulation is unlikely to be the dog for you if you are out all day at work when the dog will be left at home alone.

The rescue organisation may suggest other dogs that they consider more appropriate for you to adopt. If you are unsuitable for whatever reason for the particular dog you had your eye on, it is better for all concerned that you are turned down at this stage. It would be upsetting to choose a dog, wait with excited anticipation for it to arrive … only to discover that you can't cope with its energy levels or special requirements; but really spare a thought for the poor dog that may find itself back in another shelter.

Do not be surprised or insulted if the rescue charity asks to do a home-check on your residence, they will only want to ensure that your property is safe and secure for the animal and is common practice. They will also want to confirm that your life-style and experience is commensurate to adopting that particular rescue dog. Their primary concern is that the right dog is placed with the right owner, and that it will have a good home for the rest of his life.

Rehoming organisations may have their own rules regarding the upper age at which someone can adopt a puppy, or indeed if people with young children can adopt such a young dog which many potential adopters find incredibly frustrating. The good rescue agencies **always** have the dog's welfare uppermost in their minds.

Rescues would like the dog to go to a **Forever** Home. If someone aged 70 or above adopts a puppy, with the best will in the world, no one knows if that person's health will hold up for the lifetime of the dog, or indeed if they have the energy to run around after an active puppy. The adopter may be steered towards a more mature animal, which might be easier and safer for older owners to handle. Size may also be a consideration: a smaller dog may be easier and safer for older owners.

There is often reluctance on the part of rescue charities to allow a young family to adopt a pup – it's a given that puppies will mouth which some children will misinterpret as biting and become upset, when the parents are led to believe that the dog has "bitten". Many owners will be responsible and strictly supervise children-puppy time, and provide adequate training and chew toys for the puppy. There are sadly a percentage of people who think that puppies come fully-trained in everything at 3 months, with an in-bred knowledge of how to behave with children who may not have been taught how to interact in an appropriate way with dogs. All of which can have catastrophic consequences for the poor puppy – at best, it'll end up homeless in a shelter; at worst, it's a one-way trip to the vet.

Think very carefully if you are able to cope with a dog, particularly a youngster that will require a lot of time and care, on top of your commitments to your children and home.

And PLEASE, PLEASE, do not be surprised if the rescue charity asks for an adoption fee or donation for the dog – I can't tell you how many people contact our rescue charity and are shocked that we would have the audacity to ask for money for a stray dog! "But it's homeless – we're doing you a favour by offering it a home", and I love this one: "But you got the dog for free"!

Caring for dogs in a shelter comes at a high cost to a rescue agency – from food, vaccinations, neutering, and anti-parasite treatments, to expensive vet bills. Fees don't always cover the charity's cost of looking after a dog, with the deficit being recouped from donations and fund-raising by hard-working volunteers.

Basically, if something is worth having, it's worth paying for. An adoption fee is a small price to pay for giving a shelter dog a loving home, to experience the special companionship and love that dog will give.

CHAPTER 3

Choosing The Right Dog

So, you've considered all the pro's and con's, and have decided that, yes, the time and circumstances are right to add an additional four-legged member to your family.

The next step is just as important to consider: choosing the right dog. This is doubly so when you have decided to adopt a rescue dog. As the majority of these unfortunate dogs have lost their homes through no fault of theirs, it is vital that you make your decision with the serious intention that you will care for your chosen dog until the end of its natural days.

Working in a shelter, personally I become frustrated with people that come with preconceived ideas of the type of dog they want. Generally, it's a certain breed or their crosses, they've got to be "furry" or whatever, a certain colour, or it must be like a previous much-loved pet (give me a break!). Continually these people refuse to consider those dogs that we know to have the sweetest natures that will make wonderful companion pets.

When looking for a loving companion to join your home, try to keep your mind open to all the lovely possibilities that may dwell in a shelter. For me, a rescue dog is quite simply one that needs a loving and understanding home. Remember that no two dogs will ever be the same, so looking for a replacement for a much-loved childhood pet will be a fruitless search which will more than likely end in disappointment for you – and the poor dog that may end up back in the shelter.

Some adopters will just see "that" dog and know that he or she is The One, whether it is the look in the eye or how it behaves towards them that is enough to persuade them to adopt without hesitation.

While this is great in theory, in an attempt to reduce the risk of the heart-breaking disappointment of a failed adoption, a prospective owner must also think very carefully about whether this special dog will actually fit in to their home and life, and match their ability, energy level or experience of handling dogs.

It can be confusing to see so many happy, expectant faces with their toothy smiles in a shelter, all begging the visitor to take them. I really do feel that shelter dogs know when they're "on show" and do their best to attract the visitor to notice *them*.

Many dogs demonstrate their sociability by approaching the front of the kennel run with a loose and wiggly body, a wagging tail, soft, squinty eyes and a relaxed open mouth. These are all signs that a dog is comfortable in your presence. A great number of dogs bark in the shelter environment, this can be for a variety of reasons, excitement, frustration at being in the kennel, or fear.

Some dogs find being in a shelter very difficult, this may be the first time they have ever been in a kennel and the different noises and smells they encounter may cause them anxiety. Fearful dogs may hide at the back of the kennel and avoid contact with people. These dogs often change their behaviour if given the time and space to interact with people at their own pace.

A responsible shelter should be able to advise you of the character of the dogs in their care, and any personality traits that they have noticed. It is important to understand, however, that the behaviour you see in a kennel may not be the behaviour you would see in a home environment.

If your head is still spinning from all the lovely furry choices and happy faces in front of you but you're still unsure as to which dog would be best for you, consider hiring a behaviourist or trainer who could visit the shelter with you, to assess the dogs you're interested in. Such an expert would be able to evaluate the dog's general behaviour, ie. if he's comfortable with someone touching and handling him, his general body language, how he reacts to other dogs, if he plays gently or roughly, if he's excitable – how quickly he calms down? How is he with loud noises? How does he react to strangers suddenly appearing? Or how is he when someone comes in close proximity when he's eating, or tries to take his toy?

A word of caution though, behaviour assessments over a short period of time are often very stressful for a dog. Although they can provide us with some information about a dog's behaviour they should not be considered alone. Assessments made by shelter staff over a longer period of time often give a better idea of the dog's temperament. These should be used alongside other valuable information wherever possible, such as the dog's previous behavioural and medical history, past experience and training to provide the best evaluation of the dog's personality and likely behaviour. Ask the staff at the shelter as many questions as you can about the dog you are interested in.

Every shelter, the world over, will sadly have those poor dogs that are not so gregarious, are fearful, or have been poorly socialised, that few people will consider for adoption. They're the ones staying at the back of the run or kennel, averting their eyes from human gaze, furtively running away when someone comes near them. Who knows what terrible histories they have had, if only they could talk?

While their fears may make no sense to us, to these dogs they are very real, so you will have to try to understand and accept them, and be prepared to try to manage them when overcoming them isn't possible. They would need a regular routine in the home that will provide some comfort to them. They may not be the easiest to live with when immense patience will be required.

Such a dog may never react the way "normal" ones will, and may only be able to show their owner limited affection – if they are even capable of that. The reward will be in progress that may only be measured in months or even years, with each and every little improvement a celebration and reward in itself.

With extreme behaviours, you may need to consult a qualified professional behaviourist for their help to try to tackle the problem/s. Despite your best intentions and efforts, the dog may never be the one you thought you'd end up with, but you should take comfort from knowing that you've given a good home to a dog that may otherwise never have left the shelter alive.

As a side note, for nervous and scared dogs, it might be worth investing in a dog-vest that has warning messages: Give me space; I'm nervous; Please don't pet me, etc. to alert people to the dog's disposition.

Difficult as the road ahead may be, I honestly believe that these dogs deserve their chance of a good home too. It will take a very special, very committed and very loving person to take them on, and will not be something that will suit everyone. Great patience, knowledge and understanding will be the primary attributes that such an adopter would need, plus a lot of time and effort.

In this world that seeks perfection, there are many sweet dogs that may not match society's standards of aesthetics. They have sadly been affected by accidents or disease, or have just been born with individual physical "idiosyncrasies". While such dogs may not match up to some people's ideals of beauty, none of this would affect its ability to bring a huge amount of love into a home.

One of the sweetest dogs I ever saw in a shelter was Poppy, a little chihuahua-cross who had bandy front legs, a small tumour in the corner of her eye and a terrible underbite. She may not have been conventionally cute, but she still became a bit of an internet sensation with hundreds of people using her photo as their Facebook profile photo. The most important thing is that I don't think I've ever met a dog with a more beautiful character – she was as sweet as sweet could be. Happily, Poppy was adopted, giving her new owners years of love.

If you are serious about wanting to save a rescue dog's life, give those slightly "imperfect" dogs a second look too and recognise their capacity for sharing their lovely natures.

It sounds crazy but many adopters fall in love with their dog merely from photos or little videos online, because they are unable to visit the shelter in person. Fortunately, while most of such adoptions are successful, it must be accepted that there will always be a degree of risk involved.

In some shelters, the dog may only have been assessed in how it behaves in the centre – how he interacts with other dogs, or the volunteers, but unless the dog can spend time in a foster-home, the rescue group may not know for sure how he will behave in a home setting.

Bear in mind, if you work full-time, many shelters would be reluctant to allow you to adopt a puppy. Left for so many hours on its own, a bored, lonely, young pup will happily become self-employed, the results of which may not thrill a returning owner. You would need to consider doggy day-care or a sitter to look after the little one while you're at work.

While puppies are undeniably gorgeous, they also require a lot of work over the early part of their life – to house-train, appropriately socialise, teach basic commands, exercise. They will also have to be kept entertained and happy to prevent them from developing behavioural problems, including munching their way through your belongings.

Like human teenagers, they too can experience the stroppy teenage period when they refuse to listen to anyone, and will test your resolve and house rules. Are you willing to hang tight and give them the time to work through their teenage angst? (This does pass, I promise! Mind you, it took one of mine until she was 6 before she started to act "adult", zany pup that she is!!)

Basically, if you put in the work on a puppy, you should get an obedient, loving companion that will bring much joy into your home, but they will need time and effort in the early days.

The age of the owner should also be a consideration – an older person may not have the energy required to chase after an active puppy; will they still be healthy enough to provide the dog with a long-term home? Perhaps an older dog may be more suitable as they may already be house-trained, have been taught to walk well on a lead, and received some obedience training in their previous home?

While adopting an older dog may entail more vet bills as its health declines with advancing years, they are more likely to be satisfied with less exercise, and will be quite happy to dream their sundown years away on a nice comfortable bed or sofa. A mature dog can make a wonderful, kind companion and will more than show their gratitude for the home you've given him.

If you have a deep and meaningful relationship with your couch, you might want to look for a dog that does not require much exercise, for example breeds/crosses like Pugs, Bulldogs/French bulldogs, Cavalier King Charles, Basset Hounds, Chows, Yorkies, Pekinese, and Pomeranians.

All dogs still need mental stimulation however so need to be provided with things like puzzle toys, sniffing games or fun training tricks to ensure they have the enrichment they need if they are not getting it from exploring the outside world.

The hunting breeds like greyhounds, whippets, salukis or lurchers do not necessarily need excessive amounts of exercise, and can make lovely companion pets.

Even though racing greyhounds have a reputation for running, surprisingly they would be satisfied with a 20-minute walk, following which they'll very happily keep the sofa warm for you. While being quite lazy as guard-dogs (to put it mildly), retired racing greys are generally calm, very adaptable to new situations and their short coats won't need much work in terms of grooming. While not all are a danger to other companion animals, care must equally be taken to ensure that the dog to be adopted is compatible with smaller resident furries in the home.

There are many breeds and crosses that would make lovely family dogs in homes with children. While dainty chihuahuas and their distant cross-cousins certainly wouldn't require much space, they generally appreciate a calm, adult household rather than the chaos of one with children. Puppies of smaller breeds are particularly fragile, when young children must be very careful when handling them.

As gorgeous as the larger breeds are, they may not be the right dog for you if you have small children, or a small property. Like small acorns, what look like small puppies can grow into big dogs that could knock toddlers and even older people over. Have you the strength to deal with a large, strong dog, especially (dare I say it?) if you're knocking on in years?

Not too keen on barkers? Then the guarding breeds may not be the right ones for you as their instincts are to guard their family and home.

If you enjoy an active, outdoor life, equally there are umpteen breeds that will happily accompany you on your adventures – pointers or terriers for example, and even more lovable mixed-breed mutts lolling around in shelters that would love to keep you company on your adventures.

No matter the breed, all dogs will still need exercise to a greater or lesser degree.

Don't get carried away by those gorgeous gussies strutting their stuff around the Cruft's show-rings or on the television advertisements. No matter how beautiful they may seem, utility/pastoral/working dog breeds and their mongrel cousins (that may still carry a percentage of that DNA) were all originally bred for a particular purpose. As such, they may be high maintenance in terms of what they need to keep them happy and healthy.

There's a very good reason why Springer Spaniels are called "springers" and that those beautiful Border Collies just love to round up their families. Unfortunately, not all children (or adults) appreciate being chivvied along by having their ankles nipped!!

Lovely as all these breeds are, as the function of their breeding has been hard-wired into their DNA, the dogs will, more than likely, behave in the manner for which they were bred. They will require appropriate and sufficient exercise, mental stimulation for their breed-types. They might also benefit from additional agility and/or special work to keep them motivated. Even mongrels will have breed-specific behaviours that require commensurate care that will satisfy their requirements. Intense exercise on the sofa just won't cut it for these dogs.

Please don't subscribe to the "bad breed" theory. Evidence suggests that where breed specific legislation has been enforced, dog-bite rates haven't actually reduced so breed discrimination in terms of dog bites is unreliable. Bull breeds such as Staffies and crosses, Dobermans and Rottweilers can all make the most wonderful pets, but they should still have been rigorously assessed by the shelter, and perhaps might not be recommended for inexperienced or first-time owners.

Many owners will tell you that they find male dogs better, others that the females are the best. Really, this doesn't matter other than generally male dogs tend to be larger in both height and weight.

Much of a dog's character and compatibly with humans is down to its mother's parenting ability; how it was raised in the litter, the socialisation and training it's had, and past experiences it was exposed to, rather than being a chap or chapette. One thing that does seem more certain is the yin and yang of compatibility – generally dogs of the opposite sex tend to get along better with each other in the home – something to consider if you're planning to add another dog to your family.

Too many shelters receive dogs that were clearly inappropriate to the owner that had adopted them. Be very honest with yourself and do not take on a dog that may have handling or maintenance requirements beyond your level of expertise, or require more energy or time that you're willing to commit. **Before** committing to a particular breed or breed-cross, put in your research and understand what they will need to keep them happy and healthy.

While cats and dogs can and do live contentedly with each other, such cross-species cohabitation may not suit all. If a cat has not been used to sharing its space with a canine, some can be so nervous of even a calm dog that their general well-being will be affected. Likewise, not all dogs, especially those with high predation, would be safe to live with a cat. You would have to ensure that whichever dog you chose was compatible with felines, and both may still need time and some training to accept the other. If the dog appears very excitable around cats and can't be calmed down, it could be that you will have to keep both animals apart all the time, and get the advice of a qualified behaviourist.

Aside from deciding if your home and lifestyle suit having a dog, there are other important factors to consider.

While the gender of a dog doesn't necessarily matter, size, compatibility with children or other pets, age, character, intelligence, breed-traits and energy-levels do. Plus, finding out as much as you can about the dog's upbringing and previous experiences (where possible) should all be factors in making your final decision.

Important things to consider:

- Ensure you are choosing a dog that isn't too big, too strong, too active for you, your home, and lifestyle;
- If adopting off the internet from outside your area, take note of the height of the dog. Find a tape measure and see exactly what size he actually is. (You'd be surprised how many adopters are shocked at the size of their dog when it finally arrives with them, despite the fact that the height has clearly been included in the online description!) If you're adopting a puppy, ask what breed/s the shelter thinks he might be, and the size he's expected to grow to (often, this can only be estimated);
- Be sure to ask about the dog's temperament and character, how it interacts with people/children/cats, and other dogs. How is s/he with traffic/bicycles/noise etc? Is he calm or excitable, low or high energy?
- Ask questions so you know what, if any, medical or physical problems your chosen dog may have.

SECOND-HAND DOGS

With the wide variety of dog breeds in the world today, there is more than likely to be a dog for every lifestyle and energy capacity of the owner – the secret is to do your research rigorously and discover which breed has a character you like, and would best suit your lifestyle and activity levels.

> The most important thing to remember when bringing any dog into your lives, but particularly a rescue dog that has already experienced abandonment or been let down by humans, is that any adoption should be for the natural life of the dog.

Tasha, with Lara *(Photo: Maya)*

CHAPTER 4

Babies, Children and Dogs

Introducing a Baby

While a new baby will bring a different dynamic into your home, requiring re-organisation and introduction of certain precautions with your family dog, it IS possible to have both the baby and the dog. Generally, the simple advice is good and early preparation before baby's arrival, and consistency in following whatever system you've set up.

Have a good think about how some of your dog's behaviours may affect or impact life around your baby, if he jumps or mouths, pulls on a lead, or is generally excitable. You should address these issues in the months leading up to the birth, by either taking him to classes or talking to a behaviourist if you don't feel confident in addressing them yourself.

You should ensure that your dog is proficient in basic commands and will obey when asked, including accepting people coming close to his food bowl. Make sure that he's happy surrendering a toy by exchanging it for a nice treat, and that he knows his toy will be returned to him. Train him to enjoy being handled and touched all over – his mouth, ears, legs, toes, tail etc. It'll really help if the dog knows his "manners" and has self-control. Teach him to say "please" (basically, sitting) for anything that he wants or gets.

You're going to have quite a few months before the little one is due, so make any necessary changes to the household as soon as possible so your fur-baby can become accustomed to them.

Decide on any rules you will set for the dog, and start to implement them in the way in which you want to continue. Think about what routines or changes a new baby may bring (it's a given that the reality may bring unexpected ones) and using positive reinforcement, try to introduce them gently and as early as possible to help your dog to accept the new changes in his life.

Get the larger items you'll need for baby, like buggies, cots and baskets well in advance so your dog can get used to having them around. It would also be a great idea to introduce him to walking beside the stroller and practice walking around the garden. Treats and positive reinforcement will help him to view these things in a pleasurable light.

Put in any new stair gates you think you'll need and consistently use them before the baby's arrival. By using positive rewards, introduce the gates gradually so your pet will be able to get used to them in a gentle way, and will have happy associations with them when he's allowed into the "permitted" areas.

The various sounds of a new baby will seem so strange and even a bit frightening to a dog. There are audio recordings available with baby sounds that you could get, to play to him along with positive reinforcement and rewards training. This will really help him to accept the new noises that will come into his life.

Start this training a few months before the baby is due for just a few minutes every day, with the volume very low, rewarding the dog for not reacting, then gradually increasing the volume over time to near-normal levels.

Don't be tempted to increase the volume levels too quickly. If your dog shows any anxiety, for example licking its lips, panting, ears pressed back, go back to a point where he's comfortable, before **slowly** increasing the sound levels again until he doesn't react at all to the new sounds.

You could start to use the baby's washing powder and the bath items on yourself, to get your dog used to all the new smells associated with a baby. Let him sniff at any new baby blankets or clothing. By introducing as many new sights, sounds and smells prior to the birth, your dog will be more accepting when it's the real thing.

Invite any friends or relatives who have small babies or young toddlers (who would be calm around dogs), to visit your home so the dog can get used to having these strange little humans in his home.

The parents could be asked to throw some treats for your dog when they come, always throwing the morsels over the dog's head so he moves away to get them, and not towards the visitors. This is to prevent your dog feeling pressured to approach the visitors to get the treat.

It goes without saying to watch your dog's signals that he's not stressed or anxious with the presence of very young children, and to take him out of the situation if he looks uncomfortable with it all.

If your dog normally sleeps upstairs or with you in your room and this is going to change, make any change gradually.

Slowly start to move his bed further away from where he is used to sleeping. If he is used to sleeping in your room, consider crate training and using a crate in your room so that he can remain in there, if possible, as this will be less stressful for your dog. There are plenty of resources online, explaining how to crate train your dog but note that not all dogs will take to this practise.

Providing a cosy refuge, a safe place for the dog, will be beneficial especially when the baby starts to crawl, and walk. Gently introduce this to your dog and make it a place where he feels happy and safe.

Also consider the walking schedule. If mum is the person who normally walks the dog, she may not have the time to walk him at all after the baby is born, or the walks will have to be shortened. Perhaps another adult could take over the walking duties *before* the baby is born, gently shortening the walks so the dog gets used to the decreased length.

Once a routine has been established after the baby's arrival, always take the dog when you're going for a walk with the baby, so he learns to associate that fun things happen when the little one is around.

In the week leading up to the baby's arrival, gradually reduce the attention you give your dog. Encourage them to be calm and relaxed, and praise them verbally when they chill out by themselves. Giving them a long-lasting treat at these times would be beneficial.

The Big Day has arrived (Congratulations!!) and your family number has increased by one (or more!). When it's time to bring Junior home, it's often a good idea for someone else to hold the baby to let the excitement levels drop while mum calmly greets the dog.

Preferably make the baby-dog introduction when the baby is quiet, and the dog is on a lead with a responsible adult. Allow him to check the baby out in his own time – with his wonderful canine sense of smell, he'll be able to suss the new scents out from a few feet. Reward him for being calm.

Never try to pressure the dog to make faster progress than he's ready for. Ignore any behaviour craving attention, ie. pawing, or jumping up, and reward him when he's being quiet and well-behaved.

If he begins to get anxious or excited, the person holding the lead should gently call him back and reward with either a treat or a toy. Have a ready supply of treats handy so you can help your dog build up a happy association when he's in the same room as the baby.

> It is very important not to reprimand or punish your dog if he gets excited or fearful, raises a lip or growls, or exhibits signs of fear of the baby, as he's trying to tell you that he's uneasy or worried about this situation. Instead, calmly take him to his safe place. Punishing him will only increase his anxiety, after which he'll feel that he can't express his unease and may feel he has no option but to escalate to a snap.

When you're feeding the little one, give your dog attention. Talk to him, tell him what a good boy he's being. If he's quiet and relaxed, throw him some tasty treats so he comes to realise that he gets nice things when the baby is around. You could play little games with him so that he realises that there is still fun to be had, even with the new arrival.

It will take time and a bit of work to initiate these changes – plus patience and consistency. Such preparation will really help your dog to adapt to this big change that's going to come into his life.

Spare a sympathetic thought for your elderly dog, as the arrival of a new baby may be quite a shock to his previously tranquil existence.

Like many of us humans, aging may bring arthritic joints, aches and pains to an aging pooch when he may be less tolerant of rough play or small toddlers accidentally tripping over him. Make sure to protect him from active, noisy little ones, providing a safe haven for him to retreat to when things get too much for him to handle.

> If the dog doesn't seem to be accepting the new arrival and freezes, staring intently at the baby, calmly remove him from the room immediately, and contact a professional behaviourist.

And one more time:

NEVER, EVER LEAVE A DOG UNSUPERVISED WITH A BABY, AND ALWAYS KEEP A CLOSE EYE ON THEM WHEN THEY'RE IN THE SAME ROOM. IF THE ADULT HAS TO LEAVE THE ROOM EVEN FOR A SHORT TIME, IT'S BETTER TO PUT THE BABY BACK IN ITS COT OR PLAYPEN.

Toddlers

It's a sad fact that some owners have unrealistic expectations of their dog, believing that if they get a certain breed or type, it will automatically *know* how to behave with children. While dogs with high predation or herding instincts may not be ideal to have with small children, most dogs can be trained to accept and behave well around them. But while some may be willing to endure rough handling, it is totally unfair to expect an animal to have to put up with that kind of treatment.

A young child that suddenly begins to find its feet and move around can be alarming to a dog as the toddler's movements are jerky and rapid. He or she may not be much bigger than the dog, putting them more or less at the same eye level which may be frightening for the animal. As the child begins to discover its vocal cords, the auricular decibels increase as well, further adding to the dog's unease.

Again, (sorry to repeat this) **never, ever leave a small child alone with a dog** and continually watch the signals that the dog is exhibiting that will tell you how he's feeling.

If he appears stressed and fearful, allow him to go to his safe place, using the dog-gates to stop the toddler from following. This safe place should always be a kid-free zone, where the dog can get some peace and quiet from the whirlwind world a child can create. It's never too early to teach a little child about "personal space" that dogs also appreciate, so that they understand that even dogs need down-time, and some peace and quiet.

As most human-directed aggression comes because the dog feels anxious, afraid or threatened, the onus is on the adult/parent to watch for the signs, and what the toddler may inadvertently be doing to cause them, taking immediate action to rectify the situation to protect the child, and the dog.

Be aware of some of the signals your dog may give you if he's feeling uncomfortable:

- Licking his lips frequently, yawning when not tired.
- Ears are flattened against the side of his head, averts his eyes when the child comes near.
- Tail tucked under his body.
- Trying to sneak away, cowering, or trying to avoid the child.
- Real signs of nervousness or concern: licking or scratching himself, again when the child comes near.
- **Beware** when the dog snarls or growls when the child gets close, or
- Snaps at the child.

Once you see any of these signals, take your dog to his safe place; if this behaviour continues every time the child is around, consult a professional behaviourist.

Top canine behaviour consultant, Helen Howell, who provides dog bite prevention education, gives the following advice to teach children to respect dogs:

- Always get children to invite a dog to their space rather than invading its space. Get children to pat their leg and invite the dog over, but give him the choice of interacting or not.
- Never approach a dog that is sleeping, or in their safe space.
- Walk away from a dog that is eating its food or chewing a treat.
- Never put their face in a dog's face (including kissing).
- Children should never take anything from a dog – that is a grown-up's job.
- Dogs should not be dressed up, or sat on by children.
- They should not be hugged, or picked up by children.
- Children should be encouraged to train and play with dogs with treats and dog toys.

- Dogs should not be made to do things they don't like, or be shouted at by children.
- Children should be taught to stroke dogs from collar to tail, not on the head.
- If the dog moves away from being petted, he should be allowed to leave.

Equally, there are some other important (and rather obvious) rules for children to respect when with their dog:

- Pulling of tails, ears, whiskers or coat are absolute No-No's.
- No sticking little fingers into the poor dog's eyes.
- Stroking is much more relaxing for a dog than patting.
- The child shouldn't lean or reach over the dog, which again the dog could feel is threatening.

There is a real obligation on parents to recognise and respect the dog's limits, and to protect him from behaviour with which he's uncomfortable and will not accept. Teach children to have respect for the dog, ie. dogs are not ponies to be ridden, and they don't like having parts of their anatomies poked or pulled. This advice is not just for toddlers or small children, the same applies to older ones too.

As the toddler grows older, continue to teach it how to treat dogs kindly, which should include stranger-dogs. Little kids won't understand that all dogs are not the same. They must be protected by the accompanying adult, and as they get older and understand more, taught how to react around dogs they're not familiar with.

Older Children

All children must be taught to have positive interactions with their dogs but they must also learn to respect that dogs too have "personal space". They should recognise the body posture and signals that may indicate that the dog is feeling worried or uneasy.

It's a rather sad fact that young boys tend to get bitten more than girls as they do not appear to be as good at watching the signs.

Young boys seem to be a bit more prone to teasing not just their siblings but also their dogs, so it must be emphasised to all children to treat their pet with dignity, kindness and respect.

Children should always show caution and appropriate behaviour towards stranger-dogs:

- When with a small child, it is the accompanying adult's responsibility to tail-watch and note the other warning signals of a stranger dog. Older children should be taught that a wagging tail is not always a friendly one.
- Always ask the owner of the other dog for permission before approaching, or touching.
- Allow the dog to sniff the child thoroughly for a minute or so, before the little one touches him.
- As in the home, if the stranger-dog moves away, it should be assumed that he doesn't want interaction, in which case the child should accept the signal and ignore him, allowing him to leave the space.
- The child shouldn't lean or reach over the dog's head. If the dog looks interested in interaction, he or she should only stroke under the chin, the side of the neck, shoulders and back.

Dogs and children can quite happily live together but rules must be set for both sides that include respect and consideration for the animal. The responsibility lies with parents, guardians or adults to monitor the interaction between the two.

CHAPTER 5

Bringing Your New Family Member Home

So, all the thinking is over, the choice has been made and now it's the exciting time to welcome your rescue dog to his new home.

It's important to remember what your new family member has been through in his life. He may have been abandoned straight from his previous home, which is unbelievably traumatic for a dog. Even those surrendered to a shelter by owners will have experienced great emotional pain and anxiety. He will have lost everything he ever knew – that warm bed, the regular food, the security, and especially his beloved family. A puppy may have been taken from its mum and siblings, which will be devastating to a little one.

Most shelters in the UK do a great job in providing comfortable surroundings for the dogs, minimising stress while providing as much stability and enrichment as possible. Many overseas shelters do not have the resources, either monetary or personnel to do much more than provide safe sanctuary, food and veterinary care for the animals. Even in the best of these foreign shelters with the kindest of staff who give the dogs as much affection and attention as they can, the noise, the large number of other stranger-dogs, and a new and probably boring daily routine that contains little in the way of stimulation, will still cause stress and worry even to those dogs that may appear confident and stable.

As he's not going to understand that he's now arrived at his Forever Home, make your new family member's arrival, and first days and weeks as calm, quiet and low-key as possible. Understand what he's been through, and be patient with him.

You don't have to be told to be prepared ...

Have everything you need before your new pal arrives: a nice thick bed/mat or loads of blankets, stainless steel food/water bowls, crate (if you decide to use this equipment), baby (safety) gates, food, natural/healthy treats, a quick-release collar, ID disk, Apple Air tag/GPS Pet Tracker, no-escape harness, car harness/restraint lead, lead, slip-lead, and training lead, clicker, plenty of plush toys (of course!), and grooming tools. If your new rescue is coming from a hotter European country and has a fine coat, he might appreciate a cosy raincoat for cold, wet winter (or even summer?) days. LED light/reflective collar accessories are essential to ensure safe walking in the dark.

Getting a relaxing plug-in like Adaptil or similar, set up near his bed, or a pheromone collar might help to relax your new lad in his early days with you.

Collar, Harness, Leads

Consider using a flat collar with a side-release plastic buckle rather than one with the standard metal frame with a tang or prong that goes through a hole in the collar (see section on safety). Ensure that it's tight enough to prevent the dog slipping out of it – standard guide is 2 fingers between collar and body for larger dogs, only 1 for smaller pooches. Regularly check the fit for fast-growing puppies.

Have an ID disc with your telephone number plus the GPS Tracker disc (more about this later) on his new collar, to be put on as soon as you pick him up from the adoption centre or the moment he steps off the transport. It's possible to get flexible silicone printed name tags off the internet which, while strong, would still allow the dog to break free if he gets caught on something. Another option is a woven collar which has your contact details stitched into the fabric. (Don't forget to change these particulars both on the disk and the national database if you move house or change telephone number.)

Harnesses are recommended as the best walking equipment as they don't cause damage to the sensitive oesophageal region of a dog's throat, and are comfortable to wear.

Many harnesses have an additional D-ring on the front strap which helps with control when walking a "puller". It should be of good quality with padded straps, but **the most important thing is that it's the right size for your dog and fitted correctly,** so it's secure and doesn't chafe the dog's skin.

It should fit snugly enough across the chest area so that the dog can't wriggle out of it, but not so tight as to make it uncomfortable, or worse still, cause injury. General rule of thumb: if you can't get 2 fingers between the harness and the dog's back, it's too tight, more than 2 – it may be well a case of 'dog-gone'.

Depending on their previous life experiences, some rescue dogs may be anxious about wearing collars or having leads clipped on around their neck, when a harness may be more suitable. It will also be safe for your dog to sleep in initially, thus avoiding the daily faff – and possible additional stress to him – of taking it off and putting on for walks.

If your new rescue dog is not confident, it might be worth getting vest or tabard with a warning message of your choice, or a collar and lead which use the Dog Traffic Light System:

- Amber = dog is a bit fearful or nervous, or not good with other dogs,
- Yellow = dog is nervous, and may be unpredictable (most widely known in the UK),
- Red = caution, do not approach, give the dog space and distance as he may be reactive.

I love the idea of this colour system (there are more available for other situations) and wish that more dog-owners would use it, and that others would understand the message they're sending out. It might promote a bit more sympathy towards those people who have dogs that need understanding and/or space, instead of impatience, anger, and at times, verbal abuse.

Leads are more a personal choice, and depend on the size and strength of the dog.

While many people like extendable leads, they do not provide good control, particularly of a larger dog, either retracting when you might need instant control of a situation, or releasing the dog when the button is inadvertently hit in an emergency situation. The tape or cord can also cause serious injury to hands or legs when trying to regain control of the animal in a chaotic situation.

It is never advised to use retractable leads on a dog when near pedestrians, cyclists or other dog walkers. Also, if the handle-barrel is dropped, it can cause a fearful or inexperienced dog to panic, triggering it to run in terror with this noisy clattering and bouncing object chasing behind it. It heightens the risk that such a frightened animal may run out in front of a road vehicle in its effort to "escape" from this noise.

A long training lead is an essential tool to have, to help when teaching recall or to keep your new dog safe when you're out in the garden or yard.

Toys

Providing a varied range of dog-toys will hopefully distract him from entertaining himself with your belongings. If you have multiple dogs in the home, make sure there are plenty of toys for all.

Do not let your dog play with any toy with small detachable parts or children's toys. Check when they've become a bit tattered, removing any potentially dangerous pieces or disposing of them completely. Have a few toys that you and he can play with together, as well as those tougher ones with which he can entertain himself when alone.

Care should be taken with balls; larger dogs should not be allowed to play with balls smaller than their trachea, to reduce the chance of swallowing them during the course of play. Also avoid rubber balls with an air hole as this can suction on to the dog's tongue.

Rotating the toys by putting some away for a few weeks, regularly replacing with others will stop him becoming bored with them (and will also provide a good opportunity to pop them in the washing machine).

Bed-time

Identify a nice, quiet, cosy, draft-free area for his bed or crate where he'll sleep, relax and feel safe. He might enjoy having a soft toy to snuggle with at night.

If you've chosen to use a crate, cover the top and sides to make it feel really snug, but keep the door open.

Don't forget to take his collar off as the buckle can catch on the bars, causing injury. However, if the new dog has handling or proximity sensitivities, it might be better to leave it on rather than subjecting him to more emotional or behavioural harm in constantly putting it on and taking it off.

Generally, with anything to do with leads, harnesses and collars, any possible risks should always be balanced against the opposing dangers.

Despite some people's reservations about crates being "cruel", once a dog has been gently introduced to it in a positive, fun way, some (but not all) view them as somewhere they can feel safe and secure.

Aside from sleeping, a dog's bed should always be a place to retreat to if things get too stressful, overwhelming or noisy for him – a place of refuge. Puppies should only be contained in a crate between 15-60 minutes, depending on their age and **only** if they're comfortable in it. Tiny adult dogs which will have teeny bladders, should be kept in a crate for a maximum of 4 hours at a time.

A note of warning, though, crates **should not** be viewed as a handy way of punishing a dog, or keeping him out of the way for hours. If you have to leave the house for protracted periods of time, ie. for work, etc. you should find a professional dog-walker/sitter, or doggy day-care for your furry friend. Neither is a crate a convenient way of containing a dog that displays separation anxiety – such confinement is likely to increase the dog's anxiety.

The use of this equipment really does depend on each individual dog as some cope better when confined, but most don't.

If your puppy has come from a litter, the sudden loss of all his siblings will be a terrible shock to him.

Puppies relish the closeness of snuggling up together – bodies and limbs tangled up, lying on top of each other, heads under or resting on bodies ... it's a wonder how they even manage to sleep in such positions! To go from the security of that to being on his own in a strange environment, must be incredibly distressing for a young animal. Which is why it is sometimes suggested to allow the new puppy to sleep with you on, or next to your bed for a few weeks. (Do I hear howls of protest?)

Look at it from the purely empathetic viewpoint: how pleasant is it to hear a small puppy crying pitifully on its own at night? And why would one want to let a little baby suffer in a strange new place, in a bed that is probably way too big for him – totally empty of comforting littermate bodies? How frightened must a new puppy be in such a situation? And so lonely and sad without his playmates. Why would anyone put a little baby through such a trauma?

So, consider putting the puppy beside you, or between you and your partner, in the middle or at the foot of the bed – fairly soon, he'll be snuggling up to his surrogate littermates. It's highly unlikely that he'll cry so not only will he be more content, but you'll also get precious sleep. You may be disturbed at times as the little fella changes position to nestle in to a warm body.

People may worry about the important matter of pooing and peeing but – assuming that the pup is at least 8 weeks old, you can implement some simple rules. No food after 7pm, and a long, active playtime in the garden just before bed-time (such activity will encourage him to do his biz anyway), and he'll sleep … well … like a little baby.

However, if puppy starts to walk about on the bed, it will definitely be time to jump into immediate action! Pick him up and instantly take outside to do his biz. If you allow him to walk out on his all-fours, he'll never make it to the door without an accident. Carry him to the designated potty area, rewarding him for completing his mission.

Don't worry that he'll become so accustomed to sleeping in your bed that he'll never go back to his own at night. Over the coming weeks as he becomes more settled and happier in his new home, you can gradually accustom him to his bed or crate through positive sessions, so he enjoys having little naps in it during the day. Then put his bed beside yours, encourage him to use it during daytime, and after a particularly energetic day, pop him in it to sleep overnight. Gradually move the bed further way until it's where you'd like him to sleep.

Dogs, even older ones, generally sleep better with company and as those first few nights in his new home may be confusing and stressful, think about allowing him to sleep in your bedroom to help him to relax. Unless you decide that you're happy with this arrangement, when you feel he's settled you can gradually move him to where the permanent sleeping place will be.

My big boy chose to sleep right beside my side of the bed when he first arrived. Given that both his coat and the floor tiles are grey, it made getting out for a pit-stop during the night somewhat "exciting"! But it made him feel better and after a few weeks, he chose to retire to his own bed.

Some adopters sleep on the sofa to keep their new rescue company for the first few nights to help them settle. However, it's not advised to allow your new adult dog to sleep on any human bed or be loose in the house overnight, until he's settled down totally and you've had time to assess his temperament.

On the subject of sleep, as it takes approximately 3 days for cortisol levels to go down after the comparative shock of his change of circumstances, it's quite normal for a rescue dog to sleep a lot during the first 3 days in his new home.

Who's Doing What?

Know who is going to do what in terms of exercise, grooming and so on, and decide on the rules that you want the dog (and children) to follow, for example, no sneaking titbits at the table, no snoozling up on furniture or in the bedrooms. Consistency in observing the chosen rules is essential unless you want to have a very confused pet on your hands.

Who will do the feeding and keep an eye on the water, and who will do that really "popular" task of scooping the poop?! And most important: what training will you give your new buddy and who will take responsibility for that?

Food

The shelter will have been feeding the dog with the best food that they could afford. But as many receive donations of different branded foods, your boy may be accustomed to eating a mixture of (generally) kibble.

In an effort to avoid upset tummies by switching foods too quickly, some rescue organisations will give you a small bag of the food they were feeding him to start you off. Or if you can find the same brand, start him on that for the first few days before introducing him to the new one.

Slowly introduce a small amount (generally ¼) of the new feed combined with the old into meals for about 4-5 days, increasing it to 50-50 for 5 days, progressing to ¾ - ¼ new-old, until your new boy is finally eating 100% of the new kibble.

Even though the shelter may have given your lad a worming tablet before he left their facility, keep an eye on his poop for a few weeks as occasionally little aliens can appear with time and stress. It's not uncommon, either, for new dogs to experience diarrhoea from the change of food.

The kibble/food should be appropriate to the dog's age, breed, size, health and life-style. Occasionally it may also be determined by the dog's own preference.

Meals should be given twice a day, at least an hour or more before exercise, or **minimum** of half an hour after a walk (the longer, the better in both cases).

We humans are becoming more conscious of what we're putting into our bodies, so why wouldn't we extend this to our beloved pets? Choose the most natural and quality brand of dogfood that you can afford, with a balanced composition that contains few or no additives or preservatives. Variety is the spice of life for dogs too so a change of kibble once in a while, introduced gradually, will be appreciated.

A newly-arrived rescue dog may be off his food for a few days while he gets used to his change in circumstance, which is entirely normal – just keep an eye out that he's at least taking water.

Establish a routine by placing food down at the designated meal times in the dog's quiet area. Allow him to eat undisturbed and **never** take away his food while he's still eating. If he's not eaten it all and has walked away from it, lift the dish up after 15 minutes.

While hand-feeding **some** food can be beneficial for bonding, eating should not be contingent on being able to take food from a human hand, as this could produce conflict and anxiety in a dog who would prefer to eat undisturbed.

If you find he's hoovering his grub up so that it hardly hits the sides going down to his stomach, you could introduce him to one of the many slow-feeders, or even feed him via a Kong, which are really useful tools to have.

Some owners swear by a raw-food diet, which can be excellent for some dogs. Others may be tempted to put their animals on a vegetarian or vegan diet but **please check with your vet before embarking on any of these alternative feeding regimes.**

As your new rescue may have existed in his previous life by scavenging, help him by taking temptation out of his reach, by not leaving food out on kitchen counters or on low tables. (Our big boy nicked two fillet steaks and 2 chicken dinners – totally our fault for leaving them within his reach – before this idea finally clicked in our very slow brains!)

Treats

Many dog treats, including rawhide, pig or cow ears, contain additives, chemicals, or excessive salt and/or fat; commercial sausages or cooked ham are generally quite salty – all of which can adversely affect your pet's health. These commercial products should only be given as a special reward on an **occasional** basis.

Always supervise your pet when he's enjoying a raw beef shin/knuckle bone, or a long-lasting chewy treat as these can break up into chunks, posing a risk of choking or blockages. Rawhide is notorious in this regard as it absorbs water in the stomach and swells, and is then unable to move through the intestines, when surgery will be required. A better option would be pressed rawhide chews which dissolve naturally.

The more "enthusiastic" of dogs may even try to ingest an ear whole. Stag horns – while natural and from a sustainable source – can cause dental damage.

Many dogs adore peanut butter, but it goes without saying to choose a brand without Xylitol in the ingredients (any product containing this substance should never be given to a dog). Avoid any meats that have been smoked as this increases the risk of cancer in dogs.

It's worth keeping an eye out for some of the growing number of commercial treats that are more natural, with fewer ingredients and a lower fat content. Did you know that 1g of fat contains a massive 9 calories … twice as much as contained in 1g of protein or carbohydrates? Does your favourite furry really need this in their diet?

Feeding animal ears that are raw or as natural as possible is generally healthier for your dog, but will pose a slight risk of salmonella contamination for humans if the products originate in countries with lower standards of preparation and hygiene. Although dogs are not susceptible to salmonella, for human safety it is important that hands and surfaces are washed thoroughly after handling.

In fact, why not make your own treats by simply steaming some chicken, or baking a variety of meats – beef or lamb (how much do you love your dog?!), ham, liver (yum yum), chopped into little pieces *et viola!* your dog will have tasty, healthy treats? Baking is a more preferable method to cook meats although some nutrients will still be lost during the process.

Avoid meat products from wild game which may contain unwelcome toxins or parasites, unless the quality can be guaranteed.

Aside from cooked meat, pieces of dried or cooked fish, tinned (reduced salt) tuna/sardines, or hard-boiled or scrambled eggs can all make tasty treats. Cheese can also be a favourite; although beware, as it can cause excess gas or diarrhoea in some dogs so best to start with tiny amounts to check if it suits.

Some dogs also love fresh fruit like bananas, strawberries, peaches, apples (minus pips), pears, watermelon, or dried/dehydrated fruit (no raisins). Like kiddies, not all dogs are so keen on eating their veggies but some do like carrots, sweet potatoes, courgettes, green beans and broccoli, so why not try these out on your best pal?

Finally ... he's arrived ...

The wait is over and your rescue fur-baby has arrived! You may have already come up with a good name but for the purposes of the following chapters shall we call our boy Panza, after Cervantes' well-known wanderer?

Safety and Security

I am starting with this particular subject as, tragically, some rescue dogs never get to settle into their Forever Homes or live long enough to enjoy their new lives.

Apart from the terrible waste of a beautiful life, I cannot tell you how gut-wrenching it is for a rescue organisation to hear that one of their dogs has managed to escape, either at the transfer point from the transporter or from its new home. And the outcome is more than often fatal.

It is absolutely heart-breaking for volunteers who have rescued that dog, cared for and loved it for the time he was in their kennels, to hear that he's perished – probably scared out of his wits and so confused in what was left of his life.

So, much of what follows may appear over-the-top but assuming that you've adopted Panza because you love and really want him, surely it is better to be safe than sorry?

Local rescue organisations will ensure the chip ownership has been transferred to your name upon adoption. For dogs that have been adopted from other countries, make sure that you arrange the transfer of ownership as soon as the dog comes into your home, a process that can be started **as soon as** you hear he's on the move.

Sadly, our shelter has had 4 escapees from their new homes, 3 of which were within 12 hours of adoption, with only 1 being happily reunited with his owner. To save a lot of worry and quite possibly Panza's life, it's well worth considering putting an Apple Air tag, or one of the GPS tracking discs on his collar that can be linked to an app on your mobile, so you can track him if he does manage a successful dart for freedom.

Most parents child-proof their house to keep their children safe, but few people think to do the same to protect their pets.

Check around your home to see if there's anything that needs dog-proofing. If you're adopting a puppy, make sure especially that electrical cords are out of range or covered with PVC conduit or cable cover. Relocate fragile/breakable/precious treasures out of the range of curious noses and mouths. Equally, any items small enough to be eaten or swallowed should be kept well out of the way.

Human property like TV remotes, clothes, eye-glasses, footwear, ear-phones, etc should all be tidied away or placed out of reach – a dog isn't going to know what is precious to their owner.

If there are children in the house, it's a good opportunity to remind them to lift their toys off the floor (*how* long have you been telling them this?!!!), to put them in a safe place, or designate a dog-free playing area. Panza won't be able to discriminate between what belongs to him or to the children. If it's within his reach and it looks like fun to play with, play with it, he will.

Many children's toys will be very attractive to dogs, but by their very nature these will not be strong enough to withstand rough play, resulting in bits coming off which, if ingested, can cause a bowel obstruction. In addition, it's not very hygienic if your dog has had your kids' toys in his mouth.

Leave Panza's new toys around so his attention can be redirected to those things he is allowed to throw around and play with.

Keep the rubbish/trash bin tightly closed or out of the way of interested noses and mouths. Dogs can take easily suffocate on plastic bags/wrap or the absorbent plastic pad that previously contained meat. If they manage to eat any of these materials, they can cause blockages in their stomach or intestines. At best, an urgent trip to the vet will be required, at worst, a horribly painful death for your beloved pet. Tin foil, chemicals, small toys, plastic bricks and the like are all potentially lethal to animals.

It wouldn't hurt for all members in the household to be encouraged to keep the lid down on the toilet.

Ensure plants in both the house and garden are non-toxic to dogs, move any that are potentially dangerous out of reach. There are some good websites online (Dogs Trust have a very comprehensive list on their site) that can provide useful information on safe plants for dogs.

Strange though it may seem, even small landscaping rocks or stones used to decorate the garden can be dangerous. Dogs (as well as humans) can suffer from pica, a psychological disorder often stemming from boredom which manifests itself in a desire to eat non-nutritive objects (which can include socks, undies, nails, screws, safety pins, or anything that fits into a bored mouth). An unstimulated, fed-up dog left in a garden or home for too long on its own may amuse himself by tossing and playing with these stones, swallowing them either intentionally or otherwise, possibly requiring surgery.

Inspect external gates and perimeter fencing to make sure they are high enough with no escape routes, including storage boxes or tables against walls/fences that an intrepid adventurer can use to escape, or zones that might be suitable for digging or chewing for freedom. Gates leading to the outside world should be secured with strong bolts or locks, with the locks situated in such a way that they cannot be opened from the outside, to deter thieves. Extra care should be taken vis-à-vis opening and closing of perimeter doors and gates to stop Panza from pushing his way out.

Some dogs, especially those from the hunting breeds, are born adventurers that cannot resist disappearing off to explore the world on their own, in which case you can never drop your guard. If your exterior fencing is not high or secure enough (err on the side of caution and imagine Panza is Houdini reincarnated), he should **always** be supervised or kept on a leash when taken outdoors, even to do his potty – which is where the long training lead will come in handy, until he knows that this is now his home, or he can be trusted not to run off (always better to be overly cautious than very, very sorry). Or you might think about erecting an escape-proof run within the garden where he can be let off safely.

Sticks provide another serious hazard for dogs, with vets regularly warning about the potential dangers of using them as play-things. Not only can a dog choke on a stick, but it can become embedded in its mouth or throat if they run on to it, or the wood splinters. At best, this may cause an abscess, at worst, requiring urgent surgery to remove and repair the tissue damage. Find another safe and appropriate toy to throw or to play with.

There's probably not a garden or yard in existence with a dog that doesn't have a tennis ball or four lying around – not so bad if you've got a small pooch but potentially lethal if he's a larger lad.

A tennis ball may be marginally bigger than a medium/large dog's trachea. Now imagine Panza chasing after a ball or jumping up athletically to catch the ball mid-air. If he snatches it but breathes in simultaneously, the ball could be sucked into his windpipe. If you're next door to the vet clinic, you might be able to save him in time, otherwise ...

Nowadays, as it's possible to get balls and toys in all sizes, for dogs it's safer to get one that's too big to be swallowed.

To avoid accidental strangulation, remove the collar when inside the property, especially if the dog is unsupervised. (Note previous advice in this regard if the dog has handling or proximity issues.) The collar can catch on furniture or other items of décor when playing, and is especially important if you have another dog that may enjoy having a romp with its pal. There is nothing more dire and dangerous for both dogs – and their owner, if one of the dogs manage to get their teeth caught either in the webbing or buckle of the collar of his playmate.

The dogs will be thrashing around, totally panicked, one may be choking in its tightened collar, the other can't break free. Total chaos ... and potentially lethal. They certainly won't be standing still patiently waiting for you to release them, as the only way to release a collar, especially one with a buckle, is to *tighten it* first – and what choking dog is going to allow that?

It is difficult to consider removing a dog's collar to enable him to play with his buddies in a public area but at the very least, look for a collar with a quick-release catch or one that will release under extreme pressure (KeepSafe Break-Away Safety Collar).

Then there's food! While dogs like to get their chops around most things, some human consumables are extremely dangerous for them to ingest:

Alcohol, onions, garlic, chives, macadamia nuts, corn **on the cob** (corn kernels on their own are fine), avocado, coffee, grapes/raisins, cooked bones, anything with Xylitol (including certain brands of peanut butter), sugar-free gum, and of course, chocolate.

As any of these can be fatal even in small amounts, you should take Panza immediately to the vet if he's managed to snaffle any.

Recent research from scientists in Massachusetts has suggested a link between tinned peas and other legumes including lentils and chickpeas with the development of DCM (Canine Dilated Cardiomyopathy), so to be on the safe side, it might be better to keep these items off the menu.

NEVER leave Panza tied up or sitting outside a shop unattended while you go inside.

Currently, there is a thriving and evil trade in stolen dogs so why make it so easy for thieves, especially as you'll have to live with the consequences of losing your beloved pet, not knowing what's happened to him, or if he's being treated kindly? In addition, keep him within sight when out in the garden, vary the times and routes of your walks, and avoid sharing too much information about him on social media.

And lastly, despite multitudes of warnings, too many dogs across the world are still tragically losing their lives in locked cars. NEVER, EVER leave your dog in a car – even for a few minutes. Even if you leave a window slightly open and the dog has access to water or you park in the shade, it can still take as little as 15 minutes for an animal to sustain brain damage in a hot car or die of heatstroke.

An ambient temperature of 70°F will quickly rise to 89°F in a car after only 10 minutes, after 30 minutes the temperature will rise to 104°, and after 1 hour, it'll be 115°. As dogs can only sweat through their paw-pads, they overheat very quickly and will struggle to cool themselves down. What a terrible way for your beloved friend to die. Even in colder climates, dogs can be susceptible to hypothermia at approximately 50°F.

It's easy to say: "I'll only leave my dog in the car for 5 minutes while I ..." but sometimes things happen – you'll stop for a chat with a friend, it's even possible to lose track of time and forget that you've got the dog in the car. It's just safer never to do it.

And continuing on the theme of heat, always be careful walking your dog on pavements or sand during periods of hot weather to prevent very painful burned paws.

Collecting your lad ...

Some adopters may have to collect their dog at a designated meeting spot like a service station but tragically too many rescue dogs manage to escape at this point. They've been cooped up in a moving vehicle for some time, they're scared and confused with no idea that this stranger who has suddenly appeared is going to give them a loving life. So extra precautions are required during the handover and at the other end when you reach your home.

Whether it's at the adoption centre or a meeting point, as soon as you can, put on Panza's new collar with the ID/GPS discs and lead already attached, and the well-fitting harness; double-lead him with the other clasp or lead connected to the harness. This is the one time when you would be advised to put your hand through the lead-loop so it is around your wrist, enabling you to keep a firm hold of him when either carrying or moving him to your vehicle.

Don't worry about giving him a walk or taking him for a potty-stop at this point. It is more important to transfer him to the safety of your vehicle as quickly as possible.

Secure Panza in the car either in a large crate, a barrier/grill between front/back seat or a special seatbelt to stop him from moving around too much during the drive home. It would really help to have another person accompany you, to sit in the back seat to hold his lead during the commute and, especially, to stop him diving for freedom when you open the door to let him out at your destination.

Don't take anything for granted or think that your new family member loves you so much, he'll follow you faithfully wherever you go. Err on the side of caution and never, ever underestimate the ability or will of a rescue dog to get free, especially in the early days in a new unfamiliar environment.

Be one step ahead and take appropriate action to prevent any potentially deadly escapes:

- Ensure that the harness and collar are the appropriate sizes and fitted correctly.
- For the first couple of weeks at least, double-lead Panza when going out for walks.
- In the home, ask family members to ensure that doors and garden gates are firmly closed and locked, and to be very careful when entering or leaving the property.
- Close windows when leaving home.
- Put Panza in another room with the door and windows closed if a visitor comes, when outer doors may be opened. Or keep him on a lead (again put your hand through the loop so the lead can't slip out of your grip if he lunges for freedom) when you go to greet the caller.
- Even if you're in the garden or yard, keep him on the training leash for the first few weeks, until you're confident that he won't want to escape.
- Begin recall training as soon as Panza joins your household, using high value treats.
- Do not allow children under 16 to walk him, unless they're in a secure area, free of other dogs or people, and supervised by you.
- **DO NOT** let him off the lead for a good run until you are very certain that (a) it's an enclosed area, (b) he'll return of his own accord, and/or (c) he knows his way home. Please do not overestimate his recall ability or take unnecessary risks at this stage.
- Always keep him indoors if there are fireworks or thunderstorms around. If he has to go out in the garden to do his "business", put him on the lead and accompany him outside.
- If you intend to take Panza with you when travelling abroad on holidays, ensure you always register his chip details including your telephone number with a local vet, and that he has a collar disc with your mobile number.

- If you live in a rural area, **DO NOT** let him off the lead in case he attacks sheep or other wildlife, until he's been trained and/or conditioned to ignore other animals.

No matter how expert a dog-owner you may be, every dog is different – which is especially true with rescue dogs that will have gone through many different experiences.

Listen to the advice the rescue charity gives you about your new family member. Other than his previous owner, they know him the best and will want you to understand his little foibles or fears, especially his capacity or desire for escape.

Please follow the above suggestions until you feel sure that Panza is familiar and comfortable with you before lowering your guard and trusting him to stay within the confines of your property, or to come back to you if he gets loose.

Immediately upon arrival

If you have other pet/s in the family, please refer to Chapter 6.

When Panza arrives at your home, let him have a little sniff around, allow him to do his potty in your designated place or on a short walk.

Puppy-Panza ...

Little puppies can only hold their pee for roughly 1 hour per month of age, so if Panza is 3 months old, he'll be able to control his bladder for approximately 3 hours.

Set him up to succeed by bringing him on regular visits to the great outdoors with plenty of rewards for successful "missions", and he should quickly get the hang of that end of things. He needs your help to master this, so if you're not taking him out regularly to relieve himself, don't blame him or get angry for any little "accidents" in the house.

Gently start to introduce Puppy-Panza to the new things that he'll encounter in his life, ie. TVs, vacuum cleaners, washing machines, hair dryers, stairs, traffic, bicycles, prams, all types of people including those of different ethnicities, men with beards, hats – everything and anything new that will help him to accept things that might pop up in his environment.

Puppy socialisation or training classes are invaluable, providing great places for him to meet other dogs, and for you to meet new people.

It's never too early to let Puppy-Panza know what the boundaries are. If you don't want him to do a particular thing, don't let him. Puppies' minds are like little sponges so begin gentle (and fun) training with him from the start.

If he hasn't had all his shots, you may not be able to walk him in the neighbourhood, but use this valuable time to lead-train him in the garden, so he'll be all ready to strut his stuff proudly once he's fully vaccinated.

Please come in ...

It's important to keep Panza's arrival low-key – no excited welcoming committee of family members and neighbours with multiple hands swamping him. Much as they may be itching to meet your new family member, ask them to wait a few days so as not to overwhelm him.

If your children haven't had the chance to meet him at the shelter, it will be difficult for them not to be excited, as doubtless they'll have been looking forward to their new furry's arrival. But they should try to keep calm and quiet – no squealing, shouting and high energy, particularly with a puppy. Discuss all of this with them beforehand, including a reminder of the rules they should follow.

Quietly bring adult Panza into your house, show him where his bed and water bowl are. Offer him a small meal – if the noise of a metal dish upsets him, either put a towel underneath it, or sprinkle the kibble on the floor and let him "scavenge", which may be how he survived in the past.

He's more than likely to be frightened and feeling very insecure in this new environment, so it may help to **keep his boundaries small over the first few days.**

Limit him to one or two rooms, including where he'll be fed, so as not to overwhelm him. Let him thoroughly explore these areas by having a good sniff around, before expanding his new world over the coming days to include the rest of the house. If you have no objection to him lounging on beds or sofa, gently introduce this as a "perk" and not a right – immediately address any indications of territorial aggression.

Keeping a trailing leash on Panza for the first few days can help to limit him to where you are, and to redirect him gently from going upstairs or on furniture. Allowing a new dog free access to all areas of your home could be a recipe for disaster, what with indoor potty-breaks and chewed-up belongings.

It's also quite possible that he'll just want to hide under a table or in his den – all part of the decompression process and very normal, so just allow him to work through this transition in his own time.

An adult male may feel obliged to bless his new home to make it 'his'. My big boy even felt the need to bless our Christmas tree several times when it first appeared, brave boy that he is … given that it has integrated electric lights! A handy mop and patience, and this phase will eventually pass.

Everyone in the household should try not to make too much of a fuss of Panza after his arrival or smother him with affection. Let him set the pace, to come to you if he wants. Keep an eye on his body language which will indicate how he's feeling.

It's very important that no one, especially children, try to kiss or hug Panza, or put their faces too close to his. Not every dog appreciates that degree of closeness, particularly at such an early stage of his new life.

Allow him to have a bit of "personal space" so he can find his paws in this new environment. If and when he looks for more attention, give it to him slowly.

During the first few days …

The rescue organisation may not have been able to give you much information about Panza's background, particularly if he came off the street rather than being handed in to the shelter by owners. In which case, it's probably better to start from Ground Zero and assume he doesn't know much about living with humans.

Every dog will react differently, depending on his past history and life – many, many dogs walk into their new home as if they've always lived there. Others may take a bit longer to adjust in their own time to the new circumstances. A few may require remedial assistance from trainers or behaviourists if it appears that they're struggling to adapt to their new life.

Keep the first few days after Panza's arrival tranquil with low decibel levels, including how you speak to him. Movements especially should be gentle and slow.

Try not to look at him directly so as not to appear threatening. Let **him** approach you when he wants, and when he does gently touch him on his chest, shoulders or flanks. Hopefully, he will soon realise that you are no threat and will start to approach more often, inviting an affectionate response through his body language – leaning in to you, a relaxed body with waggy tail, soft eyes (no whale eyes), and a relaxed, open mouth with lolling tongue.

Gently introduce his name, especially when associated with something enjoyable like stroking, treats, dinner and so on. And talk to him – even though he won't understand much (except for the favourite words: walkies, dinner, treat), he'll love the sound of your voice. Different levels can be used to either correct or praise his behaviour.

Depending on Panza's previous history, he may already be house-trained and just needs to know where he's expected to relieve himself. But even if he's never lived in a house, potty-training shouldn't be so difficult as he learns the difference between in- and out-doors.

Take him out regularly during the first days to do his "biz" in the garden or your designated spot, rewarding him for success. All household members should be on stand-by to help him to succeed by keeping a close eye out for those signals that he needs to go outside.

If he continues to have little accidents in the house which, again, is quite normal, just go back to the basics of potty-training. If he's still marking in the house, keep him on a lead until he can be trusted. Both situations are quite usual and can be sorted in days, weeks or occasionally months, but you'll get there in the end with consistency and patience.

During these confusing early days for Panza, do not force him into doing anything that he's reluctant to do or be in too much of a hurry to take him everywhere.

Resist taking him for walks outside your property during the first few days, or overwhelm him with new situations too quickly.

Put yourself in Panza's head, imagine the confusion whizzing around in there with all the sudden changes in his life. Allow him time to process and take everything on board step by step, even if this means that the furthest he's gone is into the garden. This time could be used to either brush up his lead-skills with short sessions in the garden, or to gently teach him how to walk beside you on a loose lead, using those magical treats.

Fun is the key word during these sessions as dogs learn better when they're enjoying the activity. Or just use this time to bond with him.

When you think it's time to venture into the outside world, start very carefully with very short walks of just a few meters outside your gate, only increasing the distance incrementally over the coming days – but **only if he seems comfortable**.

Praise and reward him if he's calm but at the first sign of anxiety or stress, immediately bring him back home, before trying again the following day. Gently, gently, is the key.

Dogs like to have routines – when they go out for their walks, when they have their dinner, etc. Try to organise a suitable schedule so Panza knows what is happening and when. This would also include **consistency** in the house-rules. If he's not meant to be on furniture, or lay siege to the meal-table, implement those rules from the very beginning so he'll understand what is and is not acceptable behaviour. And insist that all members of the household apply them.

If you don't want him upstairs, now would be a good time to set up the baby-gates. All it takes is one person to give in on a particular rule to blow it out of orbit.

A home with clear rules and good training, that encourages the dog to please their family rather than allowing behaviour that causes frustration or anger, will result in a more confident and happier Panza.

Following an initial decompression period, over the next 4-7 days, depending on how he seems to be adjusting, slowly introduce different activities into his life. It could be that simple daily walks through the neighbourhood will be enough for him at this stage. As every dog is different, each will adjust to his new home in his own time and way. It will really help to learn your dog's body language and let him guide you.

Some adopted dogs may have received some training in their previous life but sadly, many will have been abandoned precisely because they were untrained.

Bear in mind that some rescue dogs (especially those adopted from abroad) may never have been on a structured walk with a lead, seen large numbers of cars, buses or bikes, or people with differing appearances. Sudden exposure to any or all of these can cause reactivity, when you should gently help Panza to face his fears by being patient, positive and reassuring. Watch what your new dog is telling you through his body signals and be understanding when he displays unease about a particular situation or thing.

If he overreacts to certain things, you might need to employ counter-conditioning and desensitisation methods whereby undesirable responses to situations or stimuli are changed to those that are more acceptable by changing the underlying emotion of anxiety or frustration.

You could teach him a "response substitution" or a distraction technique. For example, teaching him a command like "watch" to encourage him to focus on you rather than those things that make him fearful, before moving on to the counter-conditioning training.

Another distraction trick might be to train him to "find" treats thrown around your feet, which can be employed when you encounter a situation with which he's uncomfortable, followed by a speedy removal from whatever he reacts to.

As Panza won't learn these new techniques overnight, accept that you may have to work at them consistently over a period of time before they finally "click" with him.

If you don't feel confident enough to address such problems yourself, please contact a professional for help. It is important to ensure that the person you engage is suitably qualified as there are, unfortunately, many people masquerading as "behaviourists" who could do more damage than good.

Panza may have arrived sporting a rather distinct pungent shelter "aroma" and "hair-style". Unless your rescue lad's coat is extremely matted and dirty, allow him time to settle and relax into his new home before attempting to groom or bath the grime of his past life off him.

Not every animal enjoys heavy grooming or being immersed in water, so it's important not to force him into something that he may find stressful at this early stage. Perhaps use a dry shampoo to clean his coat, taking the edge off that piquant fragrance, before tackling the tousled tresses when he's more confident in his new environment?

Introducing your nearest and dearest ...

After 1-2 weeks, depending on how well Panza is adjusting to his new surroundings, invite your friends and extended family to meet him in your house – either singly or a small number at a time.

Keeping the occasions quiet and unforced – allow him to set the pace to approach the visitors if and when he wishes. Some yummy treats given by them can help Panza view these newcomers with more interest and anticipation. If he is reluctant to approach them or his behaviour is concerning around them, they can toss the treats for him to take at a distance from them, rather than encourage him to come closer than he is comfortable with.

Dogs may be less likely to become territorially aggressive to people coming to the house if they've already been socialised with them while they're learning what is normal in the new home. So, it would be hoped that even if the dog does become territorial in the future, your friends and family will not be viewed as "strangers" to be defended against, and any subsequent behaviour modification required will be more successful as a result.

In the early days, keep Panza on a lead during any visits from people visiting your home to provide a service – gardener, gas engineer, cleaners, etc. in case he feels the need to "protect" his home from these interlopers. Reassuring him, reward him with treats if he's being relaxed to teach him that he does not have to fear strangers. Calmly remove him from the situation if he shows any aggression.

Give Panza a few weeks before bringing him for an introduction to your vet. His new life will already have been stressful enough without a visit to someone he'd prefer not to have a professional relationship with. Call your clinician instead to register his details, pass on whatever health information you have, organise the vaccination programme, and arrange an appointment for an examination at a later date.

Show Panza that he can trust you to protect him when he needs it most. The **first week, month and 3 months are critical times** for you and your new dog.

Start as you mean to continue …

This initial period after his arrival will be when Panza learns about his new home, and is introduced gently to the house rules. He will learn what he can and cannot do and that good, polite behaviour will literally reap rewards for him.

Set up a good routine by slowly adding activities during the first week; letting him out regularly to do his biz, encouraging him for good behaviour, having playtime, feeding twice daily. And of course, he will quickly learn where those yummy titbits are stashed.

Unfortunately, as a souvenir of the poor dog's previous experiences, it isn't unusual for **some** shelter dogs to suffer from varying degrees of separation anxiety. When you suddenly disappear off to do the shopping or whatever, Panza will be distressed by being left on his own. Adopters often report that their new dog is glued to them as they move around the house, to the extent of lying outside the bathroom door while the owner is inside, which could be an indication of the dog's unease at their new human going out of eye-shot. As most dogs will have to spend some time on their own for (hopefully) only short periods, it is important that they are confident and comfortable about being left.

Our shelter recommends that the new owner takes 2 weeks off from work to ensure that they're there to help their new companion settle during those first vital weeks. This has the added benefit of providing valuable time during which they can get to know their new family member.

From the start, Panza should be very gently introduced to being on his own by leaving him for a little time every day. The aim is for him to understand that you may leave but you will come back, the advice is to desensitise the dog to departures without using food.

Begin by leaving him in a room for just a matter of 10 seconds, keeping the door open so he can still see you, then return without a fuss or paying him much attention. Very slowly increase this time by short increments – 20 seconds, then 30 etc (it's also good to vary these absence times as dogs quickly catch on to routine), always returning, building up to 10+ minutes. Then try closing the door after you as you leave, again starting just with 10 seconds, returning, building up the absence time.

If Panza seems to be taking your absences in his stride, this exercise can then be extended so that you go out into the garden for a few minutes. If you have glass doors, allow him to watch you, before returning.

If things go well, you can try to go further afield with a short walk up your street for a few minutes, before venturing further and for longer.

At this point, it might be useful leaving a food toy to take Panza's mind off your departure. Leaving a TV or radio on can provide some additional comfort during your absence but be aware that any programmes that have loud noises may cause upset. This can be eliminated over time as he becomes more accustomed to being left.

A good walk will help to tire him out but this should not take place immediately prior to your departure, or he'll come to link walks with being left on his own.

Please see Chapter 9 (Training) for further information regarding separation anxiety.

Behaviourists advocate the Cool Departures/Cool Returns with dogs – and this applies to dogs in general. Instead of the owners radiating their high inner energy by telling their dog how much they'll miss him when they go out, he's to be a good dog and guard the house, Mummy or Daddy will soon be back – very little of which the dog will understand. All he will pick up on is Mum's or Dad's apparent excitement at leaving, which causes conflict in his head.

And then when Mum and Dad return, it's all squeals and excitement (from them) and "Did my baby miss me?", "Were you a good boy?" and so on, which really does raise the poor dog's anxiety levels. The less fuss with the comings and goings, the better, as the dog should learn that these absences are not a cause for concern.

Anyone who has adopted a rescue dog will tell you that it is all too easy to spoil them, knowing what they have previously experienced in their lives but this really isn't a good idea. You can spoil them a bit with kindness, pets and cuddles (if he looks for them) and little treats here and there but it is very important that you set up a disciplined and organised routine for him from the start.

Dogs like to know they have a strong leader in their owner, who they can trust and depend on if needed, not someone who will just pander to their fears and spoil them because they feel sorry for them.

Positive Training Strengthens Your Bond with Your Dog

It is well accepted that chaotic homes or situations cause stress for dogs, not to mention humans. Creating a calm environment will benefit all, and it's never too early to begin gentle reward-based training.

This can be very productive in so many ways, and especially enjoyable not just for Panza but for you. It will help in developing a strong bond with him and will gently ease him into his new routine. And training can reduce stress or anxiety, leading to a more confident, happier dog.

Training does not have to be a tough "boot camp". It can be as simple as rewarding Panza's desirable behaviours, while quietly ignoring or addressing the bad ones.

An easy example: if he's lying quietly, a little treat would tell him that you like this behaviour. But if he's driving you mad by constantly pawing at you, looking for attention which you don't appreciate, move away. Don't forget to reduce his daily food allowance to take account for all the treats. Please refer to Chapter 9 (Training) for information on a very effective training system, SMART x 50.

Introducing basic discipline into his every-day life will help to set up good habits for the future, for example sitting for a treat/dinner, or before going out the door/greeting visitors, will all help to make him a polite member of the household.

As dogs also love to have a sense of purpose, in time, you could even teach Panza to carry out little jobs – fetching something, tidying up his toys, or more advanced tasks like turning the lights on or bringing you the TV remote. There are so many fun things to do with your dog!

Not only will training help to exercise his brain, he will come to associate you with good things that, in turn, will encourage him to be more attentive. Once it's kept pleasurable, he will also enjoy learning thus strengthening the bond between you both. What's not to like with any of this?!

If Panza doesn't seem to be responding to your training, don't feel that you've "failed" or you're a bad owner. Don't give up as dogs learn at different paces.

Visit your local dog training classes, or contact a qualified behaviourist to help you. These people are experts in their field who can give you the skills to handle and train your dog successfully. Those first weeks and months are vital times during which to set the rules, which will help your rescue dog to settle.

Helping him to settle ...

Accepting that Panza may never have lived in a house before if he was a street-dog, you must try to step inside his mind. Imagine how he must be feeling, and have a bit of understanding of how this might affect his behaviour. Getting angry or trying to push him into doing something he's clearly uncomfortable with is not going to achieve much. Gently help him accept new experiences, and BE PATIENT.

He will suddenly be expected to adapt to new and very strange surroundings. He will have to try to accept new people, perhaps learn to understand a new language, and different sounds like radios or TV's, washing machines, dishwashers, vacuums, hairdryers. He may never have negotiated stairs before, on top of all the new smells that'll suddenly surround him. Talk about a sensory overload!

It's important to remember that just because your new dog appears upset or doesn't appear to like you, it's nothing personal.

He will not know that he has just come into his Forever Home. In his poor befuddled head, he will only see that it is one more different place, so will be unsure of what is happening to him.

I can't tell you how many new owners disappointedly report how their new dog isn't bonding with them, seems quite remote, isn't coming to them ... within the first few days! Give Panza time to get to know you, and love you.

It is more than depressing to see how many adopters do not allow their new rescue dog reasonable time to settle, giving them their marching orders before they've even had the opportunity to shake the shelter dust off their coat. Do not worry if Panza does not get the hang of everything immediately, he will get there eventually.

Don't forgot the 3 x 3's: allow the new dog

- 3 days to decompress,
- 3 weeks to get used to the new routine, and
- 3 months (or longer) to settle.

(These times are estimates and may vary depending on the dog.)

Give him time to get used to everything, be patient and understanding, and most of all, do not drop your guard in terms of ensuring that he's safe and secure in his new home and surroundings.

In the long-term, include Panza in your family activities – dogs love to be where you are and to be part of the fun, and you'll enjoy his involvement.

Take him off to the beach (be careful if it's summer when the sand may be too hot for his paws), the park, to your children's activities, dog shows or local fairs. He'll be happy to be with you so long as he's comfortable and relaxed in the different environments. Many hotels or holiday rentals now permit pets, so even if you're going on a family vacation, check ahead to see if your lodging place will take dogs, and bring him along to enjoy the holiday too.

Set aside time for a bit of daily playtime which will also help with bonding, besides the joy of having fun together. And having a good laugh with your best friend will be good for your mental well-being too.

While dogs are social creatures that generally like company, equally each one is different and as such, each will decide how much interaction they want, from whom, and when.

Some may love physical contact while others are less keen. They may have very individual preferences as to which part of their body (if at all) they want stroking. Some may hate their paws or faces being touched, preferring attention on their chest or shoulder areas.

We've had people comment that their rescue dog doesn't seem "affectionate" with them, but may still appear happy to lie close to them. Again, people – and especially children – must understand that each dog will have his own preferences regarding closeness or physical contact that must be respected. This doesn't mean that he doesn't "love" them.

Most dogs will have a little spot (or a few!) on their body which they love to have stroked or tickled and they may well present that part to you where they want some attention. One of mine loves the top of her rump to be rubbed and rotates her tail-end around for me to give it "the treatment". It would have been easy to have been a bit offended to be presented with this part of her anatomy but I love that she enjoys this attention. She also loves that area at the front of her chest, in the little hollows beneath her neck, and uses her paw to drag my hand back to work.

Like humans, massages can also be beneficial to your dog's health and can really help him to de-stress.

Basically, keep Panza's tail wagging happily and you'll know you're on the right track.

These wonderful, amazing creatures give us so much with their unending love and loyalty, yet ask so little in return. Give him a soft bed, food, exercise, our company and some of our attention, and a dog will be happy.

Dogs **will** require your time to care for them, to provide what they need in terms of physical and mental stimulation. They **will** cost money through food, insurance and vet care.

A rescue dog **may** come with "issues" – reminders of treatment or experiences in his previous life, or mental scars through abandonment that will need your understanding, patience and perhaps money in trying to remedy.

But all of this is more than compensated for by the joyful welcome upon your return home, bright expectant eyes hypnotising you into a walk you didn't want to take, the extra titbit you didn't intend giving, a satisfied sigh as he settles on the sofa or his soft bed, the quiet paw-pads of a steadfast friend to keep you company, a concerned nudge or lick on a hand when spirits are low, a ball or raggedy well-loved toy thrown at your feet in an invitation to play.

To Panza, you're going to be the centre of his new world, so even though you may be tired after work, he's been waiting patiently all day for your return. Make sure to thank him for that loyalty and love by giving him some of your time, gentle pets and kind words.

Even though to him it's all blah-di-blah, he'll love the sound of your voice and getting some of your attention.

> There is nothing on earth as sweet or rewarding as the love and companionship of a rescue dog. Be sure to return that privilege and be a loyal friend to him.

CHAPTER 6

Welcome To The Gang

Introducing Your New Dog to Resident Pets

As with humans, first impressions can be just as important to dogs when meeting other animals especially living in the same home, which can shape the basis of future relationships between them. Breed, temperament, age, status etc can all play a part in introductions, so it pays to get it right from the start.

It is a fact that some dogs cannot get along with other animals. Also, some dogs cannot override their innate instinct to hunt, and will be unable to resist chasing smaller animals with the intention to catch and potentially cause harm.

This makes it really important to take one's time when initially choosing a new dog and introducing him into the home. This should be carried out in stages, with care and close supervision.

It's important to recognise that not all cats will accept sharing their space with a dog. Even the calmest can be nervous around a canine and that anxiety could compromise their general well-being.

Separation between the animals is the key in the beginning, allowing each to familiarise themselves with the new smells that have entered their domain. Supervise any interactions between the pets closely in the early days, before slowly increasing the time they spend together. Rather than all parties just tolerating each other, the aim is to get each animal to be relaxed in the other's company.

If your new dog has very high prey-drive, **never** leave him alone with your cat. Chasing another furry is fun (and self-rewarding) for such animals but your poor cat doesn't need to be that focus for entertainment. If he appears overly excited around her, and is unable to relax when she's around, it's a good indication that they should always be kept apart.

Introducing your New Dog to the Resident Cat

> Remember never to be tempted to rush the introductions, or force the animals to integrate before they're ready.

Many cats and dogs can live together and a good introduction plan, allied with care and patience, will help both animals to get used to each other. It is likely to take at least 3-4 weeks or longer to assimilate, although this will depend on the individual animals and the age at which they are introduced.

While some may become the best of bosom-buddies, others may never reach this degree of compatibility. But it will ensure a calmer domestic life if at least the two species can co-exist peacefully and respectfully without Armageddon breaking out every time they catch sight of each other.

Step 1:

Identify two rooms with a connecting door in which both animals will initially stay separately, enabling them to smell and hear each other without risking any adverse exchanges at this early stage in the introductions. Ensure that each animal has all its necessary requirements in its room: bed, food/water, litter tray, toys, climbing/scratching station, etc. If the cat normally has access to outdoors then enable them to maintain this access as well as to other areas that they commonly use in the house.

During the first week, take a piece of bedding from each animal that has its scent on it, and place in the other's room so they can get used to the new smell. Every day or so, switch these back and forth between the two animals. This bedding can be placed next to the feeding station unless this causes either animal to become reluctant to eat, in which case place it elsewhere.

It's possible to get calming pheromone products that can help cats and dogs to relax, which might help them to be a bit more chilled about accepting a new animal companion.

Make sure to spend time with each pet, giving them individual TLC, and allow them time to relax in their respective areas, with the cat having a core area which is accessible to her but not to the dog. You could use this time to see if your new dog understands simple commands like Sit, Stay, and Leave It, and if not, gently start to teach him.

When you feel that both are comfortable with each other's scent, it is time to move on to …

Step 2:

The face-to-face meeting. It goes without saying that you should try to keep your inner energy calm during the following procedures.

It's important to go at the cat's pace, don't go faster than she can cope with. Always provide an escape route with safe areas for her in all rooms – either high perches at human eye-level or above, out of the dog's reach, ie. shelving, climbing frame, baby gate, etc. There should also be access to a private area where she can have cat me-time, and where her litter tray is. (Dogs can be quite partial to a tasty bit of cat-poo, but in addition if the dog startles the cat while she's doing her "biz", she may become afraid to use the tray in future).

Place her food and water dishes in a safe place as well. Cat food is too rich for dogs to digest, and dog food does not contain the necessary nutrients a cat needs to sustain a healthy heart and good eyesight.

The Introduction:

Before the Big Meet, take your new lad out for his walk, followed by a meal, all designed to relax him before the introductions. Allow the cat to walk around freely, protected by the safety gate, have plenty of tasty treats on hand to reward good behaviour on both sides (you might need another set of hands to help you with these introductions). Don't worry if the cat's first reaction is to hiss and/or run away – this is not unusual.

With the dog on a short lead which can be attached to your belt to prevent him from chasing the cat if she runs, allow the two animals to figure each other out safely from a distance. Stroke him, telling him gently what a good boy he's being, and reward both with treats and praise. Ask him to perform simple requests such as a "sit" or to pay attention to you. If he cannot stop focusing on her, then move him further away.

If he tries to jump towards her, ask him to "sit" or "leave it". Praise and/or reward if he obeys and desists in his efforts to reach the cat. If he becomes very excited and can't be calmed and cannot stop focusing on her, immediately take him out of the situation. Repeat the exercise later but at a further distance away and with tastier treats to distract him.

Carry out these little visits between the two animals a few times a day, allowing the dog increasing freedom on the lead but **only** if he's acting appropriately with the cat and not overly fixated on her. Do not progress any further with the integration unless there have been a few consecutive days during which both animals have shown their ease in each other's presence.

The next step will be to drop the lead but be ready to step on it if he decides to dart at the cat. Using their names, talk reassuringly and calming to both animals, rewarding both for desired behaviour. Keep the dog occupied with training exercises initially; if he cannot respond to your requests because he is too interested in the cat, he is not ready for this stage.

When you consider the time is right, totally remove the lead but supervise both animals closely. Revert back to the previous stage at the first sign of any issues, especially if your commands are not having an effect. If all is progressing nicely, increase the no-lead periods but do not leave them together without supervision unless you are very sure that there will be no problems. Your aim is to have animals that are comfortable together, not just tolerating each other. The cat should always have access to escape routes where she can get away if she wishes.

At feeding time, give them their food on either side of a closed door or baby gate, as this will create a pleasurable association of eating within the other's scent – **so long as this does not cause stress to either animal, or deters either from eating.**

Keep a close eye out for any inappropriate behaviour from the dog – pestering, any hiding or chasing, or peeing near the litter-tray needs to be addressed immediately. Be particularly alert if one pet is sending "play signals" that the other pet misconstrues. If the signal has been regarded as belligerent, treat the situation as "aggressive", and handle accordingly. Dogs can easily kill a feline, even during play – one shake and the cat's neck can be broken.

Until you are confident that the dog can be trusted with the cat, always separate them when leaving the house.

Introductions involving puppies or kittens

A cat will generally be well able to sort out a puppy – do not punish her for swatting the nose of an overly-inquisitive dog or pup. It goes without saying to keep a close eye in case the cat's claws hurt the pup. Introducing a lively pup to a kitty should be carried out when the puppy is sleepy and calm, not active and playful. Be especially careful as kittens can be easily hurt or killed. Give the introductions more care if she is on the timid side as a little puppy will not understand when he's requesting playtime that's being ignored.

Do not allow the pup (or adult dog) to chase or annoy the cat generally, reward him for good behaviour, ie. being calm and gentle around her. Discourage any bad conduct by removing him from the situation, putting him in a "time out" area, until he has calmed down. Never use punishment with any animal in these situations.

It often happens that the new puppy and cat will grow to accept each other, and even move on to that point of being friends, dreamily snuggling up together, but of course, every situation and animal is different.

And finally, be sure to have one-on-one cuddle or playtime with both animals.

As with all animal behaviour problems, contact a qualified expert to help sooner rather than later. Not only can serious injuries (or worse) occur but the longer any animosity continues unaddressed, the harder it can be to sort out.

Introducing a Puppy to the Resident Dog

The earlier a pup is removed from its mum, the less time he will have had to learn those important life-lessons on how to interact well with other dogs.

If your new arrival is a puppy, hopefully he was allowed to stay with his mum until 8 weeks old. During this time, he'll have learned enough from her and his siblings to understand their communication and boundaries. He will still have to learn how to interact well with other dogs. The initial days and weeks in his new home will be confusing for him in so many ways. He'll need you to expose him gently to different stimuli and to set the rules showing him what you expect from him.

Tidy away the resident dog's toys and chewies beforehand to reduce the chances of territorial behaviour with the new dog or pup. You should have plenty of puppy-toys available for the youngster.

Bringing a new pup into a home where there are already resident dogs can be unpredictable and should be very carefully planned beforehand. The more understanding, care and time you take, the more likely the dogs will integrate.

Some adopters have dreamy ideas that their adult resident dog will immediately bond with the new puppy and act like a surrogate parent, but it may not always work out this way. Often the older dog will growl or snap at this new interloper – which is entirely normal. Provided your resident dog is reasonably well-socialised, rarely will they attack or cause injury to the youngster.

It helps to have **realistic expectations** and not to be disappointed if the dogs do not immediately hit it off. A calm and unpressured first meeting, followed by a gentle integration of the puppy into the household should help them accept each other. This could take approximately 3 weeks, depending on the dogs.

Look at it from the adult dog's point of view – he now has to share his previously peaceful existence as the only apple of his mum and dad's eye with what, to a dog, is the equivalent of a toddler that's going to climb all over him, biting any part of his body that happens to fall into the puppy's mouth, stealing his precious property and worst of all, taking attention away from him. It is your job to ensure that this doesn't happen and your older dog feels just as loved as before.

First introductions between the youngster and your resident dog should take place on neutral turf. Don't be tempted to carry the puppy in your arms. He should meet his new friend on his own all-fours.

With both dogs on leads (enlist a helper), let them greet each other with a fairly quick nose-to-backside sniff, before taking them off together for a little socially-distanced walk from each other, far enough apart that there can be no physical interaction. With their excellent powers of perception, dogs will sense any nervousness or tension so both handlers should remain calm, keeping leads relaxed, to reduce any possible stress.

When bringing the dog and the pup into the home, keeping both animals on leads, allow the youngster to explore his new home, but keep a close eye on the resident dog's demeanour. If he's relaxed to the point of almost ignoring the newcomer, you're on the right path. Offer the puppy a little meal, show him where the water is, and his bed.

Provide enough beds in different places around the home to where each dog can retire. Do not let them share a bed or crate in the early days, and feed each in separate locations.

Resist the urge to force them into being together before they're ready. Allow them to get used to each other in their own time. Give each an escape route to a quiet area where they can get some peace and quiet when they need it.

Puppies will not have fully learned "doggish" – that sensible language socialised dogs will know that provides a firm foundation for them to co-exist, and may not always be able to read the subtle signs the older dog is sending out. They may regularly overstep boundaries by jumping at the older dog, biting with razor-sharp teeth, stealing his food or toys, or generally invading his space especially when he's resting. In all such situations, it is entirely natural for the adult dog to put the youngster in its place with a growl, snap or in extreme cases, a full rack of bared teeth. This sounds all a bit frightening at the time but the pup will soon learn its manners and the new dog-rules by which he's expected to live.

However, do not put all the responsibility on your adult dog to teach manners to your pup. It is your job to recognise the subtle signals of when the dog's patience has been exhausted, when there's a possibility of his emotions escalating to a more dangerous level. At this point, intervene to separate them, removing the pup from the situation.

> Never punish your adult dog for growling at or chastising your puppy, as he is merely trying to send valuable signals to the younger dog.

Let both animals interact positively with each other, watching the exchanges, but be prepared to act to help your adult lad if the puppy is being a little pesky.

The youngster can be removed to a quiet area (behind a baby gate, or to a different room) for a "time out" until he's calmed down.

Arrange a playdate with other puppies in your area or at puppy socialisation classes, where he can expend all of that exuberant energy, giving your adult some precious peaceful downtime.

Each animal should be allowed to retreat to their bed or crate for a bit of solitude whenever they want. Your older dog could be trained to retreat to his bed where he can get a treat, and some much-needed me-time away from this persistent little fur-nado that has suddenly invaded his world. Eventually, he will learn this coping mechanism and voluntarily go to his sanctuary to get some peace. This area should be inaccessible to your pup, put the youngster in another room, if necessary.

Often when something new is introduced into a home – a new baby or a puppy, some of the existing dog's favourite things disappear. Perhaps mum won't have time to give him that special walk in the afternoon, or his daily ball game with dad disappears. Identify a few things that your older dog enjoys doing just with his favourite people, and try to continue them without the little one butting in.

Encourage your adult dog to view this new arrival as something that can bring nice things into his life. Buy (or make) some very special food or treats, for example, duck, salmon – something that is rarely on the menu. Give to both of them **together** several times a day so he learns that sometimes nice things come from being close to this little newcomer.

Continue to supervise the dogs for the first few weeks until you feel they're more comfortable with each other, especially during any playtime. Watching their body language will help you gauge how they're getting on. You may find that after 3-4 weeks (or longer in some cases), both pup and adult will voluntarily begin to play together.

Three absolute no-no's:

1. The older dog should not be allowed to bully the youngster, neither should the pup be allowed to harass, pester or bully his older companion.
2. Definitely no fighting to be permitted – intervene at the first sign of hostility.

3. Do not leave them alone together in the house until you are very sure that they're comfortable and happy in each other's company. It's important to remember that some dogs prefer to always be left separately from the other resident dogs they live with.

And don't forget to spend individual, quality time with each dog.

Introductions to Adult or Multiple Dogs in the Household

When you go to pick up your new rescue, leave the resident dog at home. Trying to transport your existing dog with a new one coming from a shelter who may be nervous, could make that initial meeting fractious.

Again, ask friends or family members to help you with the first introductions, which should take place outside the home, on neutral ground. Ideally you need one person per dog, leads held loosely with no tension. All handlers should keep their voices and body language calm, but still try to be positive and happy.

If you're introducing new boy to more than one resident dog, introduce them individually. **Keep the others separate and out of sight**; no newcomer wants to be swamped by a load of stranger-dogs.

Initial introductions between new-boy and each member of the gang should never be rushed. Allow them to interact at their own pace and try to avoid a point where they start to posture and growl at each other. Nip this behaviour in the bud early rather than having to address it **after** it has started. Forcing things at this stage might lead to aggression or defensiveness.

Introducing your calmest dog first, allow supervised visual contact between the dogs without any physical interaction. If they both appear happy to see each other and are calm, keeping a close eye on the body language, allow an initial brief nose-to-nose greeting. Follow this with nose-to-tail, then have a short break by distracting them for a few minutes with a bit of obedience work, playing or petting, before bringing them back together for another meeting. Repeat this a few times.

Repeat this procedure separately with each of the other resident dogs, with those dogs already introduced now out of sight.

When all have been presented to each other (hopefully without any strife), with all dogs on leads, take them all out for a short, socially-distanced walk for 10-15 minutes, side by side but not so close that they can interact. Praise each for good behaviour and reward dogs away from each other.

If the dogs appear to be relaxed and happy, allow them to do what comes naturally to them, watching them all the time. If they're circling or milling around each other, raise the leads higher so they don't become entangled. Treats can be given for good behaviour during the little breaks but **only** when the dogs are slightly distanced.

Any warning or defensive signs, ie. one dog putting his head above the other's shoulders, growling/showing teeth, fixated stares, interrupt immediately with a brisk and cheerful "Let's go" and lead them away to a suitable distance. Wait for them to calm down then try again, **BUT** if the dog is still tense, do not attempt the introduction again on that same day.

If they initiate playtime or your resident dog appears to lose interest and returns to you, he has given his "thumbs up" to the newcomer.

If they begin to get excited, give them a little time to calm down before moving on again. Only bring the dogs back home when they seem calm and friendly with each other, before entering the house with the new dog first. Caution is vital here.

It's important to stress at this point that if there has been any tension between the dogs or the introductions are incomplete, restrict the new dog to a certain area of the house. Use a barrier to separate him from the rest of the dogs or keep them in different rooms until you can continue the introductions the following day.

If all has gone to plan, keeping the new lad on the lead, allow him to have a good sniff around the house without the others. Then quietly bring them in, taking them around the house together while still on the leads.

If they're calm, unleash them, still keeping all interactions or play under close observation. Bear in mind that the more high-arousal there is among the animals, the more fragile the chance of calmness, so always try to keep the atmosphere tranquil.

It is recommended to keep the new boy and the resident pets apart for the first 24 hours. Many rescue organisations expect this as part of their rehoming policy.

The newcomer will be very stressed from all these changes to his life, and meeting another dog on its turf, no matter how friendly, will just heighten his anxiety. Equally, the resident dog may view another dog coming into its territory in a different light to a casual meeting outside.

Individual areas – crates, beds or separate rooms should already have been identified where each dog can sleep, eat and have time-outs, especially when no one is around to supervise. Provide places for each to have breaks away from the others.

The arrival of a new dog can change the balance or pecking order within the group, so patience and time will be required until they sort themselves out and settle together. Your existing dog will consider your home as his den, so aggression combined with a natural territorial instinct could present a dangerous situation unless the underlying issues are proactively addressed.

> It goes without saying that the new boy should be kept separate from the other dogs whenever you have to leave the house - either in another room, or with baby gates.

Positive behaviour between the dogs should be encouraged during the first couple of weeks, with constant supervision. As things progress and everything appears to be harmonious, start to leave them together for short periods of time without monitoring, gradually increasing the length of time but **only if everything is going well**.

If there seems to be any continuing tension between the dogs, reduce the time they're together and slowly try to re-integrate them. Put a quick stop to any increase of emotions or temper by redirecting the dogs with a hand target or calling them away, before immediately separating them for a short time. Praise all animals equally when they behave well.

To reduce the dangers of fights over food, **do not** free-feed; each dog should have its own food, water and toys. Feed in separate areas, especially in the beginning, pick up any bowl with an unfinished meal. In time, when they become more comfortable together and if they've been taught some meal-time manners, the dogs may eventually be fed in the same area, but these times should still be closely supervised. Some dogs feel more comfortable being fed separately.

Be careful when giving out high value treats or bones by initially distributing when the dogs are segregated, before progressing to giving such things while they're in the same room. Always keep an eye out for behaviour that suggests one is uncomfortable with the presence of the other dog when they have a high value treat.

You should be the leader in your dogs' minds. You make the decisions for them so they should feel that they can trust you. Once they have confidence in you and behave in a manner that you like, you can, in turn, trust them more. That having been said, leaving bones or tasty treats lying around is a bust-up waiting to happen.

A useful exercise is to teach dogs that it's not always their turn, so that they should be able to come for a treat, without all the others expecting one too. There's no need to "be fair" to each dog, even if that means a little dog doesn't get the same number of treats as a big one. Please don't think of this as being cruel – rather think of the little dog's health and girth.

Over these important initial weeks, introduce different situations by having other people or families to visit, to mix with the dogs while they're together.

> It is the job of the owner to watch out for and recognise any uncomfortable emotion before it intensifies into unwanted behaviour and potential aggression between the dogs.

While dog fights are never pleasant, they need to be broken up to reduce the chance of serious injury to the participants. But the last thing that any human should do is to get in the middle of the scrap.

The first option is to try to distract the pugilists with a loud noise. If this fails, try throwing something soft like a cushion or coat. If outside, a spray of water from the garden hose (especially if it can be aimed into a mouth) or a bucket of water might persuade them to break up.

As soon as the dogs are distracted, separate them until tempers have calmed. Work out what was the trigger for the fight and amend the situation before introducing them again.

Like humans, not all dogs will get along well enough that they can be left alone together, or tolerate each other for more than brief periods of time. However, once you are willing to accept that your dogs are not going to be best buddies, it is possible to come up with ways to get them to share the same home. If relations within the canine family continue to be strained or deteriorate despite all your work and efforts, engage the assistance of a qualified behaviourist.

Supervise playtime especially if any tug-of-war toys are involved. Squeaky toys can cause possessiveness in certain dogs with high prey drive, as the squeaks can sound similar to a small animal being killed. If things become too rough, verging on aggression, calm the situation down by getting them to have a time-out. If this aggression continues through rough-play, separate the dogs for a little breather until they calm down. Supervise future exchanges until it appears that they can be in each other's company, having fun, without the excitement turning into something more worrying.

Keep a close eye on the dogs' body language (see Chapter 8: Learn a New Language), especially those subtle signals that can easily be missed: tails held high, hackles that suddenly rise, the ears that are pressed back against the head, and lip curls. If one dog's body becomes rigid and he starts to stare at the other for no apparent reason, distract him, or take him to a separate area to cool off. If it was your other dog that either misread or ignored the signals, make sure he's the one that is redirected. Any aggressive lunging or growling, separate the dogs immediately and go back to an earlier stage.

Some people think growling automatically means aggression but this isn't always the case. If accompanied with a play-bow, one dog is asking the other to play. As long as the growling doesn't intensify and it is accompanied by play signals, he's just being a noisy play-mate. So it helps to learn your dog's vocal signals.

Generally, female and male dogs will self-regulate their play-time, when the female will tick the male off if he becomes too rough or tries to get "overly-familiar" with her.

As previously stated, do not expect all the furries to get along right away or try to force them into playing together; allow them time to get used to each other.

Dogs are social creatures and generally enjoy being with others. If the initial integration period has been well-planned and carried out in a calm way, your new boy will hopefully bring his special brand of fun and love both to the human and canine members of your family.

It can be difficult not to lavish a new rescue dog with a lot of love, but be careful not to pay too much attention to him at the expense of your existing dog/s.

Give individual affection, and spend quality time with each animal in the household by walks, training sessions, special outings to the market, or local dog park.

Never forget that your new dog may display new behaviours after a few weeks or months as he settles and becomes more comfortable in his home. Creating a regular daily routine with team-time, as well as time away from each other and with sufficient exercise, can all help to keep the gang content and comfortable.

Other Pets

In addition – and this "no-brainer" is based on previous experience – ensure that any chickens, ducks, hamsters, guinea pigs, snakes or whatever, are safely secured in an appropriate dog-proof enclosure. There's absolutely no use in telling the rescue organisation that their ex-resident has just killed your "favourite" chicken (that was roaming loose in the garden) and how "its sister is now grieving her loss"! Dogs will do what comes naturally to them, including catching themselves a fresh chicken dinner.

> Protecting all your animals, ensuring that they're safe is entirely YOUR responsibility.

CHAPTER 7

Fearful Dogs

Even that poor dog that's hanging around at the back of the kennel – scared, anxious or shy, refusing to make eye contact – can make a very special pet, one equal deserving of a second chance of happiness.

Such dogs would need patient and very understanding homes with experienced people as they may not be easy to live with. While some dogs may adjust quickly to their new circumstances with time, love and care, other could take longer, perhaps months or years to make any progress. But any tiny improvement will provide rich reward to the owners. Working with a scared dog may prove to be one of the most challenging things an owner will do, often frustrating, but one that will provide the most fulfilling experience.

Unfortunately, we live in a world that is happy to pre-judge without actually knowing any of the circumstances. Owners of traumatised dogs may be judged harshly on the behaviour of their dog. They may be accused of abuse by people who don't bother to stop to ask questions or understand, which can be so upsetting and heart-breaking for loving owners trying their best with a psychologically-damaged dog. So, a tough rhino-skin may come in handy!

Without doubt, a dog's fear could be the product of previous physical abuse, but in other dogs that fear could stem from a mum that wasn't well-socialised herself or highly stressed during her pregnancy. It could have been down to poor or inadequate socialisation during his puppyhood when his young brain should have been exposed to new experiences which would have helped him to cope with life – something not limited to rescue animals. Dogs are often afraid of things or situations they have never experienced or had the opportunity to learn to feel good about them.

The fears are very real to these dogs, and there's no point in trying to force them to face something that you might consider "silly", as this will only increase their fear and add to their general distrust of humans. They should not be given unrealistic targets, and be allowed to go at their own pace.

Routine is very important to fearful dogs as knowing what's going to happen will provide comfort to them. Until you know that your dog is ready, you risk making the problem worse by forcing them into a new situation. Respect your dog's fears; they are not unfounded or senseless. Your dog is also not a coward or stupid.

Patience is not just a virtue but a must when dealing with a fearful dog. Losing one's temper or expecting the dog to learn or adjust to a situation faster than it's capable of, will be counterproductive. They may require more expertise than a new owner possesses; in which case the assistance of a trained behaviourist may be required.

Sadly, despite all the hard work, effort and best intentions, it may never be the case that that a fearful dog will become as warm and affectionate as an owner may want. But the pure joy of those victories, no matter how large or small, together with the knowledge that you've given a home to a vulnerable dog will feel like the best thing in the world.

So let's give those fearful dogs a second look as they may well change your life in ways you never imagined. Bear in mind that the right home situation and good experience in owning dogs would be recommended before taking on a troubled one.

CHAPTER 8

Learn a New Language

Dogs are a very clever species as their behaviour and physiology have adapted over thousands of years in order for them to survive and thrive and especially, how to live successfully with humans, including learning some of our language.

The average dog can learn approximately 165-200 words and signals, more than enough for them to live happily with us and understand the important things in life ... like treats, dinner and walkies!

The top 20% of canine linguists have been known to learn up to 250-300 words, with some owners claiming their dog knows even more. With an approximate IQ of 100, this would place dogs on a par with a 2-year-old child. Not content to learn the spoken human word, dogs are as astute in understanding cues gleaned from our physical body language, and emotional moods.

> Fun fact: Trained by researcher John Pilley, a psychology professor at Wofford College, a very clever border collie called Chance was reported to know 1000 words.

Many owners complain that their dogs "don't listen" to them – well, mainly that's because the animals may not have received much or any training so don't understand what's being said to them or what they're being asked to do. Why don't we humans return the favour and learn a bit of Doggish to help us better understand how our dogs are feeling and trying to say to us?

Dogs have their own quite sophisticated social system which, when sufficiently learned by all canine parties, enables them to co-exist with their fellow canids in a very civilised and amenable way. Their language can be vocal with barks/growls, or as subtle as a head tilt, an ear or tail twitch, communicating with the mouth or through their eyes, body, coat – either used independently or in conjunction with the other signs.

The advantage of silent signals such as ear or tail positions is that these can be seen by others from a distance, who will instantly understand the emotional stance and intention of the sender (so long as the other party has good comprehension of these signals. They can give appeasement gestures in order to diffuse a potentially dangerous situation with both humans and other dogs, very important for their own safety and survival.

Basic canine communication using vocal and body signs is first learned while in the litter, which is why it is important to leave the pups with mum for at least 8 weeks, or longer. As the pups get a bit older, they still need to mix with other (stranger) dogs to allow them to further develop a full range of canine signals.

When they move to a human home, they then have to learn a whole new set of communication skills on their own, but will use any opportunity through contact with other dogs to continue to learn. They may even imitate sounds or barks they hear their pals making to increase their own "vocabulary".

Dogs constantly 'talk' to us even if many of us don't realise it. Being able to read their signals can really help us to understand how they're feeling in particular situations, especially if they're fearful, in pain, anxious, unhappy or unsure about something – or their intention to act. Ignoring signals may increase their unease, and at worst, result in a bite … which could lead to something much more permanent and drastic for the poor animal.

This "language" is particularly important for children to learn as research suggests that children are most at risk of lethal bites. They're smaller, closer to the dog's mouth, and more likely to do undesirable things to a dog, eg. pulling their tails, ears or whiskers, trying to ride on them.

Begin your linguistic journey (which will be fun) by watching your dog closely to identify what is his "normal" body language when he's relaxed, confident, happy – his neutral position and take it from that point. Observe the signs he's giving in different situations that show that his emotional stance has changed, so you can act accordingly, especially removing him from circumstances that cause him unease. A well-socialised dog will know the important pacifying signals another dog is sending out that will help to de-escalate a potentially dangerous situation such as turning their head away, turning the body to face away from the threat. He will also use these same signals during interactions with humans that are causing him unease.

Your dog's mouth will, in part, indicate his emotional state, be that fear, frustration, aggression, general tension, pain, or relaxation.

A soft relaxed mouth that almost looks like a smile, perhaps with a tongue slightly showing or lolling, shows that the dog is content and calm, and doesn't see anything that might be of concern.

A closed mouth with no tongue or teeth on view indicates interest or attentiveness, usually when he's looking in a certain direction. His head and ears may be held slightly forward – he's not worried or bothered but is trying to work out the meaning of what he's seeing, assessing what action may be required.

Tensed lips, usually pulled back (prior to tense panting), will indicate fear and in cases of aggression will be puckered forward (just before a growl). When displaying a big goofy (submissive) grin when greeting someone, generally in conjunction with a loose, wiggling body, a dog is telling them that "I'm no threat to you".

We yawn when we're bored or tired, but dogs also use yawns when they're uneasy about a particular situation, or as a calming signal to others – animal and human.

Licking lips and salivating is often misinterpreted. While dogs may lick their lips after a particularly delicious meal or drool in anticipation of a tasty treat, they will flick their tongue out to their nose and draw it back into the mouth when fearful or uncomfortable in a particular situation.

Other indications of increased anxiety are panting when the dog isn't hot or hasn't done any exercise (the tongue tip will sometimes curl too); an inability to settle, pacing back and forth; red around the eyes, dilated pupils, and whale eyes; or his ears are pressed back along the head.

Stressed dogs may also lose their appetite, or bark or howl when they normally wouldn't. There are other obvious signs, such as trembling, cowering or backing away from a situation or person they're unsure of, tucking their tail under their bodies, defecating in the house and/or diarrhoea.

Reading signals can be confusing as confident dogs will express their annoyance, anger or fear in similar but subtly different ways to those shown by more fearful animals. The degree of dental weaponry on show, ear position, mouth shape, nose wrinkles, how intense and open the eyes are, not to mention accompanying warning growls will all indicate the emotion levels of the dog – from issuing an initial warning that he's feeling threatened or annoyed to the very extreme stage of warning the perceived threat to back off.

Make no mistake: the threat of attack from either the confident or fearful dog will be the same if signals are not heeded and the situation de-escalated. Generally, the more teeth on show, the greater is the signal to the other party to BEWARE.

In such a case, it is wise to heed the warnings you're being sent and retreat immediately from the situation:

- Do not move any closer to the dog.
- Avoid direct eye contact to diffuse a situation the dog feels to be threatening.
- Try to stay calm, slowly blink your eyes a few times accompanied by a yawn – both of which are appeasing signals to indicate that you're not a threat.
- Turn sideways to make yourself appear smaller, before slowly backing away from the danger.
- Even though your flight-instincts may understandably kick in, resist the urge turn tail and run as this could provoke an instinctive pursuit reaction in the dog.

What is your dog's tail is telling you? Position, shape, direction and velocity of the wag will say a lot about the dog's emotional state. However, all tails are not the same as certain breeds will hold their tails differently in the neutral position, eg. herding dogs, and Italian Whippets (tails low), sled dogs (high), French Bulldogs (absent or coiled), Chow-Chows (curled over their backs).

Even if you have a mixed-breed, understand that its neutral tail may be different to that of other dogs. A wagging tail is not always a friendly one but means that emotionally the dog is aroused, be that through excitement, or from confidence, stress, fear, frustration or anger. It's important to learn the wag!

A study has shown that, interestingly, dogs tend to wag their tails more to the right when their emotions are positive, and more to the left side when faced with something they consider negative. And a helicopter tail, whirring around in a circle? An extremely happy greeting to a much-loved person.

Eye contact is an important mechanism for a dog by which to communicate their emotions and intent, and can go either way. It could be a soft gooey, gaze at a much-loved human, an intimidating stare to put its target "on alert", and everything in between.

Avoiding eye contact with a subject is a good indication that your dog is feeling uncomfortable or stressed. A soft look shows they're happy or calm, but eyes that turn "cold", or have a hard, fixed gaze, will indicate a negative emotional state. Perhaps they're guarding a resource they consider precious or are feeling aggressive for whatever reason, but this message should be heeded. When a dog breaks eye contact and looks away, they're sending a calming signal to the other party.

If your dog is turning his head away from you, showing "whale eyes", he's showing his increased level of discomfort. How many times do we see photos on social media of owners hugging their dogs, while their dog is leaning away, perhaps turning his head, displaying whale-eyes and looking away? The person may be enjoying the photo-op, but their favourite furry is sending a very clear message that he isn't.

Similar to humans, the pupils will tell a story but will indicate *changes* in how the dog is feeling rather than if his feelings are negative or positive. They can increase in size as much when your dog is happy to see something or someone as they can when they're upset and angry. Years ago, children were often asked not to stare at a dog – very wise advice, as an unwavering eye-to-eye stare can be viewed by a confident canine as a threat, or cause dread in a fearful one.

A dog's ears are wonderful mobile transmitters for messages, and while erect ears are easier to read as they can be seen from a distance by both humans and other dogs, lop-ears will also communicate its owner's emotions, albeit more subtly.

Are his ears erect or slightly out to the sides, upright, flicking back and forth, or are they flattened against his head? Used in combination with other physical signals, they will continually convey tell-tale signs as to his emotional state. That is what makes it so heart-breaking that still, in the 21st century, there are cruel individuals who still think it's acceptable to cut a dog's ears – or its tail for that matter, as these are such important communication tools for a dog.

The body is the largest part of a dog's anatomy and by using its coat, body position including paw placements and weight distribution (which will give indications as to mood and intention) your dog will be communicating his mental state. Generally, an assertive dog will hold his tail higher – almost like a flag, showing his confidence, but it can also point to aggression, depending on the stimulus he's reacting to.

The dog that appears to be trying to make himself larger, perhaps with his hackles raised (*piloerection*), and a highly held, twitching tail can indicate an arousal. It could be that the dog is worried or upset, or interested or excited at whatever it is that has grabbed his attention.

The obvious signs of a fearful dog are when he makes himself as small and as close to the ground as possible, he may roll onto his back to diffuse conflict. However, when pushed, he may still bite if his back-roll hasn't stopped the unwanted interaction and he continues to feel threatened. Ryan Dillon of Oxford Animal Behaviour and Training says that he has "seen too many people getting bitten by a dog rolling on to its back" because they misinterpreted this signal.

If the dog is relaxed and happy and does this in front of someone he trusts, he's just requesting an enjoyable tummy-rub!

Even though you won't understand the vocal "words" your boy is using, he will still be telling you what's on his mind. Every sound will have its own meaning which you should learn to decipher and recognise. Understand the difference between a vocal invitation to play, expressions of concern or alarm, a warning to stop whatever it is you're doing to him, or to keep your distance.

Over time, we've stopped "listening" to our dogs. In the past, when someone ventured near a dog that growled at them whilst eating, it would have been the human that was chastised, not the dog. Nowadays, it's the poor dog that gets punished, or worse still, put to sleep for merely expressing its emotions.

Your dog *has a right* to tell you how he's feeling, and it's your duty as a caring owner to listen to him.

We've also stopped allowing dogs the right to say "no". They have no right to indicate their feelings, or refuse to do something with which they are uncomfortable. It seems that they're now expected always to be sunshine and light, or run the risk of being considered "aggressive".

Dogs are sentient beings and experience emotions in particular situations that, just like humans, will elicit an appropriate response which we should recognise as their right.

Understanding Doggish can not only help you understand your own dog's state of emotion but also that of a stranger dog and can also strengthen the precious human-dog bond.

Unfortunately, too many owners nowadays do not understand normal dog-to-dog communication. They may have suppressed their own pet's ability to express itself, or interfered in social canine introductions when on walks then furiously accuse the other owner of having a "badly-behaved" dog when they react negatively.

Get to know the signals and be proud of your rescue dog. Do not be afraid to stand up for him especially if you feel he's behaved in an acceptable way, but equally protect him if he's in a situation that is making him nervous. If other stranger dogs come too close for his comfort, don't be afraid to ask their owners to give you space. You'll probably be tagged as a "bad owner" or of having a "bad dog" but hey ho! if you've protected him from a stressful situation, that will be a result.

The above information is no more than a brief outline but those owners who are interested in improving their canine linguistics could do worse than to get a copy of a good picture book "Canine Body Language" by Drenda Aloff.

To have a happy, content companion to share your life, it will pay to listen to what your dog is telling you through his own language.

CHAPTER 9

Training

The subject of training has been raised more than once in this book. The reason? It's IMPORTANT! Too many dogs lose their lives in shelters around the world because their previous owners couldn't be bothered to train them even to a basic level. It isn't hard and doesn't have to take up a lot of time, but the result of having a mannerly, obedient dog will make such a difference in the home, and beyond.

Training your dog using positive methods will strengthen the bond you have with him and will also give him confidence, which can help reduce the likelihood of future behavioural problems.

It's a "no-brainer" – dogs can't possibly understand what you want from them or how you want them to behave … unless you show them. If you don't teach them what you want them to do, they'll very happily do their own thing. Dogs really do want to please and are happy to learn if it's made fun – especially if there are some nice treats involved.

Give Panza lots of praise (and treats) for good behaviour. Training can even take place throughout the day with acceptable things that he does. If he's just lying quietly in his bed, tell him what a good boy he is. Basically, reward the good behaviour, ignore the bad, use positive reinforcement (treats, praise, petting, play with toys) rather than harsher methods.

Only train when you're both relaxed and calm. If you've had a stressful day, perhaps just have a good play with him instead, and wait until your mood is better.

Set aside a little time every day for training in a quiet area where there will be no distractions. Only train puppies for about 3 minutes at a time, adult dogs will be happy with approximately 10-15 minutes per session but quick, concentrated ones throughout the day can be just as productive.

Only work on one command per lesson, new commands can be introduced separately in other sessions during the day. Keep these times fun for Panza, and always end on a positive note. If he isn't quite getting the hang of what you're trying to teach him, finish the session by asking him to do something that you know he's good at so he can feel good about himself. Give him a treat and have a little play with him at the end of his classes, which he'll love – a bit of mummy or daddy time

Start with the basic commands:

- Sit
- Down (lie down)
- Up
- Stay
- Come (recall)
- Leave it (not to touch or pick up something off the ground. Can also be used in other situations)
- Drop or give (something they've got in their mouth)
- Off (ie. furniture, jumping on people)
- Walk to heel or on a relaxed lead
- Two slightly more advanced commands:
    – Watch (eyes on the handler), and Touch (basically targeting the hand or another part of the body, ie. arm or leg) are good instructions to distract him from uncomfortable situations, even a vet examination

It's a good idea to always ask Panza to say "please", basically by sitting every time he wants something, or to do something in return for a treat or something nice that you're doing for him.

The Sit command can be really useful to utilise throughout the day, ie. when putting Panza's leash on or off for a walk, sitting before exiting through the door, when meeting people or before crossing a road.

It's a bit impolite if you allow Panza to jump up on people. Not everyone will appreciate a paw print design on clean trousers or a dress, no matter how artistic or neat it may be. So gently encourage him out of this by ignoring the behaviour when he tries it with you, walking away from him.

Teach him to stay calm when the doorbell rings, or visitors come to the house. In both cases, the "sit" and "stay" request will be very useful in controlling any excitement.

"Leave It" could literally save Panza's life and an emergency trip to his favourite vet. It might seem innocuous but it's a command that can steer him away from danger – sharp objects, glass, hazardous food or rubbish, yucky poo (who enjoys seeing their beloved fur-baby scoffing down a big dollop of some other animal's poo?). It could even be used to take your dog away from an inter-dog "pawticuffs" in the local park.

There's an excellent training method called **SMART x 50**, developed by renowned animal behaviourist, Kathy Sdao. SMART x 50 is an extremely effective and simple training method that works by catching and rewarding Panza's naturally occurring good behaviours. An additional benefit is that it also makes the owner more alert to what their dog is doing. Many owners notice when their dog is being "naughty" or "bad" but overlook them when they're being good.

SMART stands for See, Mark And Reward Training.

What you need:

- 50 low-cal treats in a container or bowl, placed in a convenient place (but out of reach of Panza) where you and he spend the most time.
- A clicker or your chosen marker word, for example "yes", "good".

What you have to do:

It's easy! Keep an eye out during the day for the positive behaviour that you want from him, especially when he's doing something without being asked, like:

a. Lying quietly, perhaps playing with a toy
b. Not reacting by barking when someone passes outside the house
c. Sitting or lying down, instead of jumping up
d. Going to their bed without being asked
e. Any other good behaviour that you want to encourage.

When you see him doing something you like, mark it and immediately reward. Repeat 50 times a day.

Even if you initially don't see enough good behaviour to reward 50 times, you will start to notice an improvement in just a few weeks, as Panza twigs that if he behaves in certain ways, something tasty appears, which will encourage him to repeat it.

Be sure to gently expose Panza to as many different situations and settings as possible, to help him to accept and be comfortable in the world around him. The more experiences or sights he becomes accustomed to, the more accepting he will become. Visit the local park or take a walk-through town, praising him for being calm around other dogs, and mannerly with people who may stop to pet him.

> When you are socialising your dog, it is important to keep an eye on his body language to make sure that he is not uncomfortable with the experience. If you notice him looking anxious – some signs to look out for are a tucked tail, ears back, lip licking or turning away – remove him from the situation and try again to introduce him to the new thing on another day from a greater distance. Some dogs are very nervous of new situations, when they need very gradual introductions in a calm controlled manner to avoid future behaviour problems.

Obedience classes would be a wonderful way of really bonding with Panza. He'll enjoy meeting other dogs and learning new things, and you may find that you have a doggy-Einstein in the family if he shows a particular talent in agility, obedience or tracking. Crufts, there you may go!!! But at the very least, you'll have a nice, obedient dog to share your life.

Some dogs love the sound of their own bark but as the neighbours may not appreciate it quite so much, try to encourage Panza not to bark without a genuine reason. There are ways of teaching a dog not to bark without the assistance of lemon-spray collars, etc.

It is absolutely no fun being dragged around the local neighbourhood, so teach him to walk to heel, and to a loose lead.

Even though children and dogs can be best friends, and Panza is considered "safe" or "good with children", what if he comes across a child that isn't so good or respectful of dogs? This is the time when you'll have to step in to stand up for him, taking him away from an unpleasant situation.

> Always watch your dog's body language if he is approached by children. If he looks uncomfortable in any way, ask the child not to pet him, or remove your dog from the situation.
> One more time: never leave small children and dogs alone together unsupervised, no matter how "good" the dog is considered to be with kiddies.

Dogs are really happy if they're doing something. So give Panza little jobs to do, like carrying the paper, or fetching something.

Taking it to a more advanced level, it's even possible to train a dog to empty the dryer, put away their toys, turn on lights, bring the TV remote. There are a myriad of different tricks and activities you can teach him that will keep his brain active, leaving him happy and with a sense of purpose – while helping you!

It wouldn't hurt Panza to learn that nothing in life is free and he should do something in return for a treat, for example a high-five, shake paws, On Trust (basically waiting for the code-words "Paid For" that signal that he can take the treat).

Remember that as he gets the hang of all the commands you're teaching him in your quiet area, you should get him to carry them out in different settings – in the garden, while you're out walking with him – so he learns to obey them wherever he is, even with distractions around. And like we humans, dogs can forget, so regularly practise all the commands Panza has learned to keep them fresh in his mind.

Training Puppies

As puppies' minds are like little sponges so begin gentle (and fun) training with Puppy Panza as soon as he arrives in the home.

It may sound a bit strange, but pre-plan what you are going to teach your pup in a lesson. Without him being there, practise how you're going to teach him, and the signals/commands you'll use. Go through the motions so you know exactly what you're going to do. The clearer you are in your mind, the clearer the lesson will be for your puppy, and the more successful training will be.

In a quiet, familiar area with minimal distractions, keep lessons short and simple – just a few minutes at a time for a young pup, which are divided into short sets. So he doesn't get confused, only teach one command/action per lesson.

Don't rush him by trying to do too much. You want Panza to gain confidence by getting it right, so he can feel good about himself.

A plentiful supply of yummy treats or a favourite toy will help to motivate your young lad and keep him focused, ensuring that he'll also enjoy his training. Varying the types of treats will reduce the chance he'll become bored.

If you make your own treats, cut them into finger-nail size, dividing them into sets of 8-10 treats each so you can easily see when a practise set is over when he gets a little break, when you'll have a fun game with him.

If Puppy-Panza looks like he's getting confused by what you're trying to teach him, take a break and have a little play with him before returning to the exercise. If he continues to have difficulty learning something, stop to think about how you're teaching the lesson. Perhaps you could make it simpler and clearer for him to understand? Always end lessons with a success, something that the pup does correctly.

All dogs are different and will learn at different paces so don't worry if Puppy-Panza is not progressing as fast as your friend's new pup. As he improves in his exercises, move the location of the lessons so he knows that he's expected to carry out your instructions wherever he is.

Generally, edible treats can be used for those exercises where the dog should be relaxed and calm, and toys can be used for more energetic ones like recall. To reduce the chance of him putting on additional weight, deduct an equivalent amount from his daily food allowance.

And don't forget: it's really enjoyable to do things with your dog – be sure to have fun with yours!

Separation-Related Problems

When left alone, a dog may become destructive or disruptive, bark or howl, relieve themselves around the house, chew objects including furniture and soft furnishings, or try to escape.

Separation-related problems can be defined in many different ways. They can be subdivided into issues relating to absence of a person/isolation, and those that are not strictly to do with absence such as noise phobia or boredom, which can occur *during* absences.

There is a new understanding of some separation-related problems that cause a dog frustration when left behind barriers such as doors. It is not the *absence* of a person that causes the anxiety, but rather the *frustration* at not being able to get to them or whatever is behind the closed door.

Dogs can have more than one type of anxiety and any dog, of any age or breed, can suffer from this phobia. While trying to avoid anthropomorphism (applying human characteristics to non-human/animal subjects), it could be compared to a panic attack, and is basically an anxiety or extreme fear related to being left alone.

Separation anxiety can also stem from confinement anxiety, reaction to external stimuli, poor housetraining or chew-training, or noise phobias ranging from the old "regulars" – thunder or fireworks to high-pitched digital beeps within the home. Such anxieties will not decrease or disappear with time if ignored. The fear the dog is experiencing is very real to him, causing him immense emotional pain.

While arrivals to a new home could experience "transitional stress", which may present as a separation-related problem, sometimes a dog may follow his owner around for no other reason than he wants to be with them.

In such circumstances, allow Panza one or two weeks to adjust to his change in environment. Avoid long absences from the home in the early days, gently introduce him to brief departures, slowly building up the time he spends alone.

Hiding tasty treats in other rooms will encourage him to go off and safely explore on his own, which will boost both his confidence and independence.

Accustom him to your departures by leaving him in a room for just a few seconds, keeping the door open so he can still see you. Then very slowly increase this absence time by short increments, always returning, building up to 10 minutes or more. If Panza does try to come after you, decrease the time you're out of the room to a point where he appears content to stay on his own, and rebuild the time from there.

A good exercise to help him to learn that he doesn't have to be at your side all the time is to set up baby gates (for safety) to create "virtual" absences **prior** to your real absences. This will allow him to see and smell you, even though he cannot be beside you.

Ensure that he has everything he needs to be comfortable when left in a room, ie. that he's been out to do his toilet, has access to water and his toys.

As dogs are masters at identifying patterns or routines but are not good at discerning randomness, it's important to vary the periods when you're in or out of the room, anywhere between 5-10 seconds to begin with. A reward can be given **so long as he's relaxed and calm when you return.** He gets nothing if he's tried to follow.

As Panza becomes used to your comings and goings, move on to the next phase by closing the door after you as you leave, again starting just with a few seconds, following the same procedure above.

This exercise can then be extended so that you go out into the garden for a few minutes. If you have glass doors, allow him to watch you, before returning. Provided things are going well, you can try to go a little further afield with a little walk up your street before returning/treating, before venturing further and for longer.

So long as Panza's anxiety **is not** isolation distress/separation anxiety, a special treat might help to take his mind off your imminent departure. Leaving a TV or radio on can provide some additional comfort during your absences. These distractions can be eliminated over time as he becomes more accustomed to being left.

A good walk will help to tire him out but this should **not** take place immediately prior to your departure, or he'll come to link walks with being left on his own.

However, if it seems that Panza's anxiety is much more acute than can be helped by the above exercises and that true anxiety may be the problem, the first port of call should be to the vet for an examination to determine if there is an underlying reason that may be causing him distress.

If there are no medical reasons for his behaviour, you should immediately contact a behavioural expert who can help to initiate a training plan to identify and address his problems, as no one would want their dog to suffer emotionally in such a way. The good news is that separation anxiety IS treatable with time, total commitment, patience and hard work on behalf of the owner.

Set up a safe space for Panza where he can feel comfortable and secure, such as an open crate (provided he has been gently introduced to it and is happy to use it) or cosy bed, with an Adaptil diffuser plugged in nearby to help to relax him. The crate or bed should be placed in a location where he enjoys being, for example in the living room.

Training for more serious separation anxiety will comprise of a series of tiny steps, habituating Panza to accept the leaving cues that may initiate the distress for him and teaching him to accept and cope with being left alone. Initial training will take place for minimal periods of time – which may be just a matter of seconds. The aim is to work below the point at he starts to show distress. These little periods of absences will be slowly increased over a period of days, weeks or months as the dog becomes accustomed to being on his own. As every dog is different, it's impossible to say how long training may take so it's best not to have any expectations as to a speedy resolution but regard each tiny improvement as a mini-victory.

Some of the mistaken myths about preventing or tackling genuine isolation distress/separation anxiety include:

- leaving a radio or TV on to provide background noise may not help as either medium could create triggering sounds for the dog that can't be controlled if the owner is out of the home,
- having other companion animals in the home will not necessarily be able to quell the dog's fear, neither will tiring him out with exercise,
- leaving treats/food, or leaving owners' clothing around to "comfort" him,
- care should be taken when contemplating the option of crating which can **possibly** help if Panza is already in love with his crate, but often confinement just intensifies the problem. You'll need to determine which environment is best suited for him,

- punishing, using shock or spray collars, or being angry with him is definitely not going to contribute anything to his mental well-being but will, more than likely, make his anxiety even worse. This phobia is in his head and will need to be sympathetically handled and treated.

It's also very important not to take away affection from your troubled dog as such removal can have the opposite effect, by increasing his anxiety. Receiving love, underlined with a sympathetic understanding of his fears during re-training are more likely to help him to become confident and well-adjusted in the long run.

Make a strong commitment to Panza not to leave him on his own while undergoing remedial training as any stressful absences at this stage, other than those planned ones during the sessions, will cause significant setbacks to any progress. He should only be left alone for the absence duration that he can comfortably cope with. An owner may have to go out but they need to do some serious pre-planning, recruiting the assistance of a dog-friendly neighbour, friend or family member to sit with the dog while they're gone, or doggy day care (if the dog enjoys it and the owner's bank balance allows). Investigate online grocery delivery options until there's been sufficient progress in his re-training to allow for longer absences.

Obviously, owners will be distressed if the dog is causing a lot of destruction to their property during an anxiety attack. Experts advise leaving most of the house open to the dog, perhaps using a baby gate to restrict him to certain areas, while closing off access to bedrooms and bathrooms etc.

In extreme cases, pharmaceutical medications could be considered as an option to be **used in conjunction** with the training, when your veterinarian will prescribe appropriate products. Owners should not feel that they've failed their dog in some way or that such medication is "bad" or dangerous. There is always a place in responsible animal health-care for such treatments.

For a more detailed and experienced guide, expert behaviourist Dr Susannah O'Hanlon recommends: Separation Anxiety in Dogs (Next Generation Treatment Protocols and Practices) by Malenda DeMartini-Price. While geared mainly towards professional trainers, the book will still give lay-people a good understanding about separation anxiety and provide a guide as to how to carry out remedial training. Another good book is Be Right Back, by Julie Naismith.

Owners who feel they need more guidance and support should engage the services of an expert, but please, please, don't give up on your stressed dog as he really needs your help.

You could be his last chance.

CHAPTER 10

Why Adopt?

Why should people adopt, rather than shop? It's a question that appears to challenge many people but to me, the answer is very simple.

Since humans first began to domesticate *canis familiaris* over 12,000 years ago, employing the animals' skills for their benefit in so many different ways, dogs have remained faithfully by our sides every step of our way through history. They have happily served and worked for us without complaint: saving lives, searching out criminals, drugs, explosives, or even diseases. They have been employed as hearing or seeing guides, home helpers, herded our flocks, defended our homes, consoled flagging spirits, or just brought their warm hearts to the coldest of homes.

Other than those adventurers who enjoy nothing more than a good self-rewarding gallop out of owner's eye-shot before returning foot-sore and tired out, it is to their eternal credit that dogs never abandon us – even those who mistreat them so brutally. Quite simply, dogs want to be at our sides, which makes it an absolute disgrace and to our eternal shame that such noble and faithful animals are treated so carelessly, and with such cruelty around the world.

Some information contained in this chapter may make for difficult reading and for that I apologise but tragically what is described is the horrendous lives and endings of hundreds of thousands of innocent dogs that caring animal lovers should be aware of.

There are estimated to be as many as 600 million stray dogs in the world.

Countless millions of hapless dogs are relinquished to shelters or abandoned each year in countries across the world, only to have their unfortunate lives snuffed out in hard, unforgiving environments. They are given up for no other reasons than their owner became seriously ill or passed away, poor training, or they quite simply had become surplus to requirements.

It should come as no surprise that it's nigh-on impossible to get exact numbers of euthanasia, as which country or council would want to highlight the number of healthy animals it slaughters. Tragically, this number will increase due to the devastating effects of Covid and the current economic downturn on families and individuals across the globe over the last few years. It also includes those unwise enough to adopt puppies or dogs (against advice) without thinking ahead as to how they would be affected when their lives returned to some kind of normality.

Aside from those dogs put to sleep due to serious injury, old age, poor health, or aggression/serious behavioural issues (particularly in dogs under 2 years of age), the other main reasons for euthanasia are for breed (particularly the so-called "dangerous" breeds like pit-bulls, Staffis etc.), colour, size, also unclaimed chipped dogs or those with non-current chip information.

Lack of space in overcrowded shelters or a shortage of helping hands/volunteers will also dictate the longevity of surrendered animals. Black dogs are generally high on the list of those first to die, so a black member of the so-called "bully breeds" certainly wouldn't last long in a shelter with a euthanasia policy.

Let's do a little snap-shot of how some countries around the world handle their stray dog "problem" …

While things are slowly improving across most states in the US due to enhanced microchipping/neutering programmes and increased adoptions, the ASPCA report that approximately 670,000 blameless dogs are still unnecessarily being killed each year. Twenty-five percent of the animals surrendered are registered pedigrees but unfortunately for them, most are Pit Bulls, of which 93% will be killed.

In the UK, the 2019 Dogs' Trust survey showed that "UK owners abandoned more than 69,621 dogs of which 46% were either unclaimed or could not be reunited with their owners, with more than 5,000 being put down. PETA (People for the Ethical Treatment of Animals) estimates that there could be as many as 100,000 dogs without homes at any one time, with approximately 21 unfortunates being put to sleep **each day** – almost 1 per hour. Municipal pounds put down dogs within 7 days if not claimed or a rescue charity doesn't take them.

Romania tops the European chart for having the most stray dogs, estimated at approximately 2 million by ESDAW (European Society of Dog and Animal Welfare). This problem was initially caused by the industrialisation drive of dictator Nicolae Ceaucescu in the 1980's when people were forced to leave their homes in the country to work in cities where they had to live in small urban apartments, resulting in owners being forced to abandon their dogs. Unsurprisingly with a situation of unneutered dogs being dumped, the numbers quickly burgeoned to today's astronomic numbers.

Despite animal welfare legislation in 2008 which ruled that no healthy animal should be killed, following the death of a boy in 2013 – reportedly by stray dogs (subsequently revealed to be incorrect), the government wasted no time in whipping up hatred against them. Since then, they've been savagely slaughtered in ways that have been frequently criticised by animal welfare organisations and even foreign governments.

Despite the French claiming to love their dogs like family members, it still doesn't stop around 100,000-200,000 pets being abandoned every year, many of which will be euthanised (ref. BBC News, 8 Aug 2020). Reasons for abandonment vary from new partners who don't like pets, new baby/house, going on a holiday when *horreur des horreurs*, the owners suddenly discover that hotels charge extra for a pet, and a boarding kennel will also leave them out of pocket. In addition, owners are surprised that vets actually have the audacity to *charge them* to treat their pets. *Sacre bleu!!* Stylish as the French are reputed to be, sadly they also regard their pet as a fashionable accessory. When trends change, out goes their beloved pet as yesterday's must-have item, to be replaced by the latest in canine style. It remains to be seen if new laws being considered will have any effect in making owners more responsible for their pets.

After the 2015 economic collapse in Greece, it was estimated that more than one million pets were abandoned as their owners struggled to feed themselves, let alone their pets, and thus began the country's surge in stray animals.

It's more than a bit ironic that the Greeks smugly claim that they do not euthanise animals, while at the same time operating a widespread and daily practise whereby stray (or even owned) domestic animals are "dealt with" by using any convenient method to eradicate them. That could be rat poison, strychnine, farm pesticides or herbicides, even crushed glass (ref. Oipa.org) – all blindly accepted by Greeks as a "solution". There's a national refusal to acknowledge the true nature of this poisoning programme that indiscriminately slaughters cats and dogs in such an excruciatingly slow and brutal way, and yet citizens show no inclination to stop this carnage.

Neutering programmes for domestic pets are not accepted as a method to control reproduction due to an archaic and ignorant belief that the procedure interferes with the animals' natural life, with the resultant puppies or kittens abandoned to their fates on the roads or dumps. The fact that the current "population control" being employed in which the animals suffer a very **unnatural** demise is conveniently overlooked.

Despite the country having adequate animal protection laws, it is indicative of that society's views on animals that they are rarely enforced, (ref. Oipa.org). Pet owners devastated by the brutal extermination of their pets are reluctant to report the crime to the police, and have little trust in the judicial system.

For a country with such a rich cultural history, what a terrible reflection it is on Greek society and all of those in authority – from the police to the national Government and council officials – that there is so little compassion towards animals and zero interest in educating its populace as to responsible pet ownership, and encouraging humane population control. Those brave voluntary advocates, deeply concerned with animal welfare, who dare to speak out are frequently castigated, ridiculed, intimidated and generally disregarded by both citizens, media and government officials alike. Unless Greeks change their mentality on animals, these caring people will always be banging their collective heads against a very stubborn wall. Meanwhile, dogs will continue to be slaughtered.

How many tourists seeking a fun-sun holiday have been temporarily "adopted" by a little canine stray on the beach that follows them around faithfully in the vain hope that they may bewitch their new friend into giving them a Forever home? The average life-span for a stray dog in Greece is less than **2 YEARS**. Most die during the months after the tourists have departed when the restaurants and hotels have closed for the winter (ref. Oipa.org). The next time you are happily sunning yourself in Greece or on one of its beautiful islands, spare a thought for that sweet, raggedy stray gazing at you with soft brown eyes – that may not make it through the coming winter. Perhaps those tourists with a conscience who care about animals should talk with their feet by choosing alternative holiday destinations which have better animal welfare and some kind of compassion?

Thailand follows a boringly familiar pattern with an estimated 8.5 million dogs in the country. When fickle owners refuse to pay the costs incurred with pet care, the dogs become too old or they become bored with them, out they go – thus contributing to an already large population of 850,000 stray dogs, of which 100-300,000 are in Bangkok alone (ref. Wikipedia). These dogs live a short and generally extremely unpleasant existence. Alone and unwanted, they have to fend for themselves on the streets where they face cruel humans, illness, road traffic, and lack of food. As with so many other countries with excess dog populations, the cause is simple – irresponsible owners who refuse to care for all their animals' needs, fail to neuter or spay, then dump them to breed with other strays.

In Spain, ESDAW estimate there could be as many as 800,000 stray dogs living on the streets.

A cultural reluctance to neuter results in unwanted puppies – some as young as 1 or 2 days old – being left in plastic bags by or inside trash bins, dumped beneath hedges, or abandoned near motorways presumably by people who think that the passing traffic or the searing Spanish sun will finish the job for them. While the lucky ones are rescued and brought to one of the many over-worked rescue charities, it doesn't bear thinking about how many innocent animals perish in this callous way.

In early 2023, the Spanish Congress approved legislation to strengthen laws regarding care and mistreatment – intentional or otherwise – of domestic animals. A comprehensive animal identification system will be introduced, combined with an education programme for new owners which will include lessons on basic handling, and how to be responsible and knowledgeable pet owners. Only time will tell how effective this legislation will be. However, due to political/vote concerns and special interest group pressure, certain animals are not covered by this legislation, ie. bulls (bullfighting), **hunting dogs** and marine animals (dolphinariums). So there is still a considerable way to go before all animals in Spain are provided the adequate humane protection they need.

Aside from those dumped in the countryside, it's difficult to determine the exact number of hunting dogs – the *galgos* and *podencos* – that die each year. Because of unfettered breeding by *galgueros,* no one actually knows how many animals are born annually. As each hunter uses approximately 5 dogs each season, those surplus to requirement need to be disposed of. It's possible that between 50,000-100,000 *galgos* and approximately 150,000 *podencos* are brutally killed each year (ref. National Geographic, 2016).

Both of these unfortunate breeds will have lived truly dreadful lives for about 2-3 years, often chained up in isolated locations, or living in darkness, in sub-standard, crowded and filthy *zulos* which are rarely, if ever, cleaned. Males and females are kept together, allowed to mate uncontrollably. Feeding consists of little more than leftovers or stale bread as hungry dogs are more interested in hunting prey, with the dogs receiving scant affection or kindness, let alone stimulation. The physical condition of the animals is abysmal – skeletal from lack of food, their skin afflicted with eczema and a multitude of body sores from lying on filthy ground. With puppies sometimes being sold for minimal amounts, it's no wonder that these unfortunate creatures have little or no value to the hunters.

These animals are recklessly overbred in a search for the "Holy Grail" of *galgos* – a champion dog that can run for hours without tiring (oh, pleeassse). "Training" involves dozens of dogs being tied behind a vehicle and made to run for up to 20 miles; those that tire too quickly, or trip or fall are dragged to their deaths. The fact that the *galgueros* refuse to accept that these sighthounds are physiologically designed only for sprinting, and that that amount of distance "training" is nothing more than animal abuse, highlights the worrying ignorance and lack of care on behalf of these so-called "sportsmen" who profess to being "animal lovers".

Despite the stronger legislation against animal cruelty in the country, blind eyes are applied to the hunters as, aside from the inhumane conditions in which the dogs are forced to live and the so-called training methods, dogs still suffer horrific deaths when they've outlived their usefulness. If the unfortunate dog has hunted poorly, the *galgueros* consider that torturing and killing them will wash away the dishonour and shame the poor animal has brought to their owner.

They are used as target practise, given to fighting dogs, doused with acid, dragged to their deaths behind cars, skinned or buried alive, thrown off cliffs or into rivers or wells, their legs intentionally broken and left to die in forests or mountains. Or they suffer the infamous "piano-dance" whereby poor unfortunates deemed to have performed poorly are hanged from a height on a tree where their paws can just barely touch the ground, so they scrabble on their toes to try to stop themselves being killed, resulting in a slow, agonising death which sometimes takes days. The "good" performers are rewarded with a quick death by being hanged from a bridge or thrown down a well or off a cliff – if that's any consolation to anyone. It's a sad aside that these "hanging trees" often die after all the years of death and agony delivered from their boughs.

The only small protection these unfortunate animals have comes from the dedicated, hard-working and over-worked volunteers in the myriad of charities trying to tackle this industry (while no one in authority listens), who do their best to save as many dogs as possible from truly horrendous lives and deaths.

Again, holiday makers might want to take action by refusing to holiday in country that refuses to tackle such cruel practices, making sure that they inform local Embassies of their stance and the reason.

The so-called "sport" of greyhound racing in Ireland or the UK should not be overlooked. While fewer people are enjoying a fun "Night at the Dogs" at their local greyhound track these days, the unconscionable but very lucrative worldwide betting industry perpetuates this objectionable business.

This is an industry which encourages the over-breeding of the dogs. In 2017, a report commissioned by the Irish Greyhound Board revealed that approximately 16,000 greyhounds were bred annually for the Irish and UK racing industry – the UK imports around 6,250 (83%) of its racing dogs from that country. A yearly average showed that 5,987 (37.5%) dogs were culled or destroyed in Ireland for not making the qualifying times or declining performances, so of the original 16,000 dogs born, just 3,750 dogs (23.4%) managed to stay alive in the country of origin. According to the Irish Society for the Prevention of Cruelty to Animals (ISPCA), thousands of greyhound puppies born are never registered and simply disappear.

Racing dogs are kennelled for 23 hours every day, generally 2 to a kennel (which may not be very large, comfortable or clean), muzzled to prevent injury from fights which causes great stress to the dogs, not to mention the muzzle and crate sores caused during such incarceration. Their racing life lasts for 3-4 years or approximately 50 races with 1 in 3 dogs receiving on-track injuries, many of which will have their lives ended "humanely" because their owners refuse to pay the associated vet costs or accept the cost of recuperation while the dogs are not earning their keep. The "official stats" will not include those dogs which weren't registered, or which are officially 'retired' from GBGB licenced tracks to continue to race elsewhere.

Hounds First Sighthound Rescue report that "over 10,000 dogs "vanish" each year" in the UK with most known to be killed just because they didn't make the grade, often being illegally slaughtered by bolt guns in abattoirs for as little as £10, beaten or starved to death, or thrown into the sea by their owners to die. These poor dogs are used like money-making machines, only a small percentage of which will ever experience the love and comfort of a home, and are literally being bred to be killed. And yet the greyhound industry will have you believe that it is, indeed, a very honourable, reputable sport, one to be admired for its humane care of its animals.

There is a tiny glimmer of light for the breed as over the past number of years there has been an increase in greyhound rehoming charities that provide rehabilitation before finding new homes for a small number of lucky dogs, but much of this depends on a small number of racing owners prepared to "retire" their racers. There are still far too many dogs that are never afforded this luxury.

Once a dog's racing life is finished in its home nation, countries like Ireland, the UK and Australia sell the dogs on for hunting or racing purposes but also as breeding machines to countries with dubious to non-existent animal welfare laws, such as Morocco, Spain, Portugal, Russia, Pakistan, Mexico, Argentina, Romania, Middle-Eastern countries and to probably the worst of them all – China.

Once sold on to countries like these, the general welfare of these unfortunate animals will now take a further, very severe nosedive in standard. The vast majority will "disappear" into some black hole, never to be accounted for or seen again. Of those sent to China, after they've outlived their usefulness, some will be sent to wildlife parks as live food for the big cats, providing the sickest of entertainment for the public at feeding time. Perhaps they are the "lucky" ones as their demise might be mercifully quick. Not so lucky are those poor miserable unfortunates that end up at the infamous Chinese meat markets where dogs are crammed into impossibly small cages, dragged out and tortured because the Chinese have a very erroneous view that fear before death tenderises the meat, so the dogs are beaten, hung, boiled or skinned alive. All designed to make men more virile ... presumably these cruel, ignorant people have never heard of Viagra.

Is it any wonder that no government appears to be prepared to tackle this greedy, cruel and arrogant self-regulated, multi-million pound/euro racing industry when it raises millions in tax-revenue annually for state coffers, and huge profits for the bookmakers, owners and trainers? If there were any politicians with even a modicum of decency in any of these countries, they should hang their heads in shame at such a brutal and inhumane business which purports to be providing "sport" or "entertainment", while innocent animals pay such a high and very painful price.

And yet that "venerable" institution, the EU, which introduced tracking and animal welfare directives for farm animals that are going to be slaughtered for food, refuse to do anything substantive to protect so-called working dogs. In fact, despite introducing legislation that states "since animals are sentient beings, (the Union and Member Countries shall) pay full regard to the welfare requirements of animals". The reality is that bureaucrats apparently snooze rather than ensure compliance with these rules. EU funds are even being used to massacre stray dogs in unimaginably savage ways (Romania) instead of ensuring the animals' safety and humane care.

Not only do dogs appear on menus across other Asian countries (also Nigeria and Switzerland) with equally terrible meat markets, but their pelts are used in apparel manufactured in those countries – something which consumers in the West should be aware of and if they really have a conscience, refuse to buy. It is important for shoppers to take a very strong stand and tell the retailer why, as customers, they will not buy products that literally have blood of thousands of animals on them.

Not even that age-old and esteemed "sport" of British Fox-Hunting is exempt from enacting extreme cruelty not only on foxes but also on its unfortunate hounds. While theoretically banned in law in 2004, this gung-ho bunch of bloodthirsty Hurray Henrys and Harriets still participate in this so-called sport through their deceitful interpretation of the law. They employ duplicitous methods to enable them to continue with their bloody entertainment by carrying birds of prey with them without ever letting them loose, or laying "artificial" trails – using real fox scent, close to where foxes are known to live (ref. Ash Murphy, The Conversation, 30/1/19).

This organisation massively overbreeds foxhounds, killing those puppies that are considered too small or weak by smashing their little heads off walls or floors. Considered too old at (on average) 7 years old – half of the average expected age for the breed – healthy adult hounds are killed. And woe betide that younger hound that has the temerity to bay or move before instructed on a hunt. Such a crime will guarantee death for the poor animal upon return to the kennels. Every year, thousands of healthy hounds that are not considered "fit enough" are shot or clubbed to death. At long last, there are a few rehoming establishments for foxhounds, offering either young puppies or older adults that have been rehabilitated but there are still too many animals "disappearing" without account.

It should be a huge embarrassment that so many countries have so-called "cultural" traditions that involve extreme mistreatment of animals: British Fox-hunting, the Spanish hunters with their "Pianist" method of disposal (which also involves betting and much amusement while an animal suffers), the disgusting spectacle in Bulgaria of terrified dogs being swung across a zip-line for human "merriment" should turn the stomachs of anyone with an inkling of a heart, while the indescribable savagery of Yulin Festival and the live markets need no further discussion.

The despicable so-called "sport" of dog-fighting all over the world seems to be impossible to eradicate. What a truly awful indictment on a species that gets its "kicks" from watching one animal tear another to pieces.

While testing of **cosmetics** on animals is – in my humble view – completely unacceptable, the ethicality of medical research using animals – among which are Beagles, is always a debate fraught with strong emotions on both sides. But the fact remains that these unfortunate little Beagles are doomed by their very docile, sweet natures and size, and are bred in vast numbers specially for experimentation – all in the name of so-called human beauty. Many are used multiple times for various experiments and tests, living miserable lives until they're finally euthanised.

It is unsurprising that such so-called traditions and practices continue to exist considering that too few countries have sufficient laws governing the treatment of animals. An equivalent lack of animal welfare organisations to investigate and prosecute perpetrators of neglect and/or animal cruelty perpetuates the practices of cruelty and lack of empathy towards animals to following generations. The treatment and general welfare of dogs across the world is downright abysmal with animals facing extreme cruelty in many so-called civilised countries which rank animal welfare as non-important.

Many, many countries have blood dripping from their hands.

The human race should hang its collective heads in total shame at the number of unimaginably cruel practices it perpetrates on dogs. It is often difficult to decide which, in fact, are the animals. For all their faithful companionship throughout the millennia, humans have really let down this noble species – "man's best friend" in every way possible.

It's generally agreed by global authorities that spaying/neutering, canine vaccination programmes and encouraging proper, responsible treatment by owners are the most effective ways to handle dog-related problems. Instead of instituting strong laws that would make owners and breeders responsible for the good and humane welfare of their animals especially those used for so-called sporting purposes, many countries "deal with" unwanted dog "problems" in brutal ways. Too many dogs really do deserve better humans in their lives.

So, to answer that question posed at the beginning of this chapter: Why Adopt?

Quite simply, to save a dog's life.

Pippi *(Photo: PeaJayz)*

GLOSSARY

Adaptil diffuser® : Plug-in device that emits a dog-appeasing pheromone (DAP) in fine, odourless mist. D.A.P is a synthetic hormone that imitates the pheromones released by a bitch nursing her puppies very early in life. Can ease anxiety and help puppies and adult dogs to relax and stay calm in new environments or stressful circumstances indoors, ie. when staying alone, visitors, loud noises like thunder and fireworks, and other fears. May not work for every dog but is helpful for some.

Air-biting : Snapping at the air if feeling threatened or anxious. May be used to warn another animal or human, but can escalate to a bite if the warning hasn't been heeded. Can also be a sign of behavioural or neurological problems, obsessive-compulsive disorder, or seizure activity (with repeated incidents) when a vet should be consulted.

Bach flower remedies : An alternative or complementary treatment for emotional problems and pain. Made from watered-down extracts from the flowers of wild plants.

Behaviourist : Expert behaviourists are Applied Animal Behaviourists who have earned an MS, MA or PhD in animal behaviour. Are like psychologists who modify or change an animal's behaviour, teaching them how to better manage their emotions.

Behaviourists understand the normal behaviour of a species, how and why a particular behaviour is abnormal, and how to change it. They will work closely with the owner, teaching them how to understand the behaviour, and how to interact with their pet.

A **veterinary behaviourist** is a qualified veterinarian who has specialised in behavioural problems. Is like an animal psychiatrist. They deal also with behaviour modification and deeply understand the behaviour of each species being treated.

Campo (Span.) : Countryside, country, or field.

Canine cognitive dysfunction : A disease similar to dementia or Alzheimer's disease in humans, causing loss of memory and earlier learned training, confusion, abnormal sleeping patterns, motor function.

CBD : Cannabidiol, a compound found in marijuana. Can be used to treat anxiety and other conditions such as neuropathic pain, as well as helping to control seizures. As the use of this product for pets is unregulated, it is important to consult a vet prior to use.

Clicker/clicker training : A small hand-held device that emits a click when pressed. Is used to signal immediately to the dog that they have performed the desired behaviour or action which is then rewarded with a treat. Can assist in refining a final response more effectively than a verbal marker. The dog must be conditioned to the sound prior to training commences.

Cognitive deficit : An inclusive term to describe the loss of different area/s of reasoning. Not limited to any particular disorder or disease but may be one of the indications of an underlying condition.

Conformation : The overall appearance and structure of a dog.

Coren, Stanley : Born 1942, Dr Coren is a psychology professor, neuropsychological researcher and writer on the intelligence, mental abilities and history of dogs. He has made a career of research into dog behaviour that has led him to national television and into international media, and has written numerous books on dog-related subjects.

Counterconditioning : Changes a dog's negative emotional response or attitude towards stimuli by re-associating whatever causes the problem with a positive experience.

Desensitization : Same as counter-conditioning but involves a longer period of time to change the response. The dog is exposed to its (fear) trigger in a slow and systematic way, through gradually escalating steps.

Crate : A metal enclosed pen, large enough for the animal to stand up and turn around. Can act as the dog's bed and a place of sanctuary but also secure him when no one is around to supervise. Also comes in plastic, often called a flight kennel.

Dutch Shepherd/Bardino : A herding dog of Dutch origin, used by shepherds and farmers. Are loyal, reliable, independent and intelligent with a strong character.

Exposure therapy : See Desensitisation.

Free feed : Leaving a bowl of dog food down for hours at a time, if not all day long.

Galguero (Span.) : Spanish hunter.

Galgo/a (Span.) : Spanish hunting dog, similar to a greyhound.

GPS Pet Tracker® : Small devices that attach to the pet's collar that generally use a combination of GPS and cellular signals to keep the owner informed as to the current location of their pet.

Guardia (Civil) (Span.) : The most powerful police force in Spain.

Halti® : A head-collar/halter that fits over the dog's head and muzzle. Also known as a "gentle leader". Is used to prevent pulling, or to gently redirect the dog's attention to their handler.

Hand targeting : Dog is trained to touch handler's hand. Useful command whereby a dog can be requested to do certain things, ie. get off the sofa, into the car, even to keep the dog still during vet treatment. Can be used to bring the dog's focus from an outside stimulus back to the handler.

Harness : A piece of equipment consisting of series of straps that go around the dog's neck and body. Used to lead, hold and lift the dog. Reduces tension on the throat area if the dog pulls, and allows him to breathe more freely during walks.

High predation/High prey drive : An inbred instinct to pursue prey. More common in tracking and hunting breeds but any dog can have a compulsion to chase smaller animals.

Home-check : A visit to the home of a prospective adopter, to check that the environment is safe and suitable for a dog, ie. electrical outlets, perimeter fencing, etc. and that the dog will have a loving forever home. It also provides adopters with the opportunity to ask questions about their chosen dog, and for the adoption agency to give advice on settling in the new dog.

Hypoallergenic (dog) : One that is less likely to cause an allergic reaction. Dogs with tight curly coats or which don't shed may be more tolerated by allergy sufferers.

Lemon-spray collar : Main purpose is to stop a dog's nuisance barking. Collar reacts to barking by squirting out a fine mist of citronella liquid near the dog's face, right under their nose. Is controversial equipment and experts would recommend investigating why the dog is barking in the first place, ie. boredom, or are they trying to alert their owner to something?

Macho (Span.) : Male

Man-Trailing : A sport which utilises a dog's natural hunting ability to track a person in a safe and controlled way. Provides a fulfilling and fun activity for owner and dog to do together.

Marker-training : Similar to clicker training, marker-training is a simple method that teaches the dog to perform desirable behaviours or actions in exchange for a reward. Markers can be a clicker, verbal markers such as "yes" or "good" or even a pen-light to signal a deaf dog. More than one marker may be used but the animal must be conditioned to them before training begins.

Mastin/Spanish Mastiff : Spanish Mastiff or Mastín Español, originally bred to be a guard dog, its specialized purpose is to be a livestock guardian dog protecting flocks and/or herds from wolves and other predators.

Mouthing : Normal behaviour particularly in puppies or young dogs. Can also be associated with fear or frustration and indicate problems with aggression.

Naya (Span.) : Spanish word for an open area for dining. Can also apply to a glassed-in dining area.

Nylabone : Made from a durable nylon, these bones satisfy a dog's natural urge to chew, encourage positive chewing habits, while providing long-lasting enjoyment. Bones come in a variety of textures and flavours.

Pavlov, Ivan Petrovich : B.26.9.1849, d.2 Feb 1936. Russian and Soviet experimental neurologist, psychologist and physiologist known for his discovery of classical conditioning (training) through his experiments with dogs. This concept became known as "conditioned reflex". Nominated over 4 successive years for the Nobel Prize in Physiology or Medicine. He was finally awarded the prize in 1904 "in recognition of his work on the physiology of digestion, through which knowledge on vital aspects of the subject has been transformed and enlarged". His research on gastric function which involved experiments on dogs and homeless children evoked criticism in some areas of the scientific world about how the trials had been executed.

Perrera (Span.) : Spanish dog pound, many of which are kill stations (euthanise unclaimed/unwanted animals). This may change under new legislation introduced.

Perrito (Span.) : Puppy, dog, doggie, usually used in an affectionate way.

Pica : A compulsive urge to eat non-edible items, for example, rocks or stones, clothing, or dirt. Generally seen in adolescent and adult dogs, the cause can be either medical or behavioural. Is a disorder also seen in humans.

Pheromone collar : Calming collars that typically contain DAP (dog-appeasing pheromone). Can help dogs with mild anxiety to deal with stressful situations including fireworks, thunder, separation, but are unlikely to help animals with severe anxiety. Collars can also have herbal or essential oils although care should be taken as some are toxic to pets, especially felines.

Podenco/a (Span.) : Small to large-sized hound from the Mediterranean region, particularly Portugal and Spain. Bred to hunt, there are many different types. One of the oldest breeds of dog in the world, descending from the ancient Pharaoh Hounds of Egypt. Often referred to as 'Invisible Dogs' or 'The Great Forgotten', they are the most abused dog in Spain. Kept in squalid conditions, these dogs are not protected under Spanish law.

Podenca-Pastor (Span.) : Pastor Aleman is German Shepherd in Spanish, so is a Podenco-GSD-cross.

Positive reinforcement/reward/training : Method of encouraging desirable behaviour from the dog and a love of learning through rewards like treats, toys, petting or praise.

Reactive/Reactivity : An overreaction to a stimulus which could be another animal, object or person. Behaviour that may be construed as aggressive is generally a sign of a frustrated or insecure dog.

RelaxoDog®/RelaxoPet : A wireless sonic tranquilizer which provides soothing, subliminal sound waves (inaudible to human ears) to help anxious dogs.

Response substitution : Changing an undesirable behavioural response to a stimulus or situation to one that is desirable. The objective is to reinforce only those responses that are wanted.

Rottie : Familiar term for a Rottweiler.

Separation anxiety : A behaviour caused when dogs that are overly dependent or attached to family member/s become anxious and distressed when separated from the guardian/s.

Señora/s (Span.) : Lady/ladies.

Snozz : Humorous reference to a nose. Film buffs might recollect the actor, Jimmy Durante, who was famous for his large proboscis.

Socialise/Socialisation : Process by which the dog learns key life skills to enable it to be comfortable with places, people, other animals, and activities and enjoy interactions. Ideal socialisation period is between 3-14 weeks for puppies. Poorly socialised adult dogs can also be helped with behaviour modification methods.

Squeaky bum time : A colloquial British saying to reflect a particularly tense period of time (originally and chiefly in sporting contexts). Ref. OED.

Staffi : Familiar term for a Staffordshire Bull Terrier.

Trainer : Will train dogs to perform specific tasks or actions, but also not to do certain things. Some will incorporate the behaviourist side of things and work with animals with behavioural issues, but may not be capable of tackling more complex problems, at which point they should refer the pet owner to a qualified Applied Animal Behaviourist.

Underbite : A dental or skeletal condition where the lower teeth protrude farther than the upper front teeth.

Whale eyes : Term used to describe a dog's body language when the whites of the eyes (the sclera) are visible in a half-moon shape either at the outer or inner side of the eyes, or occasionally all round. The dog will turn his head away slightly but his eyes will remain fixed on the perceived threat. Indicating stress, fear or unease, it is an appeasement gesture to show that the dog is not a threat and needs more space. Is important that such a signal is heeded as an anxious dog may escalate to a bite.

Xylitol : Preservative and sweetening agent used in food but highly toxic to dogs.

Zulo (Span.) : Lit. a cache. An underground bunker, place used to keep hunting dogs.

BIOGRAPHIES

DR SUSANNAH O'HANLON, PhD MSc

Having fostered over 60 dogs over the last 10 years, Susannah has a particular interest in the rehabilitation and rehoming of rescue dogs, early-stage development of puppies and adolescents, and maintaining welfare in a dog's senior years.

Susannah is a qualified Clinical Animal Behaviourist, registered with the ABTC, and Full Member of the Association of Pet Behaviour Counsellors (APBC) and The Canine Behaviour and Training Society (TCBTS). She runs Cambridge Dogs which has a team of experts offering a variety of private and group classes, in addition to full behaviour counselling and one-to-one remedial training. Susannah also teaches as Associate Lecturer in Animal Behaviour at Anglia Ruskin University on a range of animal welfare and behaviour topics.

HELEN HOWELL, BSc (Hons)

Helen has a BSc (Hons) in Canine Behaviour Management from the University of Hull, UK, and is a member of the International Association of Animal Behaviour Consultants. She is also a member of the UK Register of Expert Witnesses, with her expert opinion on behaviour and breed type accepted in both criminal and civil cases.

She runs bite prevention education at pre-school and primary levels in schools and community groups, to teach children how to safely interact with dogs by understanding the reasons a dog may bite, and how the animals use body language to communicate with us. She presented The Family Dog, which launched "Stop The 77", an online dog-safety campaign for families on how to live safely and happily with dogs.

As a Behaviour Consultant, Helen travels to all parts of the UK to work with pet dogs and their owners, providing behaviour and training consultations, and carrying out behavioural assessments and breed identification of dogs both in their homes and in police custody. She previously spent time in the United States, working with game-bred American Pit Bull Terriers and Pit Bull-type dogs.

Working with rescue dogs is very close to Helen's heart and she has worked with street dogs in India and Spain, helping to rehabilitate dogs that have been rescued, often following mistreatment.

Helen is currently undertaking a PhD at the University of Lincoln, UK, her subject of research is the assessment of the risk of human directed aggression in dogs.

RYAN DILLON, BSc (Hons) in Animal Behaviour and Welfare, MSc.

Owner of Oxfordshire Animal Behaviour and Training (OABT), Ryan has worked with over 1,000 clients and their pets. He brings his special brand of enthusiasm and upbeat approach to the very popular puppy classes and behaviour rehab training sessions he runs, in addition to individual behaviour consultations.

A qualified dog trainer with the Professional Association of Canine Trainers (PACT) and a recognised animal training instructor with the Animal Behaviour and Training Council (ABTC), Ryan earned a distinction in the BSc (Hons) Animal Behaviour and Welfare degree at Oxford Brookes University, and a distinction in the Clinical Animal Behaviour Master's degree at the University of Lincoln. He is also a lecturer at Oxford Brookes University and Abingdon and Witney College, teaching on animal behaviour-related degrees, and is a tutor and assessor at PACT, teaching and providing support to students working towards becoming qualified dog trainers.

PAULA JONES

Paula has had a deep love of animals all her life, but it took an early retirement to South-East Spain to introduce her to the world of rescue dogs through her work as a volunteer with the Casa del Sol Shelter.

For over 10 years, she performed every and any duty required to help care for the dogs from committee work, cleaning out, walking, training, grooming, transporting and home-checking prospective owners and much more. This experience has given her a deep insight into the plight of rescue dogs, and what is required to improve their lives. Adoption by three abandoned dogs over the space of 7 years allowed her to discover the pure joy of living with these special animals, each one of whom has gently taught her how to understand them more, and especially how to serve them in the manner to which they quickly became accustomed.

She completed a Diploma in Dog Behaviour which helped to fill in some of the gaps in her canine knowledge that her dogs had preferred her not to learn.

CONTACT LIST

Rescue/adoption organisations:

- The Dogs Trust, https://dogstrust.org.uk/ Multiple centres in the UK and Republic of Ireland: All breeds/sizes, pedigree & crosses
- Battersea Dogs' Home, https://battersea.org.uk: All breeds/sizes, pedigree and crosses
- RSPCA (or respective national animal protection societies) www.rspca.org.uk/home: All breeds/sizes, pedigree and crosses
- AA Dog Rescue, UK, Website: www.aadogrescue.org.uk: All breeds, pedigree and crosses
- Protectora Animales Perros del Sol (PAPS); Murcia, Spain. Facebook: Support Abandoned Dogs/PAPS in Spain: All breeds/sizes, mainly cross breeds
- PAPS Germany: Facebook: Casa del Sol/PAPS Bewohner suchen ein Zuhause: All breeds/sizes, mainly cross breeds
- 1001 Patas de Marta, Murcia, Spain. (Facebook): Mainly large dogs, particularly Spanish Mastins
- Paradise Kennels, Benferri, Spain. Website: http://paradiserescuekennels.com: All breeds/crosses, including mastins, galgos and podencos
- Pat's Rescue Retreat, Malaga, Spain (Facebook): Mainly mixed breeds
- Last Chance Rescue, Romania: https://www.lastchancerescueromania.com; Mixed breeds

- The Tanzie Project: https://www.the tanzieproject.org supports the forgotten pets of Boznia, Herzegovina and the Balkans.
- The Fairy Dog Fosterers, UK (Facebook): specialises in Pointers
- Blue The Grey, provides lists of world-wide charities helping sighthounds, Website: www.bluethegrey.com
- Candy's Hound Rescue International: Website: https://candyshoundrescue.org
  e-mail: rescue@candyshoundrescue.org: Greyhounds, especially from China
- www.greyhoundprotectionuk.co.uk: Greyhounds
- www.actionforgreyhounds.co.uk: Greyhounds
- Forever Hounds Trust: https://foreverhoundstrust.org: Greyhounds, Lurchers
- Foxhound Rescue: http://www.foxhoundrescue.org: Foxhounds
- Foxhound Welfare UK: https://foxhoundwelfareuk.jimdofree.com
- Greyt Exploitations: www.greytexploitations.com: Lobby group

As the above list is merely a snapshot of organisations involved in dog rescue, welfare or activism, please research associations in your local area from which you can adopt your next rescue dog, or support.

Trainers/Behaviourists:

- Dr Susannah O'Hanlon, PhD, MSc, Cambridge Dogs, e-mail: classes@camdogs.co.uk
- Helen Howell, (UK) BSc (Hons), Canine Behaviour Consultant, Expert Witness, "I Speak Doggie" safety programmes, e-mail: info@dogbehaviourexpert.co.uk
- Ryan Dillon, BSc(hons), BSc(hons) MSc, Oxfordshire Animal Behaviour and Training (OABT), https://www.oabt.co.uk/
- Ramona Noack,(Germany) Trainer/Behaviourist, Tierzentrum Leuthen, www.tierzentrum-leuthen.de

- Animal Behaviour and Training Council (ABTC): UK regulatory body that represents and maintains registers of animal trainers and behaviourists fulfilling accreditation criteria and belonging to approved member associations, https://abtc.org.uk/
- Association for the Study of Animal Behaviour (ASAB): (UK) an independent organisation which accredits Certified Clinical Animal Behaviourists (CCAB), a standard identical to the certification mentioned above, https://www.asab.org/ccab-register

If there is a rescue charity or shelter near you, why not volunteer your services to help out, or donate?

Remember that the most important thing is to ... **Adopt, don't shop!**

www.ingramcontent.com/pod-product-compliance
Lightning Source LLC
Chambersburg PA
CBHW081613100526
44590CB00021B/3425